The Yukon

BOOKS IN THE
RIVERS OF AMERICA SERIES

RIVERS OF AMERICA

Edited by Carl Carmer

As planned and started by
Constance Lindsay Skinner

Associate Editor Jean Crawford

Illustrated by Bryan Forsyth

The Yukon

BY RICHARD MATHEWS

HOLT, RINEHART AND WINSTON

NEW YORK CHICAGO SAN FRANCISCO

Quotations from the Florence Hartshorn diary are by permission of the Editor, *Alaska Sportsman,* and Ethel
Anderson Becker; those from *I Married the Klondike* by
Laura Berton by permission of Little, Brown and Company; those from *Alaska Native Secondary School Dropouts: a Research Report* by Charles K. Ray et al. by
permission of Dr. Ray, Dean, College of Behavioral
Sciences and Education, University of Alaska; and that
from *The Random House Dictionary of the English
Language,* copyright 1966, 1967, by permission of Random House, Inc.

Designer: Ernst Reichl
8717407
Printed in the United States of America

To my wife, Ella—

Who made good bannock, typed, scaled inconnu, plucked ducks, edited, navigated, translated Jesuit Latin and Canadian French, transcribed folk tales related in broken English and pitch darkness, and was pretty good about living on a straight diet of pike washed down with sugarless tea when the grub ran low.

Contents

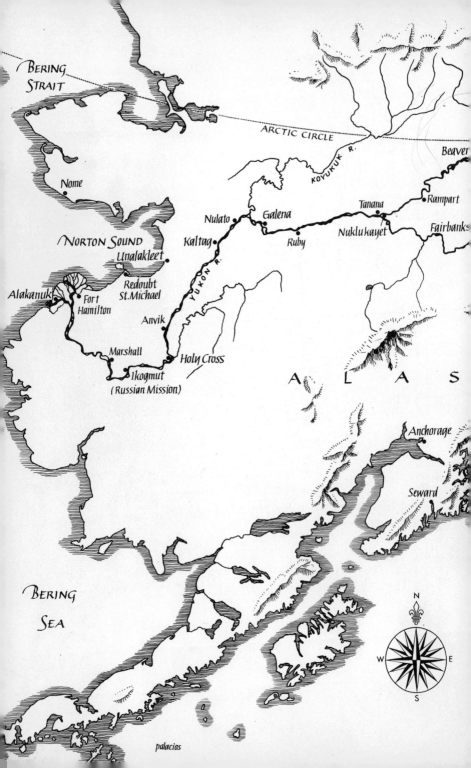

Acknowledgments: A word of thanks, first of all, to some of the people living on the river who were particularly helpful: Joe Ward, a retired trapper; Miss Teresa Barling, a student of the Kutchin dialect; and Rev. Murray Trelease, all of Fort Yukon; Mrs. Martha Taylor of Dawson City, who related many folk tales, including the one at the beginning of this book; Mr. Alan Innes-Taylor of Dawson, Whitehorse and half a dozen other places, who still knows far more than I about the upper river but who was most generous in helping to narrow the gap between us; Mr. Billy Williams of Anvik, both for what he told me and what he told Dr. Cornelius Osgood, the anthropologist to whose work Chapter III is so much indebted; Mr. Terrance Wharton and Mr. William Chase, also of Anvik; Rev. Jules Convert, S.J., a French Jesuit formerly of Kaltag whose advice on Chapter XX was most helpful; and to Mr. Jake Aloysius of Paimiut.

I am also indebted to: Rev. William J. Loyens, S.J., of the Department of Anthropology, University of Alaska, who kindly put his Ph.D. dissertation on Nulato, his House Diary translations, and his sound advice at my disposal; to Paul McCarthy, Archivist, University of Alaska; Rev. Wilfred Schoenberg, S.J., who collected so much Yukon material for the Jesuit Archives at Gonzaga University, Spokane, which he heads; Rev. Henry H. Chapman of Asheville, North Carolina, for making available the letters of his father; Mr. William Doolittle of Newtown, Pennsylvania, and Mr. Richard Actis-Grande of New York City, for their editorial suggestions and encouragement; Mr. Daniel Holder, my brother, for his skill as a boatman and *bricoleur;* and my sister, Miss Nancy Mathews, for her extra supply of bug repellent and good cheer.

R.M.

Goldens Bridge, New York
April, 1968

The Yukon

1 Lot of Water

Yukon (yōō′kon), *n.* 1. a river flowing NW and SW from NW Canada through central Alaska to the Bering Sea. ab. 2000 mi. long.

—*Random House Dictionary
of the English Language*

At the north end of Dawson City, Yukon Territory, Canada, eight uniform cabins squat in a row not a hundred feet from the river. They were all built at the same time and are all painted a uniform shade of bright pink. Each shares its tiny, bare plot with a litter of woodchips, empty Coca-Cola bottles, broken-down plastic toys and cheap furniture, a half-dissected outboard motor or two, and a varying number of chained-up sled dogs. The polyethylene and plywood tacked up in place of windowpanes long shattered give the row an aspect of forlorn shabbiness. So do the cabin walls, for they need a fresh coat of pink paint. The drab scene is brightened, though, by the long clotheslines flapping with strident reds and blues, and by the deep-orange slabs of salmon flesh that hang drying in the warm summer sun. And if the exteriors of the cabins are grim, the interiors, full of life and people, are much less so. Poverty, like sin, is less disturbing from the inside out.

A very old woman by the name of Mrs. Martha Taylor lives in one of the cabins of the row. This was not the name she was born with, but it is the one the Anglican missionary priest entered into his baptismal register. It is also the name used by the welfare

1

disbursers of the Indian Affairs Branch who built her pink house.

Mrs. Taylor has lived a long time and seen many things. She has been told of many others. The following, which she related to a visitor one bright summer morning, is one of them:

One time long ago, Beaver-Man he's traveling around, a-traveling and a-traveling. The sun he was real hot, and Beaver-Man he get thirsty, you know, real thirsty like when you don't got even spit to swallow. He need something to drink real bad. One man he's a-traveling with, he fall down dead he so thirsty.

Beaver-Man pretty soon he say to himself, "What I going to do?" And he start thinking, and pretty soon he say to the people he's a-traveling with, "I going to make you some water so you better get ready to drink."

Then Wolverine say, "There's no water. How you going to make some?" And they all get mad at him, think he's crazy, just want to make big show. Especially Wolverine, he's real mad.

Beaver-Man he take and cut willow stick and he tie willow stick to his walking stick with a piece of . . . how you say in English? . . . that string you make from caribou. Then he go down in a little valley, at the top end of it, and he say again, "I going to make you some water, so you better get ready to drink."

Then he stick willow stick into ground. Pretty soon lot of water coming out. Lot of, lot of water from good clean spring. All these people with Beaver-Man, even Wolverine, they so happy they put their whole head right in the water.

After that each time Beaver-Man and his people they get thirsty, he go up to top of little valley, stick in willow stick, and water come out. Lot of water. He done this many times. Each spring it make a stream, and after long, long time these streams so many they big enough to make Yukon.

All that, it happens long time ago. That's the end of the story.

Mrs. Taylor says her father knows the exact spot where Beaver-Man first struck water. "He told me," she explains, "but I'm old woman now and I forgot so many things." A frown deepens the wrinkles of her bronze, walnut-textured face as she chases a fugitive wisp of memory. Then, giving up, she puffs on her cigarette and turns to stare vacantly out the window at the swift, roiling current of the Yukon. God knows how many hours of her long life she has spent staring at the river like this. She was born along its banks, though in just what year she can't say, and she has never once left its valley; now she guesses she has "probably 'bout a hundred" grandchildren and great-grandchildren living along it. She turns suddenly from her reverie by the window, focuses her eyes sharply on her visitor, and says irritably, "No, I forgot where it was. All I know is how Beaver-Man done it. What more you want from old woman?"

Mrs. Taylor has never seen the sea, and Beaver-Man may not have either, but the Yukon, like all rivers, arises there. There, and in the sun. For forty million years the Yukon has come down to empty into the sea, yet it has never arrived nor ever been emptied. The sea itself and the sun have made the journey interminable: the sea that supplies the water, the sun that raises it up by evaporation to renew the river at its sources. This ceaseless journey is given form by the earth's convulsive inner turmoil, and by the river itself, which sculpts the land that forms it. For the river holds nothing it can touch inviolate. It washes down the loose Quaternary gravels of the Kaiyuh Flats where salmon fishing camps stood the year before, and it abrades the hard Pre-Cambrian schists of Rampart Canyon that are older than life on earth. It erodes the debris of Tertiary volcanoes and the remnants of Eocene peat bogs; it rifles the Pleistocene graves of woolly rhinoceroses and giant ground sloths, and the Carboniferous embalmments of semitropical forests. Down to the sea the Yukon carries the slow wreckage of the face of the earth; back to the sea whence come all land forms and all life.

Beaver-Man was a practical sort of fellow who wanted to make a stream of clear drinking water, not a whole water cycle. Perhaps, therefore, he first poked his stick into the ground among the spiked granite massifs of the Coast Mountains in what is now British Columbia. For it is here that the Yukon's water begins its fall back to the sea. It is magnificent country, rugged, difficult to penetrate, totally unspoiled. The mountains are sharp, sheer, angular, in the prime of geological manhood. They are stark and barren, for the harsh climate at sixty degrees north latitude has pushed the timber line down to the bottom of their flanks. Above twenty-five hundred feet there are no trees, only mosses and lichens which cling to the bare grey rock, and tiny junipers which creep forth hesitantly from refuges provided by rare pockets of soil in a landscape of stone. There are white spruces here and there as well, but they hardly count as trees, dwarfed and deformed as they are, a foot or two high after a century of life. In early summer blue-purple lupines and pink wild roses manage somehow to bloom, but they can never quite dispel the prevailing somberness of this realm of dark greys and black-greens.

The peaks of the Coast Mountains clutch the glaciers and snow fields wedged into their cleft valleys as a miser grips his treasure. But in May come the long warm days, and pilferage begins. It is petty at first: a matter only of microscopic pocks of liquid in the crystalline mass, of a silent deliquescence seeping away without trace. At night frost comes to the aid of the miser and locks his treasure up tight. But the pilferage resumes, and becomes more serious with each day of the advancing season. By June it is flagrant, a virtual pillage. Everywhere drops drip away, form trickles, splash down, coalesce into rivulets. The rivulets descend, find last year's watercourses under the ice, join other miniature rivers from other miniature watersheds. They converge, grow, become brooks. And the brooks coruscate down over the broken, falling landscape of alpine tundra, pause momentarily in little rockbound ponds which transmute the whiteness of rushing water to a deep, clear aquamarine. Streams plummet from the ponds, conflow, concresce, plunge onward and downward, become little rivers. Soon they fall off past the first trees, scraggly forward sentinels of the great boreal forest of North America through which their waters will flow for the next two thousand miles.

Just below the timber line they pause again. They have reached the Yukon Plateau and begin a slow, aimless meander through the trenchlike lakes—Atlin, Bennett, Tutshi, Lindeman, and Taku Arm—which lead to the beginning of the Yukon River proper. It is as though these mountain watercourses have descended so recklessly that they have taken the wrong route; now they are reconsidering. Their sources are a stone's throw from the fiords of the Pacific Ocean, yet they have embarked on a two thousand mile journey that will take them north to the Arctic Circle and across thirty-six degrees of longitude. They will reach salt water not in the blue Pacific but in the slate-grey waters of Bering Sea hard by Siberia.

The geology that decrees this tortuous fate is dominated by two continental mountain chains, the Pacific and Rocky Mountain cordilleras. Crescentic in form, and roughly parallel, both chains begin in Mexico and terminate in the Bering Sea. In the Western United States they form the two sides of the vast interior valley known as the Great Basin; two thousand miles to the northwest, they delimit the basin of the Yukon River. The subdivisions of the Rocky Mountain cordillera that mark the northern border of the Yukon watershed, the Mackenzie Mountains of Canada and the Brooks Range of Alaska, are not particularly high. In places, as along the international boundary, they nearly peter out. The Pacific cordillera, on the other hand, hems in the Yukon valley with a solid wall of granite bastioned by the six highest peaks in North America. The Yukon cannot breach it, and so the two run parallel, the river a few hundred miles north of the mountains. Since the chain continues to the northwestern limit of the continent, so does the Yukon. The two fall away together at about the 166th meridian, the Pacific cordillera into the Aleutian Islands, the Yukon into the Bering Sea.

Where the Pacific cordillera reaches the apex of its arc and elevation—where it is crowned by Mount McKinley—it has retreated from the coast. Five hundred miles to the east of this, however, it straddles the very rim of the continent, and it is here that the Yukon rises. From the summit of White Pass one can plainly see Lynn Canal, an arrow-straight fiord of the Pacific shimmering in the sun fifteen miles away and twenty-six hundred feet below. All the watercourses in between plummet down to meet the sea next to the decayed gold rush town of Skagway. Just to the east of the pass, a scant mile by the old miners' trail, a somber tarn called Summit Lake perches on an eastward-sloping ledge of bare grey rock. Its frigid water is bound for the Bering Sea.

The mountain systems that confine the Yukon basin also define it. The barrier formed by the Coast, St. Elias, and Wrangell Mountains, and the Alaska Range, all subdivisions of the Pacific cordillera, is one of climate as well as topography. It seals off the interior, the Yukon basin, from the warm air brought by the Japanese Current to the entire Pacific coast of Alaska. At Skagway a —20° F. cold snap will remain a topic of complaint for the rest of the winter, and at Sitka, a little farther down the coast, an average year brings only two sub-zero days. On the other hand, Fort Yukon, which lies across the mountains in the heart of the river basin, experiences 130 sub-zero days and in January the *average* temperature is —19° F. At a place called Snag, Yukon Territory, the airport thermometer fell to —81° F. one December night, the lowest temperature ever recorded in North America.

The climate of the Yukon is dry as well as cold, and for the same reason: the mountains block out the exceedingly moist air of the Pacific littoral. While the average annual precipitation at Juneau is sixty inches, a little to the north in the upper tip of the Yukon basin, it is a fifth of this. And the central part of the basin receives only 6.5 inches a year, less than Phoenix, Arizona.

The Yukon was the last major American river to be discovered by white men. It was most likely the first known to men, however, and these men were in all probability among the very first Americans. The aridity of the river's basin no doubt had much to do with this. During the last, or Wisconsin, glaciation, the Yukon valley was hemmed in by glaciers, but due to low precipitation it remained ice free. It was thus a corridor leading from the edge of Asia toward the heart of America, and during at least two periods, each lasting thousands of years, this corridor was connected with another similar one leading down east of the Rockies to the southern part of the continent where the glacial ice never reached. The Wisconsin glaciation caused so much of the earth's water supply to be locked up as ice that the sea level dropped by at least two hundred feet below where it stands today. As a result large portions of the shallow Bering Sea became dry land, and a wide bridge connected Siberia and Alaska. In all probability man, and many other mammals, reached the New World via this bridge, and penetrated the continent by following the valley of the Yukon. No doubt he came at many different times and as many different peoples, a sort of random sampling of the races that happened to be living in northeast Asia at the time. He was no conscious colonist or explorer, but a nomadic hunter led on by the animals whose flesh he ate. The date of his first arrival is no more certain than his identity, but it must have been well before 10,000 B.C., for by then he is already leaving an indisputable archeological record as far south as Mexico.

History is manifestly unfair to those who do not inscribe their deeds in words or temples. For thousands of years men lived on the Yukon, but all they left were occasional flint chips and obsidian scrapers, the ashes of their campfires and the mammoth bones they gnawed. Their chronicle is mute and they are thus only spectres in the mists of time, as incorporeal as the fog banks that drift into the Yukon delta from the sea they crossed dryshod. By the time events could be recorded in written words, 1,835 years of the Christian Era had passed and other migrants had reached the river from the other end of the earth. Thus, of all America's large rivers, the Yukon has the longest prehistory and the shortest recorded history.

2 *The Russians*

> On its banks live thousands who know neither its outlet nor its source, who look to it for food and even clothing, and, recognizing its magnificence, call themselves proudly *men of the Yukon.*
>
> —William H. Dall, *Alaska and Its Resources*

LIFE on the Yukon is hard. There is no fat on the land, nor is its scant bounty ever yielded up gratuitously. To survive, merely, is to succeed; to increase is to triumph. The region exhibits its poverty in numerous ways. In a year the sun radiates only about sixty-five thousand calories of heat per square centimeter of the land's surface, half the figure for New York State, a quarter of that for some tropical regions. The growing season is short, and nearly every part of the Yukon basin is subject to frost during every month of the year. The topsoil is thin and acidic where it exists at all, and even the bacteria that turn dead plants into humus work very slowly. In vast areas the subsoil is permanently frozen. Plants grow slowly, and it takes a white spruce, the region's most common tree, as long as two centuries to reach a diameter of fourteen inches. And since all animals depend on plants, or on plant-eating animals, they are neither so numerous nor represented by so many different species as in the ecosystems farther south. The aboriginal people of the Yukon basin have always been few and scattered; they roamed ceaselessly in search of an

8

uncertain sustenance and the memory of starvation was never lost among them.

Furs and gold. A rich dark lustre, a bright yellow glitter. Symbolic emblems of wealth, luxury, ease. No two products are less suggestive of the poverty of the Yukon, yet no others played such an important part in the first century of the river's brief recorded history. From a land where people regularly froze to death came furs to drape the silk-clad shoulders of English lords and ladies, Russian counts and courtesans, Manchu mandarins, American plutocrats. From a land where wealth was enough dried fish for the next two weeks came gold, symbol and substance of indestructible fortune, for the coffers of rich men and the treasuries of nations. At first it was furs alone that men sought on the Yukon. Then, beginning in the 1880s, and culminating in the discoveries on the Klondike, it was gold.

To the Russians, Alaska was not a proud extension of empire nor yet a monument to mercantilist economic theory. It was a fur farm. This was as true in the decades immediately following Bering's voyage of discovery as it was in the 1830s when the Russians reached the Yukon River. Only the form of the endeavor had changed. The fiercely independent *promyshlenniki*, hunter-traders of the early years, had been supplanted by a single monopolistic organization, the Russian-American Company. From barbarous and heroic beginnings, the fur quest had evolved into an increasingly well-regulated and civilized enterprise. Sitka, the center of operations after 1804, had grown from a precarious encampment of Aleut otter hunters and Russian convict laborers with native wives into an important Pacific port. Yankee captains bound for Canton called there, and packets brought in fresh food from the agricultural colony of Fort Ross, California. Sitka had a fine Orthodox cathedral, an academy complete with physics laboratory, a library and a shipyard that turned out the first steamship constructed on the Pacific. The aristocratic naval officers who administered Russian America from the 1830s on played whist, danced the quadrille and spoke Slavic-accented French. Sitka was a town of board sidewalks and neat wooden houses with window boxes full of flowers.

But despite its refinements Sitka was just as dependent on the sea otter and fur seal as any crude *promyshlennik*'s camp had been in the past. The pelts of these two marine mammals were the Russian-American Company's only product, and by the 1830s they were becoming scarce. Just as the *promyshlenniki* had nearly exterminated the sea otters on the Aleutians, so by now the company's hunters had decimated them along the coast of the Alaskan mainland. And the fur seals, which came each June to bear young and breed on the Pribilof Islands, were so reduced that the take fell from forty thousand in 1820 to five thousand in 1834. During the first twenty years of the nineteenth century the Russian-American Company had frequently paid dividends as high as 30 percent, but for four years of the following ten it had not paid a single *kopek*.

The alternative to bankruptcy was new fur sources. Since the early days the Russians had confined their operations almost entirely to the coast. Now they would extend the quest for furs into the uncharted interior. Already in 1818 a party of explorer-traders had crossed the Alaska Peninsula to the Bering seacoast where they established a post at the mouth of the Nushagak River. In 1829 a party from this post ascended the Nushagak, crossed a height of land just north of it, and discovered the Kuskokwim, a large river running more or less parallel to the lower Yukon. In descending the Kuskokwim to the Bering Sea they had—perhaps unknowingly—come within thirty-five miles of the Yukon.

Two years later Lieutenant Michael Tebenkov, a naval officer, was sent to make a reconnaissance of the Bering coast. In the course of doing so he was told by Eskimos of a large river reaching the sea just north of the Kuskokwim. The Eskimos called it the Kuikpak, "kuik" for large or great, "pak" for river. It was the Yukon they were referring to, and the Russians adopted their name for it. In 1833 Tebenkov returned to the region to establish a base for the penetration of the big river he still had not seen. Near the Yukon delta the coast is low and harborless; the best site that Tabenkov could find was a barren wind-swept island just offshore; here he built a fortified trading post called Redoubt St. Michael.

At no time did the number of Russians in Alaska even approach one thousand. The Company therefore relied to a great extent on the creoles, as they were called, the offspring of Russian-native unions. The creoles were excellent intermediaries between the Russians and the natives, for while they knew Russian and many of the techniques of the Russians, they also knew the languages of the natives and had their aptitude for such skills as driving sled dogs and living off the land. Quite naturally they supplied the Company with some of its finest explorers.

Andrei Glazunov was one of them. Beyond the fact that he went to school in Sitka, we know almost nothing about this man's early life. He was evidently quite well educated by the standards of his time and place, for he was literate in Russian, fluent in several native languages, and skilled in the use of navigational instruments. Judging by the responsibilities he was entrusted with, it is obvious that his superiors held him in considerable esteem.

Glazunov had come with Tebenkov to establish Redoubt St. Michael, and after the lieutenant had left, late in the summer of 1833, he remained there. That winter he was given command of an exploring party consisting of five Russians and three natives. His orders were to penetrate inland to the region where the Kuikpak was thought to flow and to chart a portion of its course. Following this, he was to traverse nearly a third of Alaska, all of it completely unknown, to the head of Cook Inlet, the site of present day Anchorage. Though Glazunov would not accomplish the second part of his mission, his journey was to be the first significant penetration of the interior of western Alaska. He kept a journal of the expedition, which, before it was lost, was published in a paraphrased French translation.

In January 1834, Glazunov and his eight men set out from St. Michael Redoubt by dogsled. They carried a supply of trade goods to barter for food and native goodwill, but they took little actual food, an omission that would cost them dearly. The midwinter journey, in almost perpetual darkness, was extremely diffi-

cult. The Russians were inexperienced in the use of snowshoes, dogs and sleds; the snow was deep, the trail unbroken and often uncertain. "They were exhausted with fatigue," reads the French version of Glazunov's journal, "and had scarcely enough to satisfy their hunger. . . . While they were seated around the fire and trying mutually to encourage each other, two ptarmigan flew down so near to them that they were able to seize them with their hands. This gift of God was a great consolation to them." But such gifts were rare. For days their only food was the dried fish they found in the summer caches of the natives.

After nearly two weeks they reached the crests of the low tundra hills that separate the Bering Sea littoral from the forested interior. On the eastern slope of these hills they came to the sources of the Anvik River and they followed this stream down about a hundred miles. At dusk on February 4, 1834, as they drew near the mouth of the Anvik, they sighted in the distance a large Indian village, the first they had seen. Just beyond it lay the Kuikpak—the Yukon—a white ribbon of snow-covered ice a mile across. No white man had seen this river before. Nor had the people of this village, or any other along the river, yet seen white

men. The interaction of these three elements, river, white men
and natives, would form the leitmotif of many future decades of
the Yukon's history.

The initial contact of the three was not particularly propitious.
Glazunov had felt it advisable to wait till next morning to enter
the village. His party, however, had already been observed.

As soon as the inhabitants had seen them [recounts Glazunov's
journal] they went out in large numbers from their houses and
climbed on the rooftops while shouting loudly and holding bows and
arrows in their hands. But Glazunov took care to stop out of range
of the arrows and to send one of his companions to the Indians to
show them that they had nothing to fear from such a small number of
strangers, adding that, if they [the Indians] refused to deal with them,
the Russian party would pass by the village without even entering.
This discourse quieted the savages, who lay aside their bows and
arrows, and sent toward the newcomers ten old men who invited them
to come and rest in the village.

Glazunov installed his men, their guns loaded in case of trouble,
in the proffered shelter and went himself to the kashim, the un-

derground communal house of the village men. He was given
the place of honor; from it, in the dim light of fish-oil lamps, he
counted 240 men; they had just finished their daily sweat baths
and were stark naked. Through an interpreter he delivered a
speech in which he told the assembled men of the village of
Anvik that he had been sent by his chiefs to invite them to
come and trade with the Russians at St. Michael. In exchange for
their furs, he said, they would receive many things of great value.
After the discourse Glazunov passed out tobacco and snuff, and it
is a wonder that amicable relations did not cease at once. For
some of the Indians "were so much dazed by the smoke that they
fell unconscious" while others "inhaled such a quantity [of snuff]
that they could not stop sneezing."

After the meeting in the kashim the Indians said to Glazunov,
"Tell us what you need, and we will be eager to furnish it to you,
now that we are persuaded of the good intentions of the Russians." During the rest of his stay in Anvik they supplied him and
his party with all the food, wood and water they could use.

The reaction of the people in the second Yukon village
Glazunov visited was much the same. At first sight of the Russians, they "took flight immediately and sent their women and
children to a nearby mountain." But they were coaxed back, and
again Glazunov was invited to the kashim. He gave his speech
inviting them to trade at St. Michael, and again they responded
favorably. One of the old men of the place confided to Glazunov,
"Now we shall no more believe what has been said to us of the
Russians, that their nails and teeth are of iron; we see that the
Russians are men like us, and we are thankful to know the truth.
We will come to visit your forts and are all disposed to trade with
you."

3 The Native People I

The wind blows over the Yukon.
My husband hunts deer on the Koyukon hills.
Ahmi, little one, sleep.

There is no firewood.
The stone axe is broken, my husband has the other.
Ahmi, little one, sleep.

There is no sun.
Is it hiding in the beaver house waiting for spring?
Ahmi, little one, sleep.

There is no *ukali.*°
The raven knows and lights no more on the cache.
Ahmi, little one, sleep.

Long since my husband departed.
What keeps him on the mountain?
Ahmi, little one, sleep softly.

—Koyukon Lullaby

° dried salmon

EARLY in February 1834, Glazunov left Anvik to continue his voyage toward Cook Inlet. Soon thereafter a wood carver of the village fashioned a mask depicting his strange looks and ways; it was hung in the kashim where Glazunov had stayed. The people

of Anvik concluded that the Russian and his men were reincarna-
tions of their own ancestors; they had been so long in the nether
world that they had turned pale and forgotten the Ingalik language. Only later did they realize that for them Glazunov was a
man of fate, the advance messenger of an utterly alien culture
that before too long would destory their own. The first white
man had come among them, and nothing would be the same
again.

Or at least almost nothing. True, there is still a town about
where the old Anvik stood, but even the Anvik River has
changed, now entering the Yukon a mile or two above the site.
There is no kashim any more, nor any underground houses. People live in log cabins, and though the roofs are covered with dirt
in the old way, the dirt is in turn covered over with sheets of
galvanized steel from Pittsburgh, or Gary, Indiana. In places a
sheet or two has slipped and thick clumps of weeds thrust up like
strands of unruly hair.

Backed up against Hawk Bluff is Anvik's one store. William
Chase, a tall, spare-framed man, half Indian, half white, runs it,
and what he stocks is as good an indication as any of how the
neolithic village Glazunov visited has changed. On the crowded
shelves Chef Boyardee spaghetti, Spam, Green Giant Peas and a
hundred other canned foods vie for space with fifty-pound sacks
of flour and sugar, bottles of viscous hair tonic, tubes of green
shampoo, home-permanent kits, aluminum pots and frying pans
lined with Teflon. A batch of quilted green synthetic-fiber parkas
hang from the rafters among Coleman lanterns and rubberized
raincoats from Japan. On the counter a couple of transistorized
forty-five r.p.m. record players await buyers next to a stack of
recent rock-'n'-roll releases. These are now the artifacts of Ingalik
daily life.

Nor have traditional religious beliefs outlasted the old technology. Anvik was the site of the first Episcopal church in Alaska,
and before the turn of the century most of its people had already
been converted. On Sundays the majority of villagers attend the
services in Christ Church, a fine old shingled structure between

Chase's store and the Yukon. Even the nonchurchgoers make sure that Mr. McGinnis, the amiable red-haired minister, baptizes their children and buries their elders: there are no village atheists as yet in Anvik. At the opposite end of town Miss Mary Light of Arctic Missions, Inc., offers a more fundamentalist version of Christianity. A short plump lady with a shrill voice, she fervently exhorts the villagers to "get right with the Lord." "God's just gotta take hold of this place and really shake it up," she explains. Already at least one person, William Chase's son Ernie, has been shaken, according to Miss Light; he gave up blasphemous language and strong drink, and the night he made his stand for the Lord he tossed his last pack of cigarettes out the bedroom window. As Miss Light says, "Christ came in and all that other stuff got chucked clean out."

Clearly, the Anvik of Glazunov's time has long since disappeared. There are, however, several reasons for trying to form a picture of what life was like there. For one thing, the Ingaliks of Anvik have a close racial, linguistic and cultural affinity to all other Indians living on the Yukon. Like the rest, they are of Athapascan stock* and were formerly seminomadic hunter-fishermen; they therefore serve well as a prototype of the others. Then too the Ingalik way of life as Glazunov knew it was probably quite similar to that which had been lived on the river for centuries, even millennia, of its prehistory. And finally, the Ingaliks, like other native people of the Yukon, are today domi-

* The Ingaliks are the westernmost branch of the Athapascan linguistic family. Five other branches live along the Yukon, each with its own dialect. Upriver from the Ingaliks are, in succession, the Koyukons, centered around Nulato and the Koyukuk River valley; the Tananas, between Ruby and Stevens Village; the Kutchin of the Yukon Flats; the Han concentrated near the Canada-U.S. boundary; and the Tutchone of the Canadian Yukon. The Athapascan stock predominates in much of interior northwest America, but is also represented by the Navajos and Apaches who are thought to have migrated southward in relatively recent times. For data on the distribution of the Yukon Athapascans, and for much information on the Ingaliks themselves, I am indebted to Dr. Cornelius Osgood of the Department of Anthropology, Yale University.

nated, even overwhelmed, by the conflict between their traditional culture and that of the white man; any attempt to understand their dilemma must begin with a look backward at the
ancestral past.

When Glazunov reached Anvik, the ancestors of the people
who now depend on the white man's goods and gods were living
in the Stone Age. All the crude tools they possessed they made
themselves, and the food that sustained them they snared,
speared, netted or picked in the country round about. They
hunted with birch bows and with arrows tipped with heads cut
from the tibia of the caribou. They caught fish in nets of woven
willow bark or knotted babiche thongs. Their pots were of birch
bark sewn together with spruce roots. Their knives were of stone,
bone, or the incisors of the beaver, their fishhooks of hawk claws.
They made their clothes of caribou, dog salmon or duck skin,
stitched together with braided sinew. They produced fire by
whirling a wooden drill with a thong, and light by burning fish oil
on moss wicks. They beat out their music on beluga drumheads.
Their food was fish mainly, and a favorite dish was prepared by
dumping fish eggs (which had been stored in fishskin bags or old
fishskin boots long enough to develop hard crusts) into a broth of
rotten black fish. For soap and for hair tonic they used urine. In
the winter they lived underground; in the summer, in fragile
shelters of cottonwood bark.

In Glazunov's time, the Ingaliks treated a headache by thrust-
ing the head into the snow, and an earache by burning the tip of
a ground squirrel's tail and directing the smoke to the afflicted
ear. A toothache was alleviated by nibbling at the inner side of
the dorsal fin of a grayling. To fill a cavity, one poked the end of
a sharp narrow bone into it, and then broke the bone off at tooth
level. A thong of babiche was crammed down the throat to in-
duce vomiting, and inserted into the anus to effect an enema. For
more serious ailments a shaman was called in. Lieutenant L. A.
Zagoskin of the Russian Navy, who visited Anvik about a decade
after Glazunov, describes the procedure:

In the corner [of the kashim] was seated a sick person; he had . . .
a pain in the small of his back. In front of him two oil lamps burned;

over his head lay the back of his parka; on each side of him a shaman was beating a tambourine, and behind them was an old woman with dishevelled hair. She croaked like a crow and pecked with her nose at the sick man's back . . . she changed her voice and jabbered like a magpie, barked like a dog. At last she started to howl like a wolf and started jumping at the sick man, pretending she wanted to chew at his back then that she had picked something from the same place, which she threw up into the air. The ringing of the tambourines got stronger; the old woman jumped and grabbed the parka from the sick man and shook it violently, then she took the brush-broom and began to fan the air with it, pretending that she was chasing some spirit out through the hatchway. Four others climbed up on the roof, beat their tambourines and hollered, "He run! He run! Oooh! Oooh!" The old woman fainted, or pretended to. This was the third spirit she chased out from the sick man's body, but nobody knew how many more were left inside him. If it was the last one the sick man should get better; otherwise the shamanizing would be continued at the wish of the sick man who pays for this doctoring in a big way.

The Anvik that Glazunov and Zagoskin knew was not a village of permanent residents but the occasional gathering place of a seminomadic people. The poor land could not support the Ingaliks in large, concentrated settlements. As its fauna moved over the hills and through the waters, so did the Ingaliks. And the axis of all their movements was the river itself. The name they and other Athapascans gave it clearly reflects this. "Yukon" does not mean "great river" as is often supposed, but something approximating "river par excellence," the quintessence and central reference point in that category of natural phenomena called rivers. And so indeed it was. When they traveled, they usually traveled along it; the Yukon meant hundreds of miles of navigable waterway, while ten feet from its banks began a nearly impenetrable jungle of spruce, willow and bog. Like the Egyptians, the Ingaliks seldom strayed far from their river, and when they paused long enough to call a place home the Yukon was usually in sight. As the Nile brought fertile muck to a race of farmers, the Yukon brought salmon to a race of fishermen. Each summer these fish ascended out of the Bering Sea, the three species in an unvarying seasonal sequence. The salmon run was just as mysterious

and mystical to the Ingalik as the Nile flood was to the ancient
Egyptian: each year the manna was given, from where no one
knew, nor why, though both people invented improbable explanations which they took only half-seriously. Like the Nile, the
Yukon demarcated the seasons: winter began when it froze up,
summer when the ice went out. Commerce and customs, legends
and gods, wars, plagues and news all moved along it. For the
Ingaliks, as for other people of the river, the dirty, grey Yukon
was the essential thread holding the world together, the most
fundamental of nature's constants. Heaven was at its headwaters,
all humanity along its course. And where the river ended in the
sea, so did the earth.

The Ingalik verb *esnaih* means to move, together with one's
family and possessions, not to a fixed destination, but to a place
where one stops moving. Such migrations were an essential part
of the seasonal rhythm of Ingalik life. Anvik was a winter village
only. Early in spring its inhabitants put their canoes and gear on
sleds and wandered up and down the river until they found
propitious places at which to stop wandering. Ideally, such places
had abundant sources of fish and game, good clear water, dead
trees and drift logs for firewood. For the first month or two they
caught and smoked grayling, pike, whitefish and inconnu, but
from June on they concentrated on salmon. If they had a good
year they would arrive back in Anvik with enough dried fish to
last themselves and their dogs through the winter. If not, they
were forced to *esnaih* in winter as well.

In the village they lived in underground houses, crude structures, dark and dank and subject to flooding during thaws. The
smaller winter houses were the domain of women; in them they
bore their children on grass-covered sleeping shelves, and dressed
their daughters in discarded skins and secluded them in a corner
for a whole year following first menstruation; here they prepared
their food and ate, and here they usually died.

For the men the center of village life was the kashim, a structure like the winter houses of the women, but much larger and
better constructed. They spent much of the long winter twilight
there making sleds and lamps and caribou bone arrowheads and

a hundred other crude implements. All the male *rites de passage* took place in the kashim: the ritual of naming a boy, the feast honoring him for the first eatable thing he killed, and the insertion of labrets (bone plugs) into his lower lip through holes cut with a bone awl. And the high point of every winter day, the sweat bath, was held there. A blazing fire would be built and, as the temperature rose far above a hundred, men stripped naked and shoved wads of bound-up shavings into their mouths to protect their lungs from the heat. They sat or lay quietly on the benches, sweating profusely. From time to time they would go to their birch bark urine bowls and pour the contents into their hair and over their bodies. Adolescents used the urine of their grandfathers, as it was supposed to bring wisdom and good luck. If one were plagued with lice—and the name Anvik apparently means "the place of louse eggs"—one bathed in urine that had been fortified by a few days' evaporation.

As the fire died down, the men pulled on their skin clothes and sat relaxed in the warm kashim waiting for their suppers. In time their wives would lift the bearskin at the tunnel entrance and set down bowls of fish or flesh, dried, rotten or raw, before them. As the men ate the women squatted patiently on the floor waiting to take the empty bowls back to their dwellings where they and their children would eat later. Not long after supper the men lay down on the benches along the walls of the kashim, wrapped themselves in their caribou blankets and went to sleep.

As with all people, the material and social worlds of the Ingaliks were intimately linked with a spiritual one that gave meaning to life and coherence to its events. Though people in Anvik still cling to fragments of their old beliefs, most no longer have a clear idea of the whole from which the fragments were sundered.

Billy Williams, a man in his eighties, comes as near to being an exception to this as anybody still living in Anvik. Sitting on a pillow in a stiff-backed chair in his cabin, he talks to a visitor. His voice, cavernous and husky but peculiarly sonorous, drones on into the summer evening as his mind goes back, recollecting, reliving, the things he has heard from his parents and his grandparents, old stories told and retold in the kashims of his ancestors. He stops only to tap his pipe against the heel of his boot, stuff more Prince Albert into the bowl, and relight it with a long wooden match. In the glow his hooded eyes, one of them opaque and blind, glisten slightly; they are the moist crying eyes of a very old man. The match illuminates a long narrow face, the color of unpolished bronze; the cheekbones are high and prominent. No passing Caucasian miner or steamboat man accounts for a single gene in his body. Out through the window in back of Billy's chair the last oblique rays of a long subarctic summer day incandesce in a field of shimmering foxtails. The man next door is chopping wood for his supper fire. Children's voices echo in the distance; now and then a few syllables drift up clear and distinct from the babble. It is English they are speaking, not Ingalik.

Billy Williams begins telling an old, old tale of a dying culture. It is the Ingalik Genesis. The children outside do not know it; they know only the Genesis of the Christian missionaries.

Raven-Man coming down. Nobody. Nothing. Pretty soon he see the big river, Yukon. Coming down in fishskin canoe, you know, made from dog salmon. Don't see nobody all the way down from all the way up there. Only seen Camp Robber [the grey Canada jay], that's all he seen. He don't know which way to go. Well, Camp Robber there, and he ask Raven-Man, "What do you want?"

And Raven-Man say, "You got anything to eat?"

And Camp Robber say, "I got nothing. What's 'eat' anyhow? Don't know how to eat. Never ate all my life."

"How do you live then?"

"I live on wind. When wind blow, I open my mouth. That make me live. How about you?"

And Raven-Man say, "Oh, I walk around everywhere. Sometime I find fish. That's what I live on. I got no house to live in though."

The two camp together, and Raven-Man has a supper of fish. After the meal they lie around the fire and talk.

Camp Robber ask Raven-Man, "What you going to do?"

"I don't know what I going to do. I been traveling all over the land; never seen even a soul of people. You first one I ever saw. . . . What you think, there going to be people here?"

"I don't know. Where you go now, up or down [the river]?"

And Raven-Man say, "Maybe up, maybe down."

"You better go down, with the current." He throw a stick in the water and they watch it float down. "As far as you go there won't be no people, nobody."

And Raven-Man say, "They got lots of people where you come from?"

"Oh, not very much. You go down and I go up home, but we meet here later on. I wait for you."

Raven-Man say, "All right." And he get in his fishskin canoe.

Camp Robber shove him off and he tell him, "Watch out. Take good care of yourself. If you see somebody anyplace, don't camp with them. They might eat you."

And Raven-Man say, "I been all over; never seen nobody and I won't see none now neither." And he went down the river.

Pretty soon Raven-Man he see high bank with lots of good timber. He say to himself, "Going to be village here." He take some bark from cottonwood tree and he make two arms and then two legs and then he make body of little man. Then he take some more bark, and he done the same thing for a little woman. They was real little, you know, no bigger than that cup there. He stick them in the ground up on high bank facing Yukon, and he say to them, "When I come back up river there going to be lots of people here. That's what I made you for."

Well, he get back in his canoe and he go a little way down, to where there's a high bluff on the left limit. You know, that bluff just below Eagle?* That's where it was. Raven-Man he turn around and look back to the high bank and he see smoke coming up, and lots of house, too. He say to himself, "Going to be lots of people now. Sure looked funny without no people 'round. Got to have people, anyhow."

Raven-Man he come all the way down the river doing that, making people out of cottonwood bark. He did it with his stick knife and after

---

* The left limit is the left bank of the river as one *descends*. Billy Williams had worked on a gold rush sternwheeler, the *Seattle Number Three*, and he picked up the term there. The designation is still current today though the steamboats have disappeared. Eagle is the first town on the Yukon after it leaves Canada, and the high bluff to which he refers is Calico Bluff.

making some people his knife wore out and he had to get a new one. So people along Yukon made with different knife and that's why they all talk a little different. Like them fellers down at Russian Mission. We can't understand them.

Raven-Man finally gets down to the mouth of the Yukon, turns around and starts back up again.

Pretty soon he comes to a village. They got men there, and they all look kinda funny at him.

Raven-Man says, "What's the matter with you fellers? Don't you know me?"

"We never seen you before," they say.

"Who do you peoples think you are? I made you. If I didn't make you there'd be no peoples over all the world and that sure would look funny."

Raven-Man spent two days there. It was down near the Yukon mouth at where they now call Fort Hamilton. He teach them peoples how to make bow and arrow and spear and pots from birch bark. He teach them how to catch fish and cut it [for drying or smoking] and how to hunt. After two days he say to them, "I guess you going to be all right now. Now you got to go by what I told you, else you won't get a living."

So he leave and go upriver and each time he come to a place where he made people, he see lots of people and lots of house. Underground house, you know, like we used to have. At each place he tell the peoples how to live, each village by [according to] what kind of a country it's in and what kinda game they got there.

He finally comes to the place where he and Camp Robber had planned to meet. A big village now stands on each side of the Yukon there. Camp Robber is waiting for him.

Camp Robber say, "Hello. I been looking for you all summer."

And Raven-Man say, "Oh, I been downriver making lots of people."

"Me too. I made lots of people, but upriver. Lots of people upriver now too." You know, up in Canada, towards Dawson.

And then each one went his own way, Raven-Man to continue his eternal wandering, Camp Robber to his "good home in woods where my people's at."

Raven-Man was the most important figure in the Ingalik pantheon. Not only did he create mankind; he created death and the afterlife. His motives, methods, and accomplishments illustrate the extraordinary fusion in the traditional scheme of things of the natural and the supernatural, the human and the superhuman, and the tremendous distance between the old beliefs and the ones the people of Anvik are now taught to accept.

Long ago, the story goes, no one died. This, however, posed problems for Raven-Man. For one thing, he found his mother-in-law much more attractive than his wife, but had no way of getting rid of the latter. For another, the absence of death had resulted in a grave overpopulation problem, and when he went to set his fish trap he could find no good spot that was unoccupied. For a long time he pondered these problems, but at last he had an inspiration. He put on his best parka and prepared for a journey. His wife, apprehensive, asked him, "What are you going to do?"

"I'm going out," he replied.

"Where?"

"Oh, someplace."

"When will you be back?"

"In a while, I guess. Maybe by dinnertime."

He is gone for two full years. During this time he digs a very long tunnel which comes out on the bank of the Yukon far from the village. At the end of it he constructs two summer houses of cottonwood bark. Returning to the village, he hopes to find his attractive mother-in-law sick. He is in luck, for soon after his arrival she stops eating and takes on a ghostly appearance. Raven-Man's wife goes to her and asks what the matter is. The woman does not reply, but starts to flee. Her daughter tries to grab her, but it is as though she were made of air. Raven-Man has been watching all this surreptitiously, and as his mother-in-law flees he follows, subtly guiding her to the entrance of his tunnel. The two of them enter, and for four days they walk through it, coming out

finally at the riverbank where Raven-Man has constructed the
two summer houses. Raven-Man now invites his mother-in-law to
share his bed in one of the houses, and there she stays until the
fourth day when he tells her to move over to the other house
which is to be her own. "If you want me," he informs her, "you
can come over here, and if I want you I'll come over there."
Raven-Man now has both his mother-in-law and plenty of places
for his fish traps.

From that time on, death has been as universal as life. When a
man dies, he enters the tunnel just as his coffin is removed from
the kashim after the wake. Near the entrance is a seat and he sits
down, feeling very sad. But soon he notices that he is dressed in a
fine new parka and that a bowl of fish oil "ice cream," the great
Ingalik delicacy, has been placed next to him. He is cheered.
Then, as the funeral chants attending the removal of the coffin

from the kashim begin, he gets up and sets out on his journey through the tunnel. At convenient places along the way he finds more bowls of food; they have been placed there by the efforts of his wife or a near relative who, during the four days of his journey, throws bits and scraps into the cooking fire. At the end of the fourth day the person emerges from the tunnel. If it is a woman, two sticks in Raven-Man's fireplace suddenly flare up to announce her arrival. Raven-Man goes to the door just as she stops in front of it. She notices that he is a very handsome man indeed and is delighted. If she is pretty, he spends two nights with her, if not, only one. The morning of her departure he cooks her a big meal and tells her to be on her way. If the traveler emerging from the tunnel is a man, two sticks flare up in the fire of Raven-Man's mother-in-law. A pot of water sits on top of this fire, and it now suddenly comes to a boil. The mother-in-law is old and none too

pretty, but as the water boils she jumps into the pot. When she comes out she is young-looking and beautiful. She sits on the edge of her bed until the man comes. He stays with her one or two days, depending on his appeal to her. Next to the mother-in-law's house is a stone pillar put there by Denato, the creator, to hold up the sky. When her visitors are too infrequent and she gets lonely, she shakes this pillar, causing an earthquake. It is a sure way to increase the traffic. After leaving one or the other of the houses the deceased darts like a fly to the river's edge. Here he is welcomed by the people of the hereafter who arrive in a flotilla of canoes to take him to their village. Life there is just like life on earth except that death does not exist and there is no hunger.

The Ingalik universe is divided into those forces that are harmful to man and those that are beneficial to him. Chief among the harmful ones is Giyeg. Some say that Giyeg appears as a whirlwind or a shriveled old man, but others insist that he has never been seen, for he always travels underground, his shadow alone visible on the surface. All agree that it is Giyeg who causes human beings to die. Raven-Man might have created death, but Giyeg, with his constant need for human flesh, brings it about. He feeds on men in just the same way the Ingalik feeds on salmon and caribou and he is in no way morally evil for doing so. He can only attack a man when his spirit, or *yeg*, has wandered from his body, so naturally he attempts to lure it away. This happens, for example, in dreams. Sickness occurs when Giyeg is trying to consume a temporarily *yeg*-less body. If the errant *yeg* returns in time the man will revive; if not he will die. Since the shaman alone is versed in the language of the human *yeg* he is hired, sometimes at exorbitant fees, to try to lure it back or at least to ward off Giyeg until it comes back of its own volition. All men will eventually be caught with their yegs wandering, but he who obeys an extraordinarily long and complicated list of taboos will ward off Giyeg the longest.

Giyeg has several categories of helpers, the most feared of which are the Nahoens. A Nahoen is vaguely manlike; it has eight-inch fingernails, wears a conical fish trap for a hat, has hair streaming down to its feet, and travels three feet above the ground. Nahoens are the descendants of people who, in the days before death, got lost and went insane. They are dangerous because they are fond of stealing children, but they do this only in summer; in winter they are quite harmless. If a person eats two human eyes he will turn into a Nahoen because hc will have taken in "too much power." This happens rarely, however, and then only when a person's insatiable curiosity has driven him to test whether it really will happen or not.

The Ingalik scheme of things was much less egocentric than ours. Man was in no way unique in possessing an immortal spirit. Each living thing had its *yeg*, and so did many inanimate objects. Survival was thought to be absolutely dependent on man's maintaining proper relations with the yegs of the creatures which sustained him. Of these none was more important than the salmon. His smoked flesh was the staple winter food of the people of Anvik, and of their sled dogs. His oil lit the kashim. His skin, made into parkas, protected from the elements.

According to tradition, salmon lived in three underwater villages, one for each of the three species that migrate up the Yukon. They had kashims, just like those of the Ingaliks, and they wore fine parkas. In spring the King (Chinook) salmon, the first to arrive at Anvik, would go to the village of the Dog (Chum) salmon, the second to arrive, and announce, while flopping on his tail in the kashim, that there would be a great potlatch upriver. He would then go to the village of the Silver (Coho) salmon and do the same. Returning to his own village, he and the other "men" there would load their families into canoes and paddle upriver. If the Ingalik had the right communication with the salmon *yeg*, he could place his traps and nets so that the fish thought they were potlatch gifts and entered. The salmon *yeg* did not mind this bit of trickery as long as it was well treated, and the Ingalik made sure that it was. When the first salmon of the season was caught in Anvik it was broiled on special sticks in the kashim while the men took their sweat baths. This was important, for a salmon *yeg* loved both being in the kashim and taking the bath. Shortly he would return to his village and tell those who were still there what a good time he had had. They would finally be convinced that it really was a splendid potlatch and set out immediately upriver toward the nets and traps of the Ingaliks. Each person in Anvik was given a small piece of the first salmon. He would eat a bit of it and throw the rest into the Yukon, saying, "Swim away with my sleep," for long days of hard work were now at hand.

The time for talk among Ingalik men was the evening after supper. Though the Arctic winter might clinch Anvik in its vise grip and immobilize the landscape to absolute petrifaction, the inside of the kashim was warm and comfortable. The dim light of the fish-oil lamps waved unevenly up from the floor to disappear against the roof rafters, blackened with the smoke of a thousand fires of a thousand winter evenings. The men sat back, languid with food and the aftereffects of the sweat bath. They told stories: an account, maybe, of the last bear hunt, rendered with the utmost realism and precision of detail; or a tale of long ago when the giants who stalked the coast of the Bering Sea were all slain by pygmies who chopped them down at the Achilles tendon. Or perhaps there were no stories, just a review of the events of the day and the gossip of the village. As they talked and listened their hands worked silently away at the implements of Stone Age technology.

Late in the winter of 1834 one of them was carving the mask of Glazunov. Perhaps the talk turned to the portent of his visit.

4 Nulato

A little Innuit lad, who ran before the dogs and
saw it for the first time, shouted at the sight,
saying, amidst his expressions of astonishment,
"It is not a river, it is a sea!" and even the Indians had no word of ridicule for him, often as
they had seen it.

—William H. Dall
Alaska and Its Resources

ONE HUNDRED and seventy miles upstream from Anvik a graveyard, visible for miles around, perches high on a bluff. Since it is
crowded and the terrain steep, some of its occupants are unhap-
pily beginning to slip down the bluff's rocky edges; each spring
the departing frost heaves the ground, giving them a further
push. The graveyard is a miniature city of tin-roofed spirit
houses. From its vantage point there is an excellent view of
Nulato, tin-roofed and small enough in the distance so that it too
looks like a spirit city.

Nulato is much like villages farther up the Yukon. There is little
left to suggest that a layer of history quite different from theirs
was once deposited here. A few outcrops are still visible, however. For one thing, the older spirit houses in the graveyard are
laid out precisely parallel to the river. For another, the surnames
Demoski and Sapiry are common in the village. Aside from these
vestiges, nothing remains to indicate that Nulato represented the
highwater mark of Russian settlement in the interior of North

America, nor that their post here was once the most important on the Yukon.

One of the main objectives of Glazunov's journey into the interior was the discovery of good locations for fur-trading posts. Upon his return to St. Michael in the spring of 1834, he recommended two such sites, one at Anvik and another at Ikogmut, the present-day village of Russian Mission. In 1836 or 1837 the Russian-American Company established a station at the latter site, its first on the Yukon.

Glazunov's explorations on the Yukon did not take him farther upstream than Anvik, and it was left to a fellow creole named Malakov to reconnoiter the region above. Malakov left by dogsled from St. Michael in February 1838. He traversed northeast over the Bering Sea ice to the mouth of the Unalakleet River where a well-used portage trail to the Yukon began. He crossed the trail without difficulty, and when he reached the Yukon he ascended it fifty miles to the mouth of the Nulato River. Here he found a little Indian village whose twenty-nine inhabitants were just then being visited by a trading party from another tribe. Malakov discovered that the place was a sort of local entrepôt. Indians from all over the region came there to purchase the goods brought in by the Eskimos on the coast. The latter provided not only seal and whale oil, but Circassian tobacco and copper spears bearing the imprint of a forge in Irkutsk, Siberia, that they received in barter with the Chukchi tribesmen on the Russian side of Bering Strait. In addition to being a center of trade, Nulato was known as a good fishing site; indeed, the name means "place where Dog salmon come" in the Koyukon dialect spoken there. Malakov was welcomed by the Nulato Indians and encouraged by their chief, Unilla, to establish a post. He was encouraged too by the 350 beaver skins he was able to barter by the time he left in May. He returned to St. Michael by drifting down the Yukon to its mouth and then sailing across the sixty-five miles of Norton Sound.

Nulato was obviously a propitious site for a trading post, and Malakov's superiors in the Russian-American Company supported his recommendation that one be established there. Accordingly, in November 1838 he again left St. Michael for Nulato. This time he was accompanied by Vasili Deriabin, a veteran of Glazunov's explorations, and by several others. When, early in April, the Russians reached Nulato, the village was in a deplorable state, having been ravaged by an epidemic of the "pox." Unilla, the chief with whom Malakov had been friendly on his last trip, had lost all his wives and sons. In despair he burned the village kashim and his own underground *barabara*. Then he entered a third dwelling, put it to the torch, and sat inside watching it burn until he was consumed. In the spring the starving dogs ate the corpses of their masters, for no one left was well enough to put the bodies up in tree platforms, as was the custom.

Despite the carnage, Malakov set about building a post. He planned to spend the coming winter there, but both he and Deriabin were forced the return to St. Michael as they could not possibly barter enough food to sustain them from the few Indians who had survived the pox. A man named Nordstrom was left in charge there, however, and he apparently remained until the summer of 1840. When he departed, the post was abandoned entirely. A year later, in September 1841, Deriabin returned to find all the fur company's buildings burnt to the ground, the native *barabaras* in ruins and Nulato totally deserted. He built a new post, located on the north bank of the Nulato River about half a mile to the south of the present-day village. Gradually the Indians, pockmarked and miserable, drifted back to Nulato and trade was resumed.

In 1843 Lieutenant L. A. Zagoskin of the Russian Navy used Nulato as a headquarters for his extensive and well-documented exploration of the region. He and his men helped Deriabin expand the post, which, by the time he left, included a large barracks where the four Russian workers lived, a fur storehouse, a kitchen, a new steam bath, and a hall.

Zagoskin arrived in Nulato in January with five sleds, a personal servant, an interpreter and four creole hunters. He stayed till June when he set out up the Yukon; until this expedition the river above Nulato was unknown to the Russians. Zagoskin

reached a point in the vicinity of the Nowitna River, about two
hundred miles above Nulato; here, he reported, further progress
was blocked by "rapids."* Along the route Zagoskin was careful
to make friends for the Russian-American Company by judicious
gifts of tea and sugar. He also engaged in trade, finding that
woven cloth, which the Indians had never seen before, was an
especially prized item. He and his men literally traded the shirts
off their backs, and "even our underwear" for beaver and marten
pelts.

For eight years following Zagoskin's departure, Deriabin carried on the fur trade at Nulato. Business was good, especially in
beaver, which abounded in the myriad watercourses of the
Kaiyuh Flats just across the Yukon from the village. During a
single season, Deriabin took in over three thousand of these pelts
alone, and there were marten, fox, wolf, lynx and bear as well. In
exchange for fur, he bartered such items as glass beads, needles,
knives, hatchets, earrings, cloth, copper kettles, mirrors and tobacco. He did not deal either in guns or liquor as John Jacob
Astor and the Hudson's Bay Company had done. The simple
trade goods which he offered quickly altered the primitive technology of the natives. Zagoskin observed during his stay at
Nulato that stone axes and bone needles were no longer being
made, and that the people were forgetting how to make fire by
rubbing sticks together. The overwhelming superiority of the
cheapest, crudest metal axe, for example, over the finest one that
the most consummate craftsman in stone could turn out, was such
that the Russians had no difficulty in attracting customers and
their furs. The Indians soon learned to drive a hard bargain,
however. "What exchanged before for three leaves of tobacco,"
Zagoskin lamented, "now costs one pound of it. It is just like in
our Russia. . . ."

In 1848, several thousand miles to the northwest of Nulato, the
last survivors of Sir John Franklin's third voyage of exploration

* These "rapids" were perhaps a figment of Zagoskin's imagination,
though this seems unlikely as he was a reliable and cautious observer. In
any event, if they ever existed, they have since been eroded away.

stumbled off their ships, struggled over the jagged pack ice of the Polar Sea, and perished. During the next few years numerous search parties were sent out to find Franklin or his remains. In the summer of 1850 H.M.S. *Enterprise*, engaged in the search for Franklin, dropped anchor at St. Michael. Captain Collison, in command, made inquiries of the Russian officers there and was told of vague rumors to the effect that white men had been seen in the valley of the Koyukuk River, a major tributary meeting the Yukon twenty miles above Nulato. He dispatched Lieutenant John J. Bernard to investigate the matter. Deriabin was in St. Michael at this time; he had come to get his stock of trade goods for the winter's business. Since Nulato was nearer the region of the rumors than any other post, he was ordered to take Bernard back with him. A surgeon, Mr. Adams, was to remain at St. Michael until Bernard returned. The *Enterprise*, meantime, departed.

The Indians of the area around Nulato were, and are, Koyukons. Their dialect is distinct both from that of the Ingaliks downriver at Anvik, and from that of the Tananas farther upriver. In the Russian period the Koyukons were divided into several bands. One of these centered its seminomadic activities at Nulato, while another gathered just upstream where the Koyukuk River joins the Yukon. Though the members of these two bands spoke the same dialect, frequently intermingled and sometimes intermarried, they had long been at odds. As recently as 1846 the Nulato Koyukons had raided and plundered the camps of their brethren to the north. Late in the winter of 1850–51 both bands had interrupted their hunting and trapping to gather in their respective villages to celebrate the annual Feast for the Dead. The northern Koyukons had neither avenged nor forgotten the raid of five years before.

During the same winter, Lieutenant Bernard stayed with Deriabin at Nulato, attempting to learn what he could about the rumor from the Indians who came to trade there. In February 1851, he sent a Russian named Ivan Bulegin[1] and a Nulato Koyukon, both employees of Deriabin, to invite the northern Koyukon chief to come and talk with him in Nulato.

The two messengers arrived in due course at the camp of the northern Koyukons. Bulegin, tired from the twenty-mile trip, sat down on his sled to rest while waiting for his Indian companion to return with water to make tea. As he sat there one of the men crept up behind him and smashed in his skull with an axe or a club. The next moment others set upon his sled and plundered it. When Bulegin's companion returned with the tea water, he saw what had happened and started to flee. But the northern Koyukons shouted to him, "Are you not one of us? We will not hurt you." He came back. They now stripped the flesh from the body of the Russian, roasted it and devoured it.* One of them noticed the reluctance with which Bulegin's companion joined in the feast and plunged a knife into the back of his neck.

The feast over, the men of the northern Koyukons got out their bows and arrows, put on their snowshoes, and departed posthaste for Nulato. At that time the Nulato Koyukons were living in three large subterranean houses half a mile from Deriabin's post. Altogether there were about a hundred of them. It had been an exceptionally warm February and, fearing a flood, they had cleared the snow off their birchbark canoes. Dozens of these lay about.

By the time the northern Koyukons reached Nulato it was late at night, or very early in the morning. They stole silently into the village. While some of them stood guard, others broke up the canoes, carried the pieces up to the smoke holes of the underground dwellings, set fire to them and shoved them in. Some of the men inside managed to chop exits for themselves through the walls, but only to find themselves cut down by arrows as they rushed out. Many suffocated in the smoke, others burned. Save for a few women whom the Koyukons took prisoner, and a few children who managed to flee to the woods, the entire camp was

---

*This, at least, is what the Russians at Nulato told the American explorer-scientist William Healy Dall when he stayed with them sixteen years later; the Jesuit ethnographer Jules Jetté who spent many years at Nulato at the beginning of the present century, feels that cannibalism was always totally foreign to the Koyukon, while imaginative invention was common among the Russians. Jetté does, however, accept all other elements in Dall's account, on which the present version is based.

wiped out. Since no guns were used, and the screams of the victims were stifled inside their underground houses, the massacre was accomplished so quietly that the Russians in the nearby post were not awakened.

From the ruins of the village, the Koyukon mob set upon the Russian post. The first person they encountered was one of their own band, a man the Russians called Ivan and employed as an interpreter. The attackers told him, "If you do not kill the *bidarshik* [the chief trader, Deriabin] we will kill you." Behind one of the houses Ivan found Deriabin, who had just gotten out of bed, sitting on a bench. He stabbed him repeatedly in the back. Just then one of the Russians, also an interpreter, happened upon the scene. Unarmed, he turned to the Koyukons and started to harangue them. But his speech was cut short by a shower of arrows. He slumped in the doorway. The Koyukons surged over his corpse into Deriabin's residence. Here they came upon Lieutenant Bernard, who was in bed reading. Bernard reached for the gun which hung above his bed. Twice he fired, but the shots were wild and hit the ceiling. The Koyukon shaman and his brother seized the Englishman by the arms. One of them plunged a knife into his stomach. Bernard sank back mortally wounded, his intestines protruding from the stab wound. In the melee that followed, several shots rang out, one of them wounding the shaman in the groin. The Koyukons added an Indian woman and her three children to the toll of their slaughter and departed.

They next attacked the workmen's barracks. This building was a distance from Deriabin's house, and its occupants, two Russians and several creoles, apparently did not know what had happened. The door had been barricaded as usual, however, and the men inside were awake. When they saw the mob of Indians running toward them, one of them fired a warning shot over their heads. The Koyukons paused briefly, but only to send off a barrage of arrows. The Russians now shot to kill, and when the first of the assailants was struck, the rest gave up the attack. The whole band hurriedly left Nulato for their camp upriver, their booty on sleds behind them, and the women they had captured under guard in their midst.

The Koyukons left behind their shaman. Nearly helpless and in great pain, he lay in the anteroom of Deriabin's house. In the main room, where Bernard had been knifed, lay a Russian, sick nearly to death with some sort of fever. Through negligence or pity the raiders had spared him. When they departed, his Indian wife brought him a loaded pistol and as she held him up he fired at the shaman. He was too fevered to shoot accurately, however, and the shaman managed to crawl out of the house and down to the river. There a woman of the shaman's own tribe happened by; she was towing a sled with her infant child on it. The shaman threw the baby from the sled and ordered the woman to pull him back to the Koyukuk camp. She refused, and he murdered her with his knife. She was the last victim of the Nulato massacre, and probably the last victim of the old antipathy between the Upper Koyukons and the Nulato Koyukons.

When word of these events reached St. Michael, Surgeon Adams, left there by the *Enterprise*, at once set out for Nulato. The surviving Russians had sewed up Lieutenant Bernard's wounds as best they could, and he lived for a while, but by the time Adams arrived he was dead. The surgeon had him buried behind the fort. To mark the spot, he erected a six-foot slab of spruce. On it he carved out the following inscription in neat square capitals half an inch high:

LIEUT. JOHN J. BERNARD

HBMS ENTERPRISE

killed near this place
by the Koükok Indians

FEB.ʸ 16th 1851
F.A.

Above was a large cross carved in half relief. Not twenty feet away lay Deriabin, the old veteran of the Nulato fur trade. Above him was a slab like Bernard's though inscribed with Cyrillic letters and topped with the double cross of Orthodoxy. Twenty years later a third grave was added, that of the first American woman who came to the Yukon. She too was murdered by Indians, but her story belongs to a later period.

When the Jesuit missionaries arrived in Nulato in the late 1880s they found the slab marking Bernard's grave, painted an inscription on it (in such pedantic Latin that the Jesuits there today cannot fully decipher it), and advised the lieutenant's relatives of their discovery through a notice in the London *Times*. For years the fathers maintained the little graveyard, and the neat picket fences they placed around each plot are still there, though fast rotting away. The original slabs are long since gone, and time, abetted by the rampant willows and spruces, seems intent on obliterating the rest in short order. By now few people in Nulato know where the graveyard is, though they cut cabin logs in the vicinity, and come there to hunt ptarmigan in winter.

The Indian victims of the massacre were buried by their underground dwellings, which gradually tumbled down over their corpses. Years later the Yukon cut away the bank where these dwellings stood, exposing a sort of Arctic Pompeii to remind a later generation of this day of treachery half a century before.

Since there were so few Russians in Russian America, their dominion over their native subjects was generally tenuous or theoretical where it existed at all. They could not afford the luxury of revenge after the Nulato massacre, nor offer an object lesson by chastisement. At first they simply abandoned the post, but in a few years they returned with more men and trade goods and again the Indians bartered their furs through the little window in the employees' barracks. The northern Koyukons came to trade as though nothing had happened; their headmen were treated to tea and crackers and a special deference as before. The Russians did, however, take the precaution of constructing a high, sturdy fence of upright logs around their compound. Its gate was closed each night and guard was mounted; only small numbers of Indians were permitted inside at any one time. The post was never again attacked, and the Russians at Nulato settled down to the dull routine of their commerce.

A party of American explorers who used Nulato as headquarters in 1865–67 have given us a picture of what this routine was like. At this time the *bidarshik*, or chief trader, was a man named Ivan Pavloff. Dall, one of the Americans, describes him as "a short, thick-set, swarthy, low-browed man," half Indian and half Russian. He had married the widow of a former *bidarshik* and had a sizable flock of children living with him at the fort. Generous and honest when sober, he was "ungovernable as a mad bull" when drunk, and so fond of drinking that Dall was compelled to poison the alcohol he had for preserving natural history specimens. The two Russians at the post held Pavloff in undisguised contempt because of his mixed blood and despite the fact that they were under his command. Since he was illiterate, one of them kept the post's accounts.

The wages of the Russians were extremely low, and the supplies they needed from the post's store were debited against them. It often happened that they would serve for years only to find themselves going deeper and deeper into debt, a circumstance the Russian-American Company deliberately encouraged, as no one who owed money to it could leave the colony. The few joys of such a life were centered around the samovar, the steam bath and an occasional alcoholic stupor.

The work Ivan Pavloff demanded of his employees was, it seems, more or less commensurate with the salaries they received. Frederick Whymper, an English artist who accompanied the American expedition, describes Russian methods of snow removal:

One Russian shoveled a few pounds of snow on to a hide. Two others then, with great appearance of fatigue, dragged it slowly to the edge of the bank and dropped it over. This unparalleled exertion rendered it necessary for the trio to sit down and smoke. After an interval of respose, and the "bidarshik" making his appearance, with great zeal and alacrity they started to work again. The "bidarshik," satisfied that they were indefatigable servants of the company, went in himself to take a nap, or to play a game of cards with his clerk. They repeated the process, and cleared up a few inches more; it was then time to "chi peat" (drink tea), and they adjourned for the purpose.

The monotony of the routine at Nulato was broken by the voyages to and from St. Michael where the furs were taken and the post's supplies received. In winter, travel was by dog team, in summer by *bidarra,* the boat of seal or walrus skins stretched on a light wooden frame that the Russians adopted from the Aleuts. Also, there was the annual trading expedition Ivan Pavloff led up to Nuklukayet, two hundred twenty-five miles up the Yukon.

Since time immemorial the Indians of the Alaskan interior had assembled at Nuklukayet each year to trade. A natural gathering place, it was located at the meeting of the Yukon with the third longest of its tributaries, the Tanana, a river of silty, glacial water flowing westward from Canada. As many as six hundred Indians gathered at Nuklukayet at a time, and they came from as far away as the Kuskokwim and the Koyukuk, the upper Tanana and the Chandalar. Their birchbark canoes lined the banks and their skin tents crowded the shore. Pelts and caribou pemmican were swapped, along with hunks of raw copper from the headwaters of the White River, and dentalium shells that had passed hand to hand all the way from the coast of British Columbia. The trade fair was as much a festive as a commercial occasion. Men danced long and wildly, their necklaces of wolf ears and mallard duck scalps jogging up and down to the rhythm, the sweat of the effort streaking their make-up of charcoal and powdered cinnabar. Songs were sung, dirgelike and minor in key; endless stories were told, and a year's gossip exchanged. The young men fought wrestling matches, ran races and pulled in tug-of-war contests with each tribe trying to outperform the others. The festival went on through the light of the northern night; no one took time out to sleep.

Each spring just after the breakup of the Yukon ice, Pavloff and his men loaded their *bidarra* with a couple of tons of trade goods and laboriously worked their way up against the swollen current to Nuklukayet. In the spring of 1867 Dall and Whymper joined the Russian party. Approaching Nuklukayet, Pavloff announced his arrival with a few blasts of the flintlock whaling gun he had mounted on the bow of his *bidarra.*

Upon landing, writes Dall,

we formed in a line, with blank charges in our guns. The Indians did the same. They advanced on us shouting, and discharged their guns in the air. We returned the compliment, and they retreated to repeat the performance. After ten minutes of this mock fight the tyone [chief] appeared between us. He harangued the Indians, who answered by a shout. Turning to us, he informed us that we were now at liberty to transact our business.*

Within a few days Pavloff's *bidarra* was emptied of its kettles, beads, tobacco, guns, ball and powder and reloaded with furs. The Russians then drifted back down to Nulato.

It will be recalled that the Nulato massacre was accomplished without the use of firearms, and that Deriabin was never willing to barter these to the Indians. It was a simple matter of security. The Russians found, however, that the Indians who came to Nuklukayet were obtaining guns from another source, so to compete they also had to supply them. The guns of their competitors were long-barreled flintlock muskets of English manufacture. At the time they were well known to practically every inhabitant of the backwoods from the St. Lawrence to the Yukon, and so was their supplier, the Hudson's Bay Company. The operations of this company extended from London west across the Atlantic and the whole breadth of Canada; those of the Russian-American Company stretched east from St. Petersburg across all of Asia and the North Pacific. And halfway round the world from these two cities, they met, here at Nuklukayet, an obscure and ancient trading ground tucked away in the fastness of the most remote corner of the North American continent.

* This custom of greeting by firing off guns continued on the river for years after the Russians departed, and fell into disuse only when repeating rifles became common. The early muzzle-loaders could get off but one shot at a time, and the discharge said, in effect, "You have seen us shoot into the air. Our guns are now empty. We approach as friends."

5 Robert Campbell

> Friday 6th June 1851 . . . The course of the river more westerly and its size and beauty increasing . . . it is the most splendid river I ever passed through.
>
> —Robert Campbell, *Journal*

> I never saw an uglier river, every where [sic] low banks, apparently lately overflowed, with lakes and swamps behind, the trees too small for building, the water abominably dirty and the current furious.
>
> —Alexander Hunter Murray,
> *Journal of the Yukon,* 1847–48

THE HUDSON'S BAY COMPANY established two trading posts on the Yukon; one, Fort Yukon, was located three hundred miles upstream from Nuklukayet on the great bend the river makes as it crosses the Arctic Circle. The other, Fort Selkirk, was situated five hundred miles farther upriver where the Pelly flows into the Yukon. Fort Yukon was the first English-speaking enterprise in Alaska, and today the village that has grown up around the site is the largest on the Alaskan part of the river, a rambling, down-at-the-heels Arctic slum of seven hundred souls. Similarly, Fort Selkirk was the first important Anglo-Saxon enterprise in the Yukon Territory of Canada, but it has not shared Fort Yukon's demographic boom. A few decades ago Fort Selkirk had a

hundred-odd inhabitants, but they have all left except Danny
Roberts, an Indian trapper, his large wife who is pleased to be
staying on there because "nobody bother you," and such of their
children as are not out at the residential school at Whitehorse. In
addition there are the Roberts' nine sled dogs which grow lean
and mean on a diet of straight rolled oats while awaiting the dog-
salmon run to begin later in the summer.

Up beyond Danny Roberts' cabin two indistinct mounds of
chimney rubble lie hidden by the alders that have now reclaimed
so much of Fort Selkirk's grassy clearing. It was here that the first
white men on the upper Yukon built their post for the profit of
the Hudson's Bay Company, and it was here, too, that they
suffered their first disaster in the region. The whole enterprise
was the result of the obstinacy, courage and ill luck of Robert
Campbell, a Scottish sheep farmer turned trader who believed in
presentiments, bathed under the ice each winter morning, and
once showshoed from the Canadian Arctic to St. Paul, Minnesota,
in the dead of winter. Fort Selkirk was his enterprise and his
dream, and one summer day it was literally smashed to bits.

The Hudson's Bay Company, still very much in business today,
was already a venerable organization when it engaged Robert
Campbell in 1830. Charles II had affixed his signature to its first
charter back in 1670, thereby granting the company's eighteen
shareholders ". . . the sole Trade and Commerce of all those Seas
Streightes Bayes Rivers Lakes Creekes and Soundes . . . Landes
Countryes and Territoryes" in an area that was subsequently interpreted to include over a quarter of North America. It was a
generous grant, but not remarkable for a century in which the
vibrant expansionism of northern Europe expressed itself chiefly
in the form of the charter company.

The Hudson's Bay Company's first posts were located on the
shores of James and Hudson bays, and for over a century they
did not extend beyond this region. Toward the end of the eighteenth century, however, the company began to push its operations inland. In 1789 Alexander Mackenzie discovered the river
that bears his name, and by the early 1800s the company had
built several trading posts along it. The most important of these

was Fort Simpson located where the Liard, a large river falling down the eastern slope of the Canadian Rockies, meets the Mackenzie.

Robert Campbell arrived at Fort Simpson on October 16, 1834, with heaps of dried fish in his canoe and great joy in his heart for having finally reached "the great Fur Trade country" of which he had dreamed for some time. He was twenty-six years old. Four years earlier he had been tending his father's flocks in Perthshire, Scotland, when a cousin of his, a chief factor of the Hudson's Bay Company, returned home for a year's furlough. Campbell's career as a sheep farmer was brought to a quick end by the things his cousin had to tell him. "Through him," Campbell writes, "I heard for the first time of the Great North-West and the free and active life that awaited one there; of the Hudson's Bay Company and the Fur Trade, the boundless prairies roamed by tribes of Indians and herds of Buffalo, the vast Lakes and giant Streams, the sublime majesty of the Rocky Mountains. . . . I became possessed with an irresistible longing to go to that land of romance and adventure."

"On the 2nd of June, 1830," his journal records, "I bade farewell to my Father, best and kindest of men, and received his blessing; I shook hands for the last time with my relations and friends; took a final look at the familiar scenes of my youth, and wrenched my self [sic] away to begin my journey to the New World." Now in the prime of youth, he would return many years later a middle-aged man, hardened and a little embittered, in search of "a wife to cheer my long dreary winters in the north."

After several years of what Campbell found to be rather monotonous drudgery at the Company's farm on Red River (near present-day Winnipeg), he was transferred to Fort Simpson. Here his apprenticeship in the fur trade began. He learned to grade beaver pelts at a glance and a touch, to barter with the Indians in the polyglot Ojibwa-Cree-English-French-Slavé *lingua franca* of the trade, to net whitefish and inconnu under the ice, to build good log buildings, and to live off the land. He showed himself an apt pupil. Within two years his superiors had sufficient confidence in him to place him temporarily in charge of Fort

Simpson. Campbell thus transformed himself from sheep farmer to trader; he would now become an explorer.

By the 1830s the Hudson's Bay Company had extended its operations to the shores of what are now the Alaskan Panhandle and British Columbia. In 1835, however, the Russian authorities in Sitka denied the company's ships access to important sections of the Panhandle. To circumvent this ban, the company was obliged to penetrate the area overland from the other side of the Rockies. The natural jumping-off place for such an operation was Fort Simpson, located as it was at the mouth of the westward-leading Liard River. Robert Campbell became the company's chief instrument in this thrust. He distinguished himself in difficult and dangerous explorations on the Liard and its tributaries; he crossed the continental divide to the west of its headwaters to discover the upper Stikine which flows from the interior of northern British Columbia to the Pacific. He established several new trading posts, drawing new furs and hitherto unknown Indians to the commerce of the Hudson's Bay Company.

The life of an explorer-trader in the northern Rockies was not an easy one. Campbell's nature prevented him from complaining very much, but the following diary entries give an idea of the hardships he faced:

February, 1839—Late on the third day we reached the first camp. . . . As I apprehended, their condition was no better than ours. Not a track of game was to be seen far or near. On one occasion all they had among 9 for 1 day's rations was *1 squirrel*. One great blessing they enjoyed, however, was immunity from the visits of the pillaging Indians who made our lives a burden to us.

May [1839]—As we were now ready to start & our snowshoes were of no further use to us, we removed all the netting off them, & that along with our parchment windows, was boiled down to the consistency of glue. The savoury dish thus prepared formed the "menu" of our last meal before leaving Dease's Lake. . . .

Winter, 1850—The 2 men Forbisher & Debois died of starvation & several of the Indians around; & pitiably sad to relate, some of the poor wretches had been driven by their unspeakable sufferings to commit some acts of cannibalism.

Early in 1839 Sir George Simpson, governor of the Hudson's Bay Company, concluded an agreement with representatives of the Russian-American Company whereby he leased from the Russians the entire coastline of the Alaskan Panhandle for an annual fee of two thousand land otter pelts. Since Simpson's ships could again trade in this region it was no longer necessary to explore routes to it from the eastern side of the Rockies. The governor therefore urged Campbell to direct his future explorations to the northwest. "I am quite sure you will distinguish as much in that quarter," he wrote to Campbell on June 16, 1839, "as you have latterly done on the West side of the Mountains."

In May 1840, Campbell left his post on the Liard to undertake this new series of explorations. He was accompanied by the three most loyal and constant companions of his expeditions. One of them was François Houle, a French-Canadian voyageur, interpreter, trapper, hunter, fisherman, boatman, master canoe builder and jack of numerous other trades. The other two were the young Indians Kitza and Lapie, who would never allow Campbell to face peril alone, even if he ordered them back. "Their fathers," Campbell informs us, "had told them that if they ever deserted me in danger they need never come back themselves . . . I have great pleasure & pride in recording the unselfish fidelity of these two Indian boys—a fidelity which was proved on many trying occasions afterwards."

Campbell and his men tracked and poled their boats far up the Liard and then ascended its main tributary, the Francis River, to its headwaters in a body of water he baptized Finlayson Lake. From here they crossed the continental divide, a short distance away. Just over the divide, Campbell writes:

. . . we had the satisfaction of seeing from a high bank a large river in the distance flowing Northwest. I named the bank from which we caught the first glimpse of the river "Pelly Banks" & the river "Pelly River," after our home Governor, Sir H. Pelly. Descending to the River we drank of its pellucid water to Her Majesty & the H. B. Co.

We constructed a raft & drifted down the stream a few miles, & threw in a sealed tin can with memoranda of our discovery, the date, & c., with a request to the finder, if perchance the can should fall into anyone's hands, to make the fact known. After taking possession in the name of the Company by marking a tree "H.B.C." with date, & flying the H.B.C. ensign the while overhead, we retraced our steps . . . highly delighted with our success. . . .

The date Campbell cut into the tree was July 25, 1840. He fully realized that he had just discovered the headwaters of an important river system, but he had no idea that it was the upper Yukon, nor that his note in the sealed can might be picked up and found indecipherable by the Russians then establishing their post nearly two thousand miles downriver at Nulato.

For the next three years Campbell was occupied in building and running trading posts on the eastern side of the Rockies, and he had no occasion to press forward his explorations. During the winter of 1842–43, however, he sent Houle to the place he had named Pelly Banks to build a cabin and some canoes in preparation for the explorations of the following summer. Campbell, Kitza and Lapie joined Houle in June, and on the tenth the party set off down the Pelly. This river, the fifth longest of the Yukon's tributaries, flows 450 miles west-northwest out of the low northern Rockies. It is a clear and lovely river, and Campbell, who had a keen appreciation of natural beauty, noted a "succession of picturesque landscapes" as he drifted down it. On the sixth day of his journey, June 16, 1843, he passed below a high, crumbling mesa topped with poplars like candles on a birthday cake. Just below the water widened to left and right and he drifted out into the Yukon. He named the river after J. Lee Lewes, a governor of the Hudson's Bay Company, and until recent years the Yukon above the Pelly retained this name.

Campbell and his men camped that night at the confluence of the two streams, a place they would come to know well a few years later. Early next morning they started down the Yukon. After going a short distance they came upon a large band of Indians who, though awed by the sight of white men, were friendly. Campbell indicated by signs that he planned to continue farther down the river, but these Indians warned of tribes that "would not only kill but eat" his party. Campbell's men were so frightened that he had to consent to turn back. Apparently all the belligerent Indians were not confined to the river below, for on the third day of the return trip the party came upon a large encampment of them.

They were very hostile [writes Campbell] standing with bows bent & arrows on the string, & would not come down from the high bank to meet us. I sent up some tobacco to them to assure them of our peaceful intentions, but they would scarcely remove their hands from their bows to receive it. We then ascended to the bank to them, as they would not come down to us, and our bold and at the same time conciliatory demeanour had the effect of cooling them down. We had an amicable interview with them, carried on with words and signs. It required some finessing however to get away from them; but once in the canoe, we quickly pushed out of range of their arrows & struck obliquely down stream for the opposite bank, while I faced about, gun in hand, to watch their actions.

Campbell and his men continued on upriver until the fatigue of battling the swift current forced them to stop. They pitched their tents, and all of them went to sleep except for Campbell, who sat on the branch of a tree reading *Hervey's Meditations* in the midnight dusk and keeping a sharp lookout. From time to time he would go down to the river's edge and fill his drinking horn with water. Two years later, when he had established friendly relations with the Indians of the region, he was told by them that every move he had made that night had been observed. "With the exactness of detail characteristic of the Indian," Campbell relates, "they described me sitting in the tree holding 'something white' in my hand & often raising my head to make a survey of the neighborhood; then descending to the river, taking my horn out from my belt & after filling it, turning quickly around, & glancing up & down the river & towards the hill while in the act of drinking. They confessed that had I knelt down to drink, they would have rushed upon me & made away with me & the sleeping inmates of the tent." When Campbell and his men left their campsite next morning the Indians did not follow, and the rest of the journey back across the Rockies was uneventful.

In 1844 Governor Simpson urged Campbell to return to the
Yukon-Pelly junction and establish a Hudson's Bay post there. In
preparation for this, Campbell set up headquarters at Pelly Banks
where he remained for two winters. Trade prospered there, and
since the surrounding country was rich in game, there were no
more meals of snowshoe webbing and window parchment.
Campbell was especially pleased because the post

. . . was nicely located on the bank of the Pelly, which enabled me to
enjoy the luxury of a bath in the river every morning. This practice I
kept up until the ice got too thick. As the season advanced our cook
would knock at my door to tell me the hole was made in the ice
ready for me. I would then run down with a blanket round me, dip
into the hole, out again, & back to the house, my hair often being
frozen stiff before I got there. After a good rub down I would dress, &
no one who has not tried it can have any idea of the exhilarating glow
produced on the whole system by this hydropathic treatment.

In May 1848, as soon as the ice went out, Campbell again
descended the Pelly to the Yukon. He was accompanied by nine
men including John Green Stewart, a fellow Scotsman, and Kitza
and Lapie. They arrived on the first of June. For the site of his
post Campbell selected an island, now eroded away, in the Pelly
estuary. He named the new post Fort Selkirk after the English
lord who sponsored the Red River colony where he had begun
his life in Canada. The Indians of the region who congregated at
the site were friendly, and were increasingly astounded as the
buildings took shape, for they had never before seen any structure more elaborate than a skin tent. One of the Indian visitors
was a man who five years before had lain in ambush as Campbell
sat reading *Hervey's Meditations.* Shortly after this he had become lame in one leg and concluded that Campbell's magic was
the cause. He now tried to buy off the spell with a large parcel of
furs, but Campbell wouldn't negotiate. At the incessant implor-
ings of the man's wife, parents and in-laws, he decided instead to
try his hand at doctoring. "I took the case in hand, finding the
poor fellow a truly patient subject, & I am thankful to say the

treatment proved successful; the man was soon able to go about &
hunt as formerly; he & his family & friends were overjoyed & the
story of this marvellous cure was spread far & near; as also were
accounts of the wonderful goods of all kinds we had brought with
us."

As fall approached, the men at Fort Selkirk made fish nets of
twine and set them in the lakes of the district to take in as many
whitefish, pike and grayling as they could. Hunters were sent out
after moose, caribou and bear. The results of this harvest of wild
food were so good that the storehouses of Fort Selkirk were soon
crammed full; and, as Campbell put it, "We passed the winter
enjoying an abundance of country produce."

The harvest of the following season was less abundant, but no
one starved, and Campbell reserved the complaints in his diary
for the paucity of trade goods, not food. He was no doubt justified in blaming the incompetence of company officials, but the
difficulties and uncertainties involved in transporting goods from
England to Fort Selkirk were enormous. They had first to reach
York Factory on Hudson Bay by sailing ships, and the ice-free
season was but two or three months long. From the bay they
were carried in the York boats and on the backs of the company's
French-Canadian voyageurs all the way across the North American continent. The return traffic in ninety-pound bales of fur was
just as arduous. Seven years passed between the time when a
trade good left an English port and when the pelt for which it
had been exchanged reached a London fur auction.

In April 1851, Campbell received orders from Governor Simpson to explore the Yukon downstream from Fort Selkirk as far as
he "might deem advisable." By this time Campbell had spent
nearly three years at Fort Selkirk and by his efforts the region
was now "known." The explorer in the man thus rejoiced at these
new orders; they would allow him to fulfill "a long cherished & oft
expressed wish."

He departed downriver at five o'clock on the morning of June 4
as the men he had left behind fired off their guns in salute. He
did not then know whether the Yukon would carry him to the
Pacific where the Russians were, or to the Arctic Ocean. If Simp-

son's suppositions were right, it would be the latter, for the governor thought that the Pelly and the Lewes were affluents of the Colville which empties into the Arctic Ocean near Point Barrow.

There is no darkness at this latitude in June, only a bright dusk, and Campbell traveled nearly around the clock. Below Fort Selkirk he followed the river through the deep trench it has cut between the then-unnamed Dawson Range to the south and the still unnamed cluster of four-thousand-foot hills to the north. In places the bottom of this trench is broad, and the river, not needing so much space, has filled in most of it with alluvium. Flat, forested banks a few feet or a few hundred yards wide intervene between the water and the high ground beyond. The swift current—here about six miles an hour—continually eats away at them; spruce and poplar at water's edge are undermined, then toppled over to bob up and down in the current with peculiarly machinelike rhythms. Sounds of the eroding bank punctuate the stillness of the wilderness: first there is the splash of a tree trunk; then the solid plunk, like a beaver tail slapped on the water, of a slice of bank that follows; then the almost inaudible sound of tiny avalanches of loose gravel dribbling in; and, finally, the silence again, for the low, constant shush of the Yukon's movement is so pervasive that it goes unheard. A foot or two in from the bank's edge, the trees lean precariously out over the water—the "sweepers" of Mississippi lore—but just behind them others point straight up, oblivious of the fate that already laps at their roots. In places the debris along the river's banks makes a landing impossible, though much of it is cleared away by the running ice and high water of spring. In this way lodgepole pines all the way from British Columbia reach the tundra Eskimos of the Yukon estuary; they are used for fuel and housebuilding—a magic gift from distant forests to people who know trees only as drift logs.

About forty miles below Fort Selkirk, Campbell saw the alluvial banks give way to ones of sheer rock rising two or three hundred feet straight up out of the river. Here the Yukon flows in shadow except at midday, and no doubt he appreciated this reprieve from the hot June sun. In Campbell's time, as in ours, pairs of peregrine falcons came to nest on these high cliffs. Year after year they return to the same eyries to hatch new generations out of pinkish eggs and add the bones of another season's rapt to the accumulation of former ones. As his boat passed hundreds of feet below their eyries, Campbell was likely greeted by the female swooping down with a marvelous grace and an angry *kee, kee, keeeek,* as the male perched a distance away, like a spectator at a sporting event, to watch his mate's carryings-on.

On June 5, a day and a half away from Fort Selkirk, Campbell drifted past the mouth of the first large Yukon tributary along his route. He named it the White River "from the color of its water," which is opaque and milky due to glacial silt. Until its confluence with the White, the Yukon's water has been clear, if not always pristine. Most of its tributaries have come from the low, unglaciated northern Rockies, while the few that arose in ice fields have paused long enough in lakes to allow the glacial grist to settle out. The White, however, plummets down nonstop from the St. Elias and Wrangell Mountains, among the highest and most heavily glaciated peaks in the continent. These glaciers pulverize rock to flour-sized particles which the White dumps into the Yukon. At first the parent stream refuses to accept this filthy donation, and the two rivers run parallel along a water edge sharp as a knife. But after half a mile the edge grows dull; the zone of intermingling—swirling billows of lactescence in the brown water—widens until, four miles below, it reaches from bank to bank. Only farther down do the two rivers become really homogenized, and when they do it is the White which imposes its identity. Though a relatively minor tributary, less than two hundred miles long, its silt will henceforth be kept in suspension by the current of the larger river; and the Yukon will end as a great whitish blot spreading out into the Bering Sea. By then the Tanana River, third largest of its tributaries, will have contributed the ground rock of the Alaska Range as well, but, even without this, the Yukon has become so opaque after receiving the White that it is pointless to use fishing lures—the fish cannot see them. Bathing now makes sense only if you are dirtier than the river, a question involving many complexities; unless you are somebody like Robert Campbell, the cold water (seldom above 55° F.) is apt to help you decide that you are not. Once in the water, if you look up toward the sun from a foot below the surface you see only a midnight blackness. The water is potable, however, especially if you leave a glass of it to sit overnight so that at least three fourths of an inch of sediment can settle out. With time and laziness you get used to drinking the river water as is, and soon enough the pellucid tributaries seem flat and tasteless—nothing to grit your teeth on. From the White River on down, the friction of silt against a wooden boat hull produces the sound of dry snow falling on dead leaves.

Campbell's boat had a draught of less than a foot so he didn't have to worry about the bars and boulders concealed by the opaque water. And though later, larger boats would be sunk by such hidden menaces, the Yukon's glacial tributaries would prove more a help than a hindrance to navigation because they tend to stabilize the water level. Affluents such as the Pelly, and later on the Porcupine and the Koyukuk, are fed mainly by melting snow. They rise swiftly in May and June to discharge huge volumes of water into the Yukon. But by July the snow is gone, and with little rainfall they shrink back nearly as fast as they swelled. Then, however, summer finally reaches the high mountain glaciers and the increased flow of the White, the Tanana, and the headwater streams of the Yukon itself acts to compensate for the reduced volume of the nonglacial tributaries. Similarly, during hot dry summers when the snow melts early and fast, and the nonglacial streams are low, the glacial ones are high. During cool wet summers the opposite occurs.

By October the glaciers feeding the Yukon have frozen and the river is miraculously cleared of most of its silt. From fall to spring it flows limpid and clean, hiding its regained purity under five feet of ice. Whereas in August the gauging station at Eagle, Alaska, records eighteen hundred parts per million of suspended sediment, in October this has fallen to fifty per million. In midsummer, when the glaciers are making their maximum contribution, a remarkable total of 188 tons of silt can pass the station each minute, but during winter the figure falls to as low as four hundred pounds per minute.

A few miles below the White, and on the other side of the Yukon, Campbell passed a second large tributary. He named it after John Green Stewart whom he had left in charge back at Fort Selkirk. The Stewart, like the Pelly which it roughly parallels, rises in the Mackenzie Mountains, the local subdivision of the Rockies. Though it drains an area larger than Switzerland and is just short of four hundred miles long, it is only the sixth largest of the Yukon's tributaries.

Robert Campbell was much impressed by the river he was exploring—"the most splendid I ever passed through"—but for him "the great attraction was the natives." Like the Ingaliks a thousand miles downriver they were Athapascan Indians, but of the Han and Kutchin branches. Campbell encountered a number of them encamped along the river. Though astonished at his strange appearance and the odd construction of his boat, they were invariably friendly; Campbell never passed a camp without stopping to converse in signs and smoke the pipe of peace. Stone Age people, these Indians were even less advanced than the Ingaliks who knew, for example, how to make cooking vessels of clay pottery. To boil their food they filled baskets of tightly woven root fibres with water and then dumped in heated stones. "By the time [the cooking . . .] is accomplished to the satisfaction of the 'chef,'" Campbell reports, "the water is converted into a pretty thick soup—not with vegetables like Scotch broth—but with sand & ashes conveyed into the cooking utensil by the hot stones."

Somewhere near what was then the boundary between the British and Russian empires, the Indians indicated to Campbell that before long he would encounter men of his own peculiar kind. Campbell's diary gives no indication of whom he thought the Indians were referring to, but quite possibly he expected to find Russians. After a few days of threading his way through the maze of islands and channels that make up the Yukon Flats, he nosed his boat around a bend and was astonished to see the ensign of the Hudson's Bay Company flying atop a large new trading post. As Campbell landed he was greeted not by a Slav but by William Hardisty, a good friend who had served under him at Fort Selkirk three years before. Neither the company nor

Fort Yukon (after Alexander Murray)

the men at either of its Yukon posts had known that Fort Selkirk and Fort Yukon were on the same river. It was indeed a small world.

Fort Yukon* was located just above the Arctic Circle at the top of the river's great northern arc. A mile below the site the Yukon receives its longest tributary, the Porcupine, which flows in from the northwest. This stream arises near the Mackenzie, where the Hudson's Bay Company had long been established, and provided a natural route of access for John Bell, who first explored the region, and Alexander Hunter Murray, who established Fort Yukon. Murray began work on the post in June 1847, and it was thus older by one year than Fort Selkirk; however, neither he nor Bell reached the Yukon as early as Campbell. Murray's fort consisted of three large log buildings surrounded by a stockade one hundred feet square; at each corner a bastion protruded. Its defenses were this substantial more out of the fear of the Russians than of the Indians. Murray knew full well that in building the post he was committing an act of trespass on the territory of

* Then spelled Fort Youcon, or Fort Youcan.

Russian America, and he spent his first year there in dread of an attack by them. Such an attack never materialized, and Murray had long since departed when the new American owners of Alaska evicted his successors.

Upon reaching Fort Yukon, Campbell had accomplished the basic purpose of his explorations; he had established that "his" Pelly and Lewes rivers, Murray's Youcon, and the Kuikpak of the Russians were all part of the same system. In so doing he had made an important addition to contemporary geographical knowledge about this last remote corner of North America. Since the general course of the river below Fort Yukon was known, he decided not to continue any farther down it. Instead, after a single night's rest at the fort, he started up the Porcupine to overtake Murray who had just left for the Mackenzie with the season's furs. He accompanied Murray to Fort Simpson, and from there took his old route back over the Rockies to Fort Selkirk. He arrived toward the middle of October after a summer's trek of something over three thousand miles.

Campbell's diary that winter reflects a grimly pessimistic frame of mind that was never evident before. February 22, 1852, was his forty-sixth birthday and on that day he broods on death and the meaning of his life. "For what have I been created?" he asks himself. "And what use have I made of the past year and years a merciful God has bestowed on me? . . . O how improperly I have wasted them!" For eighteen years now he had seen nothing more suggestive of civilization than a trading post of squared timbers, and during most of this time his principal human contact was with people just emerging from the Stone Age. A sense of isolation and foreboding now began to weigh on him and turn his thoughts inward. He began to interpret peculiar natural phenomena as mystical portents. On the first of May, for example, he was awakened by a magpie, a bird seldom seen in these parts, which chattered at his window. He alone heard it, and when he went to look at the bird it had disappeared. "What it had to communicate," he wrote in his diary that day, "I could not comprehend. God grant it may be the forerunner of good tidings." In later years he would assert that it was the forerunner of very bad tidings indeed, an obvious warning his stupidity prevented him from comprehending.

Early in the summer of 1852 Campbell went down to Fort Yukon again, this time to get supplies. John Stewart, left in charge as before, was kept hard at work re-erecting the post buildings which had been moved that winter and spring from the island to the mainland, where the banks were less endangered by erosion. When Campbell returned on July 26, the work was nearly finished, though a stockade had still to be erected. He brought back with him the first complete outfit of trade goods and supplies that Fort Selkirk received. He could now really test the promising fur trade potential of the country, for he had enough goods to barter all the pelts the Indians could offer. For the first time, also, the men at Fort Selkirk would have all the "luxuries"—flour, tobacco, cloth, sugar, raisins, and a swig or two of brandy—with which the company was supposed to supply them regularly. Campbell had even brought back with him, of all things, a cow, so there would be fresh milk. In a letter to a fellow trader, Campbell predicted "the commencement of a new era on the Pelly." He could now look forward to a season both prosper-

ous and comfortable in the solid little fort that he had conceived and built on the grand river that he had discovered and
named.

On July 29, three days after Campbell's return, John Stewart
and seven other men left on a trading expedition that would take
them some distance from the fort. The hunters Campbell employed to keep Fort Selkirk supplied with meat were also away;
they had gone to the rich game country up the Pelly River.
Campbell and five others remained.

On Friday morning, August 20, 1852,* Campbell and three of
his men were cutting grass for the cow in a meadow a short
distance away from the buildings of the post. Suddenly five rafts
carrying twenty-seven Chilkat Indians hove into view and made
for a landing at the post. Twice before these coastal Indians had
come to Fort Selkirk, and although they had not caused trouble
they looked upon the existence of the post with undisguised hostility. The reason for their antipathy was commercial; until Fort
Selkirk was established they had enjoyed a complete monopoly
on trade with the Indians of the upper Yukon, acting as the
exclusive middlemen between them and the Russian and British
traders on the coast. Campbell had broken their monopoly, and
they were not at all happy about it.

At the sight of the Chilkats, bristling with guns and obviously
set on making trouble, three of Campbell's men fled to the woods;
he and two others were now left to face all twenty-seven of them
alone. Campbell realized he must try to placate them; an open
fight would be disastrous. He reached the post as they debarked
from their rafts. "Though I temporized and used every conciliatory appearance to soothe them," he records, "they were like a
volcano every moment ready to burst out." The volcano did not
erupt that day and the Chilkats simply milled around the fort.
Campbell and his men spent a sleepless night in the buildings of
the post. They watched as "the infernal devils, on the move the
whole night, were trying the store doors and windows to open

* Campbell gives this date in a letter written at Fort Simpson the following November; according to his journal, however, it was August nineteenth.

them and get inside." Campbell relates the events of the next day
as follows:

Early the next morning, Saturday 21st August 1852 they were on
the move bent on mischief of every description . . .—They would thief
before our eyes—our vigilance they put at defiance; we could not turn
our head but that they had some article secured—They now became
urgent for me to decamp if I wanted to see another day, etc. Every
moment the clamour was getting louder and they more restless. . . . I
wished to take shelter in the store and defend ourselves to the last
extremity but then we had no water and they could set fire to the other
end of the house and burn us out.

In the afternoon, two of the hunters and their families, returning
from up the Pelly, approached the fort in a boat; they had no
idea of the situation there.

    . . . as the boat neared, the Chilcats rushed out with their guns and
knives, though ignorant who or how many were in the boat. Having
yet some control over them, I left McLeod to notice [i.e., guard] the
house, and to prevent bloodshed, rushed to the bank.
    The boat was passing some distance out. The Indians sprang into the
water and dragged it ashore, and amidst roaring and yelling had it
emptied of everything, and the two [Fort Selkirk] Indians disarmed of
their guns, knives, and axes in a moment. One of the principal leaders,
"Mustash the Postman" who appeared in no way excited . . . seized hold
of one of the hunter's guns, on which I [also] laid hold of it. . . .
    An instantaneous rush was made upon me, with their guns and
knives. Others seized me by the arms. Two of the guns snapped
[misfired]. One Indian as he sprung at me with a knife, ripped up the
side of a dog that came across him, and the blood off the blade
crimsoned my arms as I evaded the blow. In one of the guns aimed at
me (a brass blunderbuss) I saw four bullets put a little before the fray
began. My pistols, which were concealed in my belt, were wrenched
from me before I could fire; in fact an attempt to do so would have
been in vain, and could have ended only in the indiscriminate murder
of all.
    They were already masters. On seeing it likely to come to the worst,
I called out to our Indians to try for the store, where guns were ready

for the enemy's reception, but in this sudden onset I found myself alone and could see none of our people. My attempt to gain the store was defeated; I was dragged and pushed towards the bank, one . . . of those holding my arms warded off several knife thrusts, and I believe under Providence I owe my life to so many having hold of me, as those with the guns, though jumping round and round me, could hardly cover me alone.

In the struggle I felt sure of death, and it was with thankful surprise, though stunned with vexation, that I found myself released on the bank of the river . . .

The roaring and yelling of these painted fiends, smashing everything that came in their way—and firing—beggars description. . . .

Campbell, Lapie, and a few others managed to reach their boats and push off downstream. Next day they came to a camp of Indians who had always been friendly toward them. The chief was furious when he heard what had happened. He returned with his band to help Campbell take his revenge.

. . . we reached and surrounded the fort, never in the least doubting that the Chilcats were still there, but to our inexpressible vexation all were gone. . . .

Not a grain of powder or rag of clothing was left. Cassettes, dressing cases, writing desks, kegs and musical instruments were smashed into a thousand atoms and the house and store strewed with the wreck, a sight to madden a saint. [The floors] from end to end were slewed over with ball, shot, meat, geese, fish, pans, kettles, rice, raisins, sugar, flour, feathers, knives, paper, leather, letters, etc. etc. God Almighty what a syte in the abode of peace and comfort a few days ago.

Campbell was bent on giving chase, but was forced to abandon the prospect of "such pleasure" because the friendly Indians would not go along with him. With so few supplies left, and the winter not far off, he reluctantly decided that Fort Selkirk would have to be abandoned for the time being. He sent most of his men down to Fort Yukon, while he wearily trudged back over the Rockies along the trail he had blazed years before.

His one objective now was to see Fort Selkirk re-established as soon as possible, and to do this he needed the support of his superiors in the Hudson's Bay Company. At Fort Simpson he received a sympathetic hearing, but no definite commitments. He would take his appeal to higher authorities. Like a man obsessed, he put on his snowshoes and walked all the way to Fort Garry (now Winnipeg), over two thousand miles away, where the company's North American headquarters were located. Again he received no positive commitments, so again he put on his snowshoes and trekked to Minnesota, where he boarded a train for Montreal. Here he argued his case before Sir George Simpson, the greatest of the Hudson's Bay Company's governors, and the man who had encouraged him in his explorations for many years. "I explained to him," writes Campbell, "that the sole object of my coming thus to see him, was to obtain leave to retrace my steps at once, and re-establish Fort Selkirk and square up with the Chilcats." However, the governor was no more encouraging than the others had been. Disheartened, Campbell took his long overdue home leave to Scotland in quest of forgetfulness and a bride. The latter he found, but never the former.

A year later he returned to Canada where he further distinguished himself in the service of Hudson's Bay, this time as a trader and administrator, not as an explorer. He never again crossed the Rockies nor beheld the "most splendid river," as he described the Yukon. After forty-one years with the company, he was suddenly and unjustly (as his employers conceded years later) fired. An old man now with an Old Testament beard, he took up cattle ranching in Manitoba. He enjoyed reminiscing, but it was perhaps as expiation that he told again and again what a fool he had been not to heed the warning sent by God in the form of a magpie.

6 The Telegraph Expedition

> I had been prepared to see a large stream, but
> had formed no conception of the reality. Neither
> pen nor pencil can give any idea of the dreary
> grandeur, the vast monotony, or the unlimited
> expanse we saw before us.
>
> —Frederick Whymper, *Travel and Adventure*
> *in the Territory of Alaska*

IN THE summer of 1867 two white men reached Fort Selkirk, the
first since Robert Campbell's departure sixteen years before. In
the interval the post had been burned; only the chimneys remained, lonely crumbling sentinels visible from a mile away. The
two men camped there a few days, then returned downriver
whence they had come. Like Campbell, Mike Laberge and Frank
Ketchum were explorers, but they were blazing a trail for the
wires of the Western Union Telegraph Company, not for the fur
brigades of Hudson's Bay. And though their project too came to
nought, it did so for quite different reasons.

In 1857 the first of Cyrus Field's telegraph cables lay broken
and useless on the floor of the Atlantic. The skeptics now *knew*
the project to be impossible and the man mad. Investors suddenly
became interested in the alternate proposed by a businessman
named Perry Collins. This envisaged an overland telegraph line

that would begin in the state of Washington, traverse western Canada and Russian America, cross the Bering Straight and all of Russia, and link up finally with the European system at St. Petersburg. Collins had obtained the necessary charters from the governments concerned, and the failure of the Atlantic cable brought him the potent backing of the Western Union Telegraph Company. It was a grandiose scheme and the price tag was commensurate, but if, as expected, the line could carry a thousand messages a day at twenty-five dollars each, it would generously reward its investors.

The planners of the Overland Telegraph decided, on the basis of the little solid information they had, that the valley of the Yukon would probably be the best route for the line to follow through Russian America. Robert Kennicott, a gifted young naturalist, was given command of explorations in this vast region. His appointment to the position was logical, for at the time he was the only American who had ever seen the Yukon. At the age of twenty-three Kennicott had undertaken a three-year voyage through northern Canada and Alaska, and in the course of it he had spent most of 1861 at Fort Yukon. While there he collected such things as bird skins, mastodon teeth, Indian fire drills and dragonflies, many of which are still stowed in the deeper recesses of the Smithsonian Institution, which sponsored his work. Keenly interested in the relationship of the species of northwestern America to those of Siberia, he welcomed the opportunity to return to Alaska provided by the Telegraph Expedition.

Kennicott left New York in March 1865, and arrived in St. Michael that summer. He planned to make Nulato the headquarters for his explorations, just as Zagoskin had done twenty years before. To carry his six men and his supplies upriver from St. Michael, a small steamboat, the *Lizzie-Horner,* had been brought in pieces from the States. On reassembling the craft, Kennicott quickly discovered that some crucial parts had been left behind. The *Lizzie-Horner* thus forfeited her chance to inaugurate the long and colorful history of steam navigation on the Yukon, and seriously compromised Kennicott's plans in the process. He and his men were now obliged to spend the winter hauling supplies overland to Nulato instead of beginning their explorations.

Kennicott was a high-strung, impatient man. With all these delays and frustrations he became deeply depressed, full of dark doubts about the feasibility of the telegraph and the value of his own work. "I begin to think he is crazy," one of his men confided to his diary as the winter wore on. But spring finally came to Nulato, and it seemed to dissipate his despondency. "He began to enjoy the gradual approach of leaves, birds, and salmon," a subordinate later recalled, "and thought less of the cares and annoyances of the dreary winter season." On the twelfth of May he was quieter than usual. That night, after several sleepless hours in bed, he arose and worked on plans for the coming summer's exploration. Next morning, as usual, the six members of his party assembled for breakfast at eight o'clock. Kennicott did not appear. An hour later his body was found, lying face up on the muddy beach of the Yukon a few hundred yards from the Russian post. At his side lay his compass, and next to him on the soft alluvium was a sketch map of the nearby mountains which he had drawn with a stick.

Whether Kennicott died of a heart attack or committed suicide —he had a supply of arsenic for preserving zoological specimens—was never determined. His body was taken to Ivan Pavloff's house, sewn into an airtight shroud of skins, and temporarily buried until it could be transported to the family plot in Illinois. Robert Kennicott was thirty when he died, the first American to live on the Yukon, and the first to die there.

Earlier in the spring Kennicott had directed two of his men, Mike Laberge and Frank Ketchum, to make a reconnaissance of the five-hundred-mile section of the river between Nulato and Fort Yukon. The two left just after the breakup in the spring of 1866, stayed briefly at the Hudson's Bay post, and returned to Nulato sometime in midsummer.

The following November the Telegraph Expedition received a new leader. He was William Healey Dall, a Bostonian who at twenty-one was already an avid, and far from amateur, botanist, conchologist, geologist, ornothologist, historian and explorer. At twenty-five he would write what is still one of the best books on Alaska, and a little later he would become the dean of American scientific investigation in the territory. Dall was a calm, easy-

going sort of man, and his flexibility was much better suited to
the leadership of the expedition than Kennicott's nervous impa-
tience. A streak of fatalism was part of his nature, and in Alaska,
where a man's control over the things around him is strictly
limited, this piece of emotional equipment is as important as good
survival gear or a rugged physique. Without it men become as
dispirited as Kennicott had been, and low morale is a greater
peril than even the deep cold.

With Dall, another new member, Frederick Whymper, joined
the expedition. An English artist, he had been hired by Western
Union to keep a pictorial record of the explorations.

The four men of the Telegraph Expedition—Dall, Whymper,
Ketchum, and Laberge—spent the winter besieged behind the
drafty log walls of Ivan Pavloff's trading post. The mercury
stayed frozen solid for six days of a single week, and the little
winter sunlight that might have cheered their quarters was reduced to half by opaque seal gut window "panes." They made the
best of these grim surroundings, however; witness, for example,
the way they went about celebrating Christmas:

25th.—Merry Christmas! [reads Frederick Whymper's journal] not
the first by a good many that I had spent away from home and
kindred. We all tried to be jolly, and were moderately successful, yet
there was a slight "black current" of regret, and a tinge of melancholy
in our proceedings. We decorated our room with flags and Indian
trading-goods, and spruce-fir brush, in place of holly; got out the
newest and brightest of our tin plates and pewter spoons, [and] raised
a big fire of logs. . . . About five o'clock in the afternoon, the table
neatly covered with cotton drill . . . we sat down to a repast—to use a
Californianism—of a "high-toned and elegant nature".

Dall describes the repast:

Our knowledge of chemistry and the domestic arts was taxed to
the utmost in the production of pies, gingerbread, and cranberry
dumplings; while a piece of Ulúkuk reindeer meat, which had been
kept frozen ever since our journey across the portage, performed the
office of the customary "roast beef of old England," and a brace of

roasted ptarmigan represented the Yankee turkeys. Green peas, toma-
toes, and other preserved vegetables were produced for the occasion;
and, with the company of the bidárshik and his assistant, we sat down
to the best dinner ever eaten in that part of the continent. The day was
enlivened by the reading of several original literary productions, and
the brewing of a mild bowl of punch from a supply of old Jamaica. . . .
Altogether the occasion was one that will be long remembered with
pleasure by those who took part in it.

The literary productions included a story by Whymper, "Missing
Mummy!", whether a plaint of homesickness or an ancient Egyptian thriller, its author does not say, and a poem that Dall composed and recited for the occasion.

Dall spent the winter filling his ethnographic notebooks with
material on the Nulato Indians, preparing for the explorations of
the coming season, and collecting natural history specimens. In
the third of these pursuits he was quite as avid as Kennicott
had been, and that winter his acquisitions included both mice
and men. For the former he hired Indian boys with bows and
arrows to scour the local tussocks, and for the latter he stealthily
rifled bones from the Nulato graveyard while a blizzard covered
his tracks.

Whymper was occupied with his sketches of the people and
scenes of Nulato, even at thirty below. The problem was that he
couldn't draw with his mittens on, while without them he ran the
risk of frozen hands. He resolved this dilemma, he explains,
through resort to drawing "by installments." "Between every five
strokes of the pencil I ran about to exercise myself, or went into
our quarters for warmth . . . I . . . once froze my left ear, which
swelled up nearly to the top of my head, and I was always afraid
that my prominent nasal organ would get bitten. The use of
water-colors was of course impracticable—except when I could
keep a pot of warm water on a small fire by my side. . . ."

In the meantime Ketchum and Laberge busied themselves with
procuring dried fish, the standard dog food of the region, and
preparing their sleds for the first stage of the journey that would
take them over a thousand miles upriver to Fort Selkirk. They

planned to reach Fort Yukon, the halfway point, by dogsled and
then continue by canoe after the ice went out. After going as far
upriver as possible, they were to return to Fort Yukon where Dall
and Whymper planned to meet them during the summer. They
left Nulato about the middle of March.

Spring comes to Nulato in the form of a goose, and on May 3
Ivan Pavloff gave the traditional gift of a pound of Circassian
tobacco to the Indian who had shot the first one. Two days later
the Nulato River shunted its strait jacket of ice down onto the
still-solid Yukon, and once again ran pristine and unfettered past
the pale green buds of the alders lining its banks. On the twelfth
the first mosquitoes appeared, frail infrequent forerunners of the
hordes that would soon cloud the muskeg bogs and the spruce
forests like smoke. A week later the ice on the Yukon, five feet
thick, began to go, smashing and crashing with rage at the termi-
nation of a reign that had seemed absolute and eternal until just a
few weeks before. Every writer who has wintered on the Yukon
describes this event with awe and gratitude. With awe because of
the display of sheer physical might involved; with gratitude because nothing so well symbolizes the return of a life-sustaining
order of things: the long cold night of winter has seemed to
congeal the sap and blood of all living things into permanent
petrifaction, but now it finally ends in flowing water and nearly
endless daylight. On May 19 Whymper put away his sketchbook
and simply watched, as a "constant stream of broken ice passed
the station, now surging into mountains as it met with some
obstacle, now grinding and crushing on its way, and carrying all
before it. Whole trees and banks were swept away before its
victorious march, and the river rose some fourteen feet above its
winter level . . . there was a constant sound as of the smashing of
glass."

As soon as the ice floes had thinned sufficiently, Ivan Pavloff
and his seven-man crew started for Nuklukayet in a *bidarra*. Dall
and Whymper accompanied them in a boat manned by themselves and three Indians, one of whom was a Koyukon with a
name "so remarkably long and unpronounceable, that we decided
to call him Tom." Dall had been given to understand that game

was scarce in the region of Fort Yukon, his destination, so along the way to Nuklukayet he managed to barter for three hundred pounds of leathery dried moose meat, caribou intestines stuffed with the fat of that animal, beaver tails, and dried moose noses which, he reports, make "a delicious dish when thoroughly boiled."

Twenty miles above Nulato, Dall and Whymper worked their way slowly up past the mouth of the Koyukuk. This river, second longest of the Yukon's tributaries, flows southwestward through a basin the shape of an hourglass and the size of Ireland. Rising in the Brooks Range, the clear blue waters of the Koyukuk run 550 miles through the deep wilderness before being engulfed by the silted Yukon.

Just above the Koyukuk confluence, the Yukon passes a high bluff, called Yistletaw in Dall's day, but now known as Bishop's Rock for a missionary murdered there. At this point the river veers sharply eastward toward its meeting with the Arctic Circle five hundred miles farther up. Along the first part of this stretch the north bank is formed by the Kokrines Hills, a sere bald ridge of crumbling rock. At dusk these hills often take on a deep purple cast and they are exceedingly beautiful. The south bank is completely different, a gently undulating plain thickly forested with spruce and balsam poplar. It provides an excellent habitat for moose, and, despite repeating rifles and airplane hunters, they are probably more numerous now than a century ago when Dall bartered for their noses. Paradoxically, forest fires have helped the moose. Fires have frequently raged over this area and sometimes have been very large. In 1940, for example, a fire burned from June to August and ravaged 1,250,000 acres, mostly of spruce forest. Within ten years willows, birches and aspens, the moose's staples, had replaced the destroyed conifers on much of the huge burn. In this region moose are often seen at dusk browsing by the river, the cows with their dark-eyed, spindly-legged calves, the bulls solitary and magisterial.

At Nuklukayet Dall and Whymper left the Russians to their trading and continued on toward Fort Yukon. It was an arduous journey, especially along the first half of the route where the river

has cut a narrow, ragged slot through the Ray Mountains. This series of deep gorges, known as Rampart Canyon, compresses the river between high, dramatic walls not fifty yards apart in places, and the river makes up in velocity what it loses in breadth. In many places the current is too swift to paddle against, while towing a boat from shore—called "lining" or "tracking"—is made next to impossible by the abrupt banks.

About a hundred miles above Nuklukayet the sheer clefts of the Ray Mountains give way to the Yukon Flats, a large interior basin 250 miles long and 80 wide. The Flats are covered with a thick mantle of sand, silt and gravel washed down from glaciers in recent geological time. There is no rock to give strength or relief to the landscape, nor any feature on the horizon higher than the scraggy spikes of the spruce trees. Unconstrained, the river sprawls out all over the land, spills into myriad channels, dissipates its current in arms, inlets, bogs, swamps and dead-water

Western Union Telegraph Expedition (after Whymper)

sloughs beyond counting. It builds up innumerable islands, continuously shifts them around, adds to them, subtracts from them, divides them in halves and in hundredths; finally washes them away altogether and makes new ones of the wreckage farther down. No one has ever made a reliable map of the Flats, and nobody ever will, for they are not the same from one week to the next. So fast do the channels change that the captains of the Gold Rush stern-wheelers, though they made several runs through the Flats each navigation season, were obliged to take on pilots who had made several runs in the preceding week or two.

The myriad boggy ponds—thirty-six thousand of them by one estimate—with their profusion of aquatic plants make the Yukon Flats, like the river's delta, an important waterfowl nesting ground. About a million ducks, geese and swans are born here each year, more than in all the refuges of the lower forty-eight states combined. Lesser scaup and widgeon from the Pacific flyway swarm in by the thousands, and the canvasbacks, 9 percent of the continent's total, come all the way from Central America to nest here. Snow geese, pure white except for black wingtips, and small cackling Canadian geese (*Canadensis minima*) hardly larger than mallards fill the air with their lovely raucous music as they knife across the flat horizon. Sand-hill cranes, known locally as Alaska turkeys because of their flavor, strut with awkward dignity on the bars, the male and female inseparable. In slow meanders and oxbows diminutive green-winged teal lead their fluffy ducklings on foraging trips into the winter cress, and in the western part of the Flats pure white trumpeter swans, the largest of northern aquatic birds, hatch out their brownish offspring in nests perched atop beaver houses. A proposed dam that would drown the entire Flats under a lake bigger than Erie would of course put an end to this boggy, mosquito-infested waterfowl Eden.*

Fort Yukon, which Whymper and Dall reached on June 23, is situated at the geographic center of the Flats. The chief trader and several "servants" (as the Hudson's Bay Company still called its subordinate employees) were temporarily absent at the time, but Antoine Houle, brother of Robert Campbell's old voyageur companion, and the two Scots there showed their hospitality by offering the travelers a house in which to rest up. Fort Yukon was the most civilized place the telegraph explorers had seen in some time. "After our experience of the rather dirty Russian forts," observes Whymper, "it was quite a relief to find newly-plastered walls, glazed windows, capital floors, open fire-places, and a general appearance of cleanliness." Fort Yukon was evidently prosperous as well as clean. The Hudson's Bay Company had been in the fur business for a long time, and no organization better knew how to stimulate commerce with the primitive peoples of the northern forests. Each Indian who bought furs to Fort Yukon was given a clay pipe and a bit of tobacco, and if he was out of food

---

* Fortunately this project, which is an uneconomic make-work scheme to subsidize the Alaskan economy with Federal funds and keep the Army Corps of Engineers busy conquering nature, has been abandoned, at least for the time being.

a daily ration of moose meat as well. To the headmen of the tribes Chief Trader McDougall presented uniforms so resplendent with gilt epaulettes, brass buttons, ribbons and bangles that they would have made the *Chasseurs alpins* look like so many Salvation Army sergeants. The Indians responded to this treatment by coming to trade in large numbers; Whymper counted over five hundred of them assembled at one time, and their fusillade greetings gave the impression that the fort was under siege. By the time they left, the loft above the storehouse was "literally overflowing" with rich furs. The company took in about eight thousand marten skins a year, and many beaver, fox, lynx and wolverine as well. According to Dall a musket bartered at Fort Yukon cost twenty beaver skins or forty marten, worth about $150 in those days. The original cost of these guns was five dollars each, so even when they had to be hauled halfway round the globe, a profitable commerce was possible.

About the time that Dall and Whymper left Nulato, Ketchum and Laberge departed upriver from Fort Yukon where they had exchanged their dogsleds for a canoe and purchased some pemmican from the Hudson's Bay Company. Toward the end of June they reached the remains of Campbell's old post at the Yukon-Pelly confluence, and here they paused before starting back to Nulato. They gathered what information they could from the local Indians regarding the river above and heard reports of a large and beautiful lake, the only one on the Yukon, some distance upstream; lack of time prevented them from exploring it. Laberge, who spent many subsequent years on the Yukon, told others about this body of water, and it became known as Laberge's Lake, a name considerably easier to pronounce than the local Tutchone word for it, only partially captured by "Tlootsat-sahiya." This long, narrow cliff-bound lake of utterly transparent deep green water has retained the name of the good-natured French Canadian ever since, though whether it is properly Lake Laberge, Labarge, Leberge or Lebarge is disputed. The Geologic Survey of Canada favors the first, local usage employs them all except the first, and Robert Service, who had Sam McGee cremated on the lake's marge, favored the last.

On July 13, 1867, Ketchum and Laberge returned to Fort Yukon where Dall and Whymper were waiting. All four then embarked on the easy drift trip down to Nulato. They had reason to be well satisfied with their work, for now the basic reconnaissance of nearly the whole course of the Yukon—over one thousand five hundred miles—had been completed. The members of the Telegraph Expedition had suffered their share of hardships and privation, and the death of their first leader, but now their highly successful explorations were almost finished.

Back in Nulato a message awaited them; it had arrived there in late May, just after Dall and Whymper departed. It read:

"COMPANY HAS SUSPENDED OPERATIONS. REASON: THE ATLANTIC CABLE IS A SUCCESS. WE ARE ALL ORDERED HOME. UNITED STATES BOUGHT RUSSIAN-AMERICA FROM RUSSIAN GOVERNMENT."

7 An American River

December 1, 1867. Today mail arrived from
Mikhailovsky Redoubt [St. Michael]. A letter
from Novo-Arkhangelsk [Sitka] informed me
about the sale of the colonies to the Americans
and about plans for the deportation of all Russians. Perhaps that concerns me. Oh, Lord! So
shall it be!

—Diary of Hieromonk Illarion,
Orthodox priest at Ikogmut on the lower Yukon.

IN OCTOBER of 1867 Sitka was aswarm with Russians from all
parts of the ex-colony. Toward midsummer they had been informed that the Czar had sold the ground from beneath their
feet, and they were now packing up to leave. No doubt some
were glad to be seeing the last of this remote colonial backwater,
but apparently most were thoroughly depressed at having to
abandon the ambitions and dreams they had formed for their
future in Russian America. To an observer who watched them
stuff their belongings into crates on the Sitka waterfront, they
"seemed as though they were preparing for the funeral of the
Tsar, going about the town in a most dejected manner." On the
eighteenth, when the ceremony of transfer took place, few of
them had the heart to watch the Russian double eagle lowered
for the last time.

A number of Americans were present, however, men of all
degrees and means who had come to scout out the opportunities

75

this vast new frontier might afford them. Among them was Mr. Hayward M. Hutchinson, a Baltimore businessman who had made a modest fortune manufacturing tin cups for the Union armies. The end of the war had seen his contracts dry up, and he had come west in search of new prospects. In San Francisco Hutchinson, several other businessmen, and a sea captain named William Kohl joined together for the purpose of buying up the assets of the Russian-American Company. Hutchinson and Kohl then proceeded to Sitka. A week before the transfer ceremony they were received by Prince Maksutov, the Russian governor; the meeting lasted twelve hours, and by the time it was over the firm of Hutchinson, Kohl & Company had exchanged $350,000 in gold for the trading posts, ships, warehouses, inventories and "goodwill" of the Russian-American Company.

One of the items on the bill of sale was Redoubt St. Michael, a fortified trading post on the Bering Sea about sixty miles from the Yukon estuary. Located on an inhospitable tundra island just off the coast, St. Michael had no harbor to protect boats from the continuous arctic gales, and the sound around it was full of shoals and sand bars. Nor were there any sea otters or fur seals, only the lemmings that swarmed and died out every few years, and an occasional fox that strayed from the mainland. Lieutenant Tebenkov, who founded the Redoubt in 1833, well knew the disadvantages of the place, but he could find no better base for trading operations into the Yukon. In the years since then, St. Michael had served as the jumping-off point for all Russian penetrations of the river basin. After the American purchase, it became the principal depot for goods destined for interior Alaska and northwestern Canada. Ocean-going ships transferred their cargoes to shallow draft stern-wheelers there, and the latter then cautiously pushed their way to the navigable Apoon Channel of the Yukon delta where the upriver voyage began. The first gold of the Klondike passed down through Redoubt St. Michael—"St. Mike" to the miners—and a month later the first of thousands of gold rushers swarmed through it on their way to the new Eldorado. When traffic on the Yukon boomed, so did St. Michael. Today few boats ply the river and the boneyard of rotten hulks is the only reminder of a more prosperous era.

During the summer of 1868, when Messrs. Hutchinson and Kohl were on the Pribilof Islands organizing their tremendously profitable sealing operations, they dispatched George R. Adams, late of the Telegraph Expedition, to take possession of St. Michael. Adams ran the American flag up over Tebenkov's old hexagonal blockhouse, set up quarters in the Russian storehouse, and engaged the men of the region to hunt furs for his employers. He thus established a base for Hutchinson, Kohl & Company's future operations on the Yukon.

Already, however, a handful of Americans and French Canadians had set up a tenuous, petty trade on the river. They had almost no capital and their "Pioneer Company" was not a legal corporation at all, but a loose association of friends. Most of them had entered the country with the Telegraph Expedition or the Hudson's Bay Company, had liked it and decided to stay. Mike Laberge was among them, along with several other French Canadians including Moïse Mercier, and his brother François, a bearded giant of a man who would later become a sort of backwoods commercial czar of the Yukon. Two of the Americans were John Clark and Thomas Conlin, sketchy shadows in the river's early annals; the third was James Bean, a reckless man whose lack of good sense and tact would cost him dearly. In the fall of 1868 the Pioneers established a trading post called Nukluroyit Station, a dozen miles below the Yukon-Tanana confluence. It was the first American establishment on the Yukon, or anywhere in the interior of Alaska for that matter. This location, it will be recalled, had been the scene of annual Indian trade rendezvous since time immemorial; in recent years both the Hudson's Bay traders from Fort Yukon and Ivan Pavloff's men from Nulato had come there each June to barter furs.* The Pioneer Company lasted only a season or so, but the experience its men had acquired of the Yukon's geography, peoples, and furs proved most valuable to its successors.

In 1869 the directors of the Alaska Commercial Company (which Hutchinson, Kohl & Company had become in September,

---

* Dall refers to this place as Nuklukahyét, Whymper as Nuclukayette; in previous chapters I have simplified the name to Nuklukayet.

1868) decided to push their commerce from St. Michael into the
Yukon valley proper. That June Captain Kohl's *Fideliter* arrived
at St. Michael with a cargo including a gross of harmonicas, six
gross of agate buttons, and six hoop skirts, as well as more con-
ventional items such as flour, bacon, candles, and three quarters
of a ton of Kentucky leaf tobacco. One wonders just what clientele the company dispatchers back in San Francisco had in mind
for the harmonicas, but the huge consignment of tobacco was
undoubtedly ordered by someone well versed in Indian weak-
nesses.

The Alaska Commercial Company would hold a complete
monopoly on Yukon trade for many years, but at the beginning
it had competition. In this same month of June 1869, the brig
Commodore, belonging to Parrott and Company, also of San
Francisco, put in at St. Michael. The two firms would merge a
year later, but for the present Parrott had a decided advantage
over its competitor in the form of a tiny stern-wheel steamboat
lashed to the *Commodore*'s deck. The *Yukon* she was called, a
scanty fifty feet long and twelve wide, her homely outline sug-
gesting a small cow barn set on a scow. Early in July she was
lowered into Norton Sound and piloted down to the Apoon
Channel of the Yukon delta.

It is a dreary place, here where the first steamboat met the
river and the river meets the sea. So much so that people who live
here are beyond complaining about its dreariness; their only re-
course is to extol this very quality as the Bedouin extols his desert
wastes. The delta is a rough triangle about fifty miles across on
the seaward side. Treeless and utterly flat, a straight horizon
severs it from a usually grey sky with the cold brutality of a
surgical incision. The delta is the work of the Yukon, past, present
and future. All along its course the river has been demolishing the
land. Now it builds with the wreckage—a final creative act as it
ebbs to oblivion in the Bering Sea. There is something of every
feature of the Yukon valley here, from Mt. McKinley to the least
hillock, all of it abraded, transported, homogenized and set down
again by the endless motion of water. Too young for wrinkles or
contours, too early in evolution for a skeleton, the delta spreads

out nearly as inchoate as the sea beyond. And over it all sprawls the Yukon in a maze of unstable channels reticulated like a drunken spider's web.

Though the Yukon flows through an unbroken forest bigger than Texas, it ends as it began, in the tundra. The headwaters are treeless because of elevation, the delta because of the climatic influence of the Bering Sea. The sea water retains the cold of winter late into spring, and during the summer water vapor rising from it filters out the sun. The delta is far from lifeless, however. Five species of bush willows, freed here from the competition of the forest, thrive in abundance. They are the beginning of an important food chain that leads first to lemmings, voles, snowshoe and tundra hares, and ptarmigan, and then to such predators as the lynx, the wolf, the fox, the weasel, even the bear.

The delta is so waterlogged that from the air it resembles an island-choked lake. On the edges of thousands of shallow ponds and sloughs, wild celery, cowslip, sourdock and goose grasses proliferate, and on slightly drier ground half a dozen kinds of berries ripen in late summer. This combination of shallow water and abundant food makes the Yukon delta, like the Flats a thousand miles farther upriver, one of the world's greatest waterfowl nesting grounds. From May to September the air is alive with the cries and wingbeats of birds who migrate here from as far away as Japan and South America. Slate-blue emperor geese, Canadas, white-fronteds and snows all nest in the delta, as do tens of thousands of pintail, baldpate, golden-eye and old squaw ducks, all the species of eiders, common loons, greyheaded Arctic loons and red-eyed loons, and a dozen species of shore birds.

After a day aground on a shoal in the Apoon Channel the *Yukon* continued on without further mishap. After every ten hours of running time, she would be tied up to the bank next to a pile of driftwood. All hands would descend to saw up the four or five cords she could carry on her minuscule decks, and in a few hours she would be on her way again. If it hadn't been for driftwood, obtaining fuel would have been a serious problem. There are no trees along the river for the first 150 miles or so, still only the tundra characteristic of the delta. And the first trees that appear are dwarfed spruces and balsam poplars, which gain only precarious and intermittent purchase as a narrow fringe between river and tundra; the timber line here stands at twenty-five feet above sea level. Farther up, the trees gradually become larger and the fringe of forest broadens, becomes continuous, ascends the slopes at the expense of the tundra. Only when the river reaches the region of Anvik, 325 miles from the Bering Sea, does the timber line rise to the 2,000-3,000-foot level it will maintain in most parts of the Yukon basin. By then the tundra hare, the Arctic fox and the collared lemming have been left behind, for they cannot make the transition from tundra to forest. The moose, however, has come into his own, and since there are now spruce cones there are red squirrels which live on them and martens which live on the squirrels. Some mammals, such as lynx and wolves, are adapted to life on both sides of the ecological frontier, but this was not true of either the Eskimos or the Indians—or at least not in 1869, before wage employment and airplanes carried them across it. The Eskimos inhabited the river from the coast to Paimut, the last village surrounded by the tundra, and the Indians from a few dozen miles above Paimut to the Yukon's headwaters.

The *Yukon* entered the river's delta on July 4, 1869. The date has symbolic significance, for Captain Charles P. Raymond, U.S. Army, was aboard, and his mission was to investigate an infringement by the Hudson's Bay Company of United States territory. Back in 1847, when Alexander Hunter Murray had established Fort Yukon, he was fully aware that he was poaching on Russia territory. "I wish," he had written in his journal, that the region "was our own, I mean the Hudson's Bay Co.'s, at least for a term of years until we thinned it of its superabundance of Beaver and Martens." But it was not, so Murray, fearing an attack, set to work on substantial fortifications. "When all . . . is finished," he noted, "the Russians may advance when they d——d please." Though the Russians knew of the trespass, they had neither the resources nor the energy to put an end to it. The men of the Pioneer Company knew about it too, and complained that their trade at Nukluroyit Station suffered heavily from the efficient, skillful competition of the Hudson's Bay Company.

The upriver voyage of the *Yukon* was a great event for the native people of the river. Until then they had seen no more sophisticated evidence of the Industrial Revolution than a few mass-produced glass beads, knives, and flintlocks. Captain Raymond describes their reaction:

Our approach was usually the occasion of considerable excitement. As we drew near a village, we were accustomed to herald our coming by a vigorous sounding of the whistle, and this was usually followed by a general stampede of men, women, children, and dogs. Our little steamer, which, puffing about the bay of San Francisco, had seemed a mere toy, appeared to them a huge monster, breathing fire and smoke. Curiosity would, however, bring the more daring ones to the river's bank, and, having won their confidence by a few judicious presents, we would soon find our boat surrounded by a score or two of noisy and excited natives.

The manager of Parrott and Company, owners of the *Yukon*, had hired Mike Laberge and several other Pioneers in St. Michael, and he had purchased Nukluroyit Station, their post near the mouth of the Tanana. On the way upriver he had the *Yukon* stop at Anvik, Nulato (where Ivan Pavloff's buildings lay abandoned), and Nukluroyit Station to leave off his fur traders and a year's supplies.

From Nukluroyit Station the stern-wheeler steamed up to Fort Yukon. Captain Raymond informed Mr. John Wilson, the Hudson's Bay Company's chief trader there, why he had come. "Notwithstanding the somewhat unpleasant character of our errand," recounts the captain, "we were cordially welcomed." Raymond lost no time in setting up his instruments, and within a week had determined beyond doubt that Fort Yukon was well to the west of 141° west longitude, the international boundary line. "I notified the representative of the Hudson [sic] Bay Company," the captain reported to his superiors, "that the station was in the territory of the United States; that the introduction of trading goods, or any trade by foreigners with the natives was illegal, and must cease, and that the Hudson Bay Company must vacate the buildings as soon as practicable. I then took possession of the buildings and raised the flag of the United States over the fort."

The manager of Parrott and Company had brought along two fur traders, Ferdinand Westdahl and Moïse Mercier, just in case Raymond should issue such a decree. He now installed them in place of the British, and then departed downriver for St. Michael on August 10. This was too soon for Captain Raymond. He already knew Fort Yukon was well within American territory, but to establish its exact location he had to wait until the perpetual light of the arctic midsummer gave way to brief nights, during which he could use the stars for his astronomical calculations. He completed his work two weeks later. On the twenty-sixth he and his assistant loaded their instruments and a few provisions into the *Eclipse*, a leaky skiff of spruce planks caulked with rags and covered with pitch. They tethered the craft to the bank with a sturdy thong of moosehide, and turned in for a good night's sleep before the morrow's journey. "But in the morning," relates the captain, "we discovered that the hungry dogs of the station had eaten the moose-skin fastening, and our boat had started off on an independent voyage to the coast." No doubt the Hudson's Bay men, whom Raymond had dispossessed, relished the spectacle. The captain and his aide finally got to St. Michael, however, just before the ice set. The only food they had left during the last few days was part of a ham which they rationed out in pieces "about the size of a half-dollar" and washed down with sugarless tea.

On her maiden voyage the *Yukon* introduced the machine age and American dominion to the river, but for the next decade and a half the activity of the Americans, like that of the Slavs and Scots before them, would be limited to bartering furs, and confined to a tenuous string of insubstantial log trading posts.

8 *Leroy Napoleon McQuesten*

> . . . on the 10th May [1874] the Yukon ice
> started to run. . . . I thought it was a grand sight
> then to see the ice go tearing and smashing ev-
> erything that was in the way, and I have seen it
> every year since and I still think it is a wonderful
> sight.
>
> —L. N. McQuesten, *Journal*

IN THE old days especially, the valley of the Yukon was a magnet
for men charged with peculiar properties. They were drawn to an
exile out past the last tattered fringes of civilization. Why? "Because there one suffers more for Our Father," said Jules Jetté of
the Society of Jesus, who served for many years at Nulato. Because "I became possessed with an irresistible longing to go to
that land of romance and adventure," said Robert Campbell. Because "it provides an excellent opportunity for the study of the
relationship of North American and Asiatic flora and fauna," said
Robert Kennicott. Because "up here you can do as you goddamn
well please, and f—— what anybody says. And most times ain't
nobody round what's gonna say it," says an old fur trader who
lives in the little river settlement of Beaver. Some came to the
Yukon in pursuit of wealth, others of solitude, or anarchistic free-
dom, psychic peace or noble savagery. Some came to evade social
obligations, haunting memories, nagging wives, sheriff's posses or

83

creditors. Most came for a variety of reasons, and it was not in their natures to pause and sort out their mixed motives. In general they were not of the type that delights in self-revelation, and they were usually too busy surviving to have much time left over for introspection. They were of various backgrounds, conditions and places: among them were Anglican bishops and Catholic scholars, illiterate trappers and prospectors, whiskey peddlers, wood choppers, preachers and vagabonds. In common, they chose a life that, materially at least, was much more difficult than that to which they were born. In common, too, they found that their long experience in the wilderness rendered them unfit, or at least uncomfortable, in any other surroundings.

The current of the Porcupine River carried Leroy Napoleon McQuesten, his two partners, four sled dogs and fourteen hundred pounds of provisions down to Fort Yukon in August 1873. What motives carried him there, beyond the most unsubstantiated rumors of gold, he never revealed to others, and probably not to himself either. Indeed, for him, the journey was routine enough not to need any special motive; ever since he had left his native Maine, he had been making similar roaming voyages through the wilderness of the Northwest.

Like Robert Campbell, McQuesten was a farm boy with a romantic imagination, and he too ventured into the remote parts of Canada as an employee of the Hudson's Bay Company. Unlike Campbell, however, he spent only a year or two with the company. Thereafter he worked at times as a free trader, at others as a trapper and prospector. He rambled over large sections of what are now British Columbia, Alberta, and the Northwest Territories, never staying in one place nor with one pursuit for long.

In 1871 McQuesten set up winter trapping quarters near Great Slave Lake in the Northwest Territories. At the time, and for many years thereafter, Alfred Mayo, a barrel-chested former circus acrobat, was one of his partners. One of the few visitors McQuesten and Mayo received that winter was a Hudson's Bay employee who had served at Fort Yukon. He informed them that Alaska was now American territory, an item of news already four years old, but fresh to them. Further, the Hudson's Bay man said that gold, or what he took to be gold, had been found there. And even if the gold should prove too elusive, the country around Fort Yukon was a fabulous fur region. At the fort itself, the man told McQuesten, one "would catch a silver fox near the water hole about every night" and as for marten, they could be clubbed to

death right inside the stockade. "These stories interested us;" Mc-Questen relates, "it was just the country we were looking for."

Two years later McQuesten, Mayo, and a third man named George Wilkenson, then encamped on the Liard River in preparation for their journey to the Yukon, encountered another party with the same destination and purposes. One of the five men in this group, Arthur Harper, was to play an important part in the history of the Yukon. A tall, bearded man strong as an ox, Harper was obsessed with the search for gold. Part of his very being was a compass that pointed toward this metal—though, as shall be seen, never quite to it—and Harper spent his life following the needle. Since leaving County Antrim, Ireland, he had been on gold stampedes in California, in the Fraser Valley, and in the Cassiar District of British Columbia. He was heading for the Yukon, of course, to continue the search, and he had a good rationale for doing so. Looking at Arrowsmith's *Atlas of North America,* he was struck by the fact that gold had been discovered all up and down the Rocky Mountain chain from Mexico to northern British Columbia. Why, he asked himself, should it not also occur at the northern extremities of the range? He decided that it should and spent the rest of his life attempting to prove that it did. He never made a rich strike in all his years of prospecting, but such was his faith—his monomania, some might have called it—that he could spend decades of the most grueling toil in the most remote corners of the wilderness sinking worthless shafts and yet believe that the next one would uncover a fortune. Perhaps, though, it was the search that really mattered to him; unearthing great treasure would have put an end to the constant questing ramble that was synonymous with his life. It would have been as unsatisfying as finally arriving at the horizon.

McQuesten, Mayo, and Wilkenson reached Fort Yukon on August 15, 1873. Moïse Mercier was running the trading post there at the time. He had come to Fort Yukon with Captain Raymond four years before to establish Parrott and Company (which merged with Alaska Commercial in 1870) in the place of the expelled Hudson's Bay Company. Mercier seldom saw white men, and he was cordial in his welcome. "We were treated like kings," recounts McQuesten. "Some of us had not had such good living in ten years. It was there we saw the first repeating rifle. Mercier had no flour to sell—he let us have 50 lbs. that was for four of us [the fourth, a man named Nickelson, had joined them on the Porcupine] for a year. . . . That was quite a treat to us, as that was the first we had had for two years."

Earlier that summer Harper's party had reached Fort Yukon by the same route. One of its members, Andrew Kenseller, had accepted a job with the ACC⁰. as assistant trader at Nukluroyit Station, downriver at the mouth of the Tanana, but the others —Harper, Finch, Gestler, and Fred Hart—ascended the Yukon to the White River where they planned to do a winter's prospecting. McQuesten and Mayo thought first of trapping, however. The fur trader who had described the Fort Yukon country to them had also told them of a tremendously rich fur region in the vicinity of Rampart Canyon. They reached this area around the first of September.

We went to work and built our cabin [writes McQuesten] and then started to lay in our provisions for the winter. We killed three moose and one large bear and had plenty of geese and ducks all the time until the lakes froze up. So we had a good stock of meat in hand for the winter. We set our nets under the ice most all winter and we would catch some fish most everytime we took them [up]. . . . They were the largest and fattest white fish that we had seen in the North West. They would fry themselves; one pint of oil was very common to get out of one fish. They weighed from eight to twenty pounds each. . . . We would snare rabbits for a change.

We had no window glass for our cabin so when the lake froze up we cut out pieces about two foot square and they did very well in the place of windows. We had to change them once a week.

While living off the land was a success, trapping and trading were failures. The Indians had departed the region, and so apparently had most of the marten and beaver. McQuesten and Mayo returned to Fort Yukon in April after a discouraging winter.

In those days it was the custom of the handful of traders on the river to load the season's furs into scows and float down to St. Michael right after the breakup each spring. They would arrive there about the time the annual supply ship from San Francisco did, and receive the only news of the outside world they would get until the following year. The stern-wheeler *Yukon* would then tow them back upriver, laden this time with trade goods.

Late in May 1874, McQuesten and Mayo started down the Yukon in Moïse Mercier's scow. They stopped at Nukluroyit Station where hundreds of Indians had assembled to barter their furs to the ACC⁰. While McQuesten and Mayo waited for the commerce to be finished, Harper, Hart, and Finch, who had drifted nearly a thousand miles down from White River, joined them. "It was the first we heard from them since they left Fort Yukon [a year before]," writes McQuesten. "They killed plenty of moose and lived like Kings all winter. They had done considerable prospecting but they found nothing that would pay." Having come to Nukluroyit for supplies, and finding none available there, they decided to continue down to St. Michael in Moïse Mercier's scow. The whole group arrived there on June 25.

François Mercier, Moïse's brother, was in charge of the ACC⁰. St. Michael depot and, in fact, of all the company's operations in the Yukon basin. Wishing to expand the business, he sought to hire as fur traders every one of the members of both McQuesten's and Harper's parties. McQuesten, Mayo and two others accepted. Harper and two others, however, refused. They would continue prospecting. At Nukluroyit Station they had seen about thirty dollars' worth of coarse gold brought in by an Indian of the vicinity. The discoverer said he found it on a nearby mountain, and the prospectors wanted to investigate his report.

On July 7 the *Yukon* left St. Michael for the upper river. Harper and three others were dropped off at Nukluroyit Station to prospect, and Mayo to run the ACC⁰. post there. Fred Hart was left at Nulato to work for Mike Laberge, the company's chief trader in that village. Thus, of the men who had come in from Canada the previous summer, all were now on the lower river either trading for ACC⁰. or prospecting—all save McQuesten. François Mercier had other plans for him.

The *Yukon* stopped for a few days at Fort Yukon, then continued on upstream. "As it was the first time the Steamer [or any other, for that matter] had been on that part of the River," McQuesten relates, "we had considerable trouble in keeping the channel which necessarily delayed us some. We had only about three ton of merchandise aboard and a Whale boat in tow. We selected a location [for the new post] near Trundeck about 350 miles from Fort Yukon." They reached the vicinity of "Trundeck" on August 7, 1874, according to the Mercier manuscript, on August 20 according to McQuesten's journal. Whatever the date, the *Yukon* unloaded its cargo and started back for St. Michael two days later. The location was far upriver from that of any post then existing, and far above the farthest point Mercier or any of his men (save Mike Laberge) had ever been. The site chosen was a good one; on the east bank, it was high enough above the river to avoid the spring floods and sloping enough to be well drained; neither of these advantages existed at the site six miles upstream on the same bank where Dawson would mushroom in the mire twenty-three years hence. The "Trundeck" to which McQuesten refers—Mercier calls it the "Clondik"—later became known as the Klondike, as, indeed, did the whole region.

McQuesten and Frank Bonfield, the young Englishman Mercier had engaged to assist him, had to rush to construct a cabin and trading post before the winter set in. McQuesten hired the local Indians to float logs down to his site, and others to hunt for him. By the time the cold weather came, "We had our house and the store completed and the Indians brought in plenty of dried meat to last us all winter." They also brought in furs, and by the end of the winter McQuesten had bartered away every item in stock for them. Fort Reliance, as McQuesten had called it, was a prosperous little outpost.

In May, McQuesten and Bonfield packed their furs aboard their scow and started for St. Michael. As he had the previous spring, McQuesten encountered Arthur Harper at Nukluroyit Station. He had spent another rigorous winter of prospecting, and again he had nothing to show for it. His partners were by now thoroughly disgusted with the Yukon. They accompanied Mc-

Questen and Harper to St. Michael, where they shipped out to San Francisco. Their reports of the poor prospects for placer mining on the Yukon circulated through the mining camps up and down the coast, and no new prospectors entered the region for several years.

Harper was not so easily discouraged; he had to make a living, though, so he too turned to trading. While at St. Michael the ACC⁰. agent offered him, McQuesten, and Mayo a franchise on all trade upriver from Fort Yukon, and they accepted. Off and on for the next twenty years and more these three men would be associated in one endeavor or another; if it wasn't fur trading, it was prospecting, and if it wasn't prospecting it was selling miners' supplies or staking out townsites. They probably came to know the upper river better than anyone before or since, and they were the first whites to penetrate a number of its tributaries. They considered as their domain an area bigger by several times than McQuesten's native New England or Harper's Ireland, and for years they were the only white men in it. They were no longer, strictly speaking, employed by ACC⁰., because now they traded on commission. Their time was their own, and they were free to wander, explore, and prospect at will. They received mail once a year and were sometimes alone for months at a time, but there is no record of their complaining of loneliness. Though the company offered them free passage to San Francisco each summer, they did not avail themselves of the opportunity. Alfred Mayo died and is buried not a hundred yards from the Yukon at Rampart, Alaska, and the other two did not survive their final departure from the river by more than a year or two. Their names are now borne by streams, mountains, bends in the river, bluffs and towns, and by half- and quarter-breed grandchildren as well, for each one of them took an Indian wife.

For the first three years of their association, McQuesten traded at Fort Yukon, while Harper and Mayo ran Fort Reliance. Late each summer, after returning from St. Michael on the *Yukon*, Harper made extended prospecting trips. He found gold in nearly every stream in which he panned, but not in quantities that made it profitable to exploit. Finally, in 1877, he discovered deposits on

the Sixty Mile River (so called because it entered the Yukon
about sixty miles upstream from Fort Reliance) that he thought
rich enough to justify working. He sent out for some mercury, an
element with an affinity for gold, used to capture fine particles of
the metal that otherwise might escape in the sluicing process.
When it arrived he planned to start the first mine on the Yukon. A
conflict with the Indians, however, forced him to abandon not
only this project, but Fort Reliance itself. The trouble started
when Mayo found an Indian with a packet of tobacco that had
obviously been stolen from the post. He forcibly recovered it
from the thief, but the angry and menacing reaction this pro-
voked among the culprit's tribesmen led Harper and Mayo to
decide that the better part of valor was to close up the place and
leave. They went down to Nukluroyit Station to join McQuesten.
That summer, for the first time, there was Indian trouble there as
well.

In 1875 when Mike Laberge left to go back home to Quebec,
the ACC⁰. assigned a man named James Bean to take over his
trading post at Nulato. Alone among the early traders on the
river, Bean had brought along his wife; she was the first American woman to live on the Yukon, and, a year or two later, the first
to bear a child there. After three years at Nulato, Bean decided to
quit ACC⁰. and start trading on his own account. He wanted to
set up a post in the vicinity of Nukluroyit Station, but at this time
both ACC⁰. and a new arrival, the Western Fur and Trading
Company, were established there, and something of a price war
was being waged between them; it was hardly a good location for
a small independent trader to get started. Bean reasoned that if
he could build a post some distance up the Tanana River, he
would be able to intercept the Indians on their way to trade with
the big companies. In May 1878 he left Nulato in a large *bidarra*
loaded down with trade goods and provisions. His passengers
were his wife, his infant son and a young Russian creole girl.
They reached the mouth of the Tanana on June 7, as McQuesten,
and Harper and Mayo, who had just arrived after abandoning
Fort Reliance, were getting ready for the annual trip to St. Michael. Bean explained his plans to them.

McQuesten, the only white man who had ever been even a little way up the Tanana, told him it was a risky enterprise. The Indians were "a kind of a wild set" and not to be depended on; if Bean still wanted to go, McQuesten advised, he should at least take the precaution of leaving his family behind. Bean disregarded the advice and proceeded up the Tanana as planned. He found a suitable location about thirty-five miles above the river's mouth, built a crude trading station and went into business.

Toward the end of September two young Indians came to trade. When the transaction was completed, they asked Bean, whose wife was just then preparing a meal, if they could have something to eat. He refused, perhaps not uncharacteristically, as he was known to his fellow traders as a close sort of man. The Indians departed, and Bean and his wife sat down to eat, he facing the door, she with her back to it. Suddenly one of the two Indians reappeared in the doorway. He began to say something to Bean. The second Indian crept up behind him, raised up the barrel of his gun and fired. The bullet hit Mrs. Bean in the back. She keeled over to the floor, dead. Her husband leapt up and ran into the adjoining room to get his rifle. The Indian with the gun attempted to shoot him down, but the weapon misfired. By the time Bean loaded his rifle and re-emerged, the two Indians had fled into the woods. Apparently seized by panic at this point, he grabbed up his son and the creole girl and ran down to the Tanana to make his escape. The murderers' canoe was lying on the bank; he put the two children in it and shoved off. A moment later he had capsized the frail craft, but fortunately in shallow water. He managed to scramble ashore with the children. Just then an old Indian woman appeared. She was bringing a canoe-load of dried salmon to trade at the post, and of course knew nothing of what had just happened. Bean managed to grab hold of her canoe, and to force her to take him and the children down the Tanana to the post François Mercier was then running for the Western Fur and Trading Company.

Mercier was there when he arrived. Bean seemed to him "quite out of his mind," but managed to relate, in fits and starts, what had happened. Mercier immediately summoned Arthur Harper and Alfred Mayo from the ACC⁰. post at Nukluroyit, seven miles downstream. They arrived several hours later, and Harper and three of his Indian employees started up the Tanana to fetch the body of Mrs. Bean. She was found lying in a pool of blood on the floor. They brought her back to Mercier's, where she was "washed and dressed" by Indian women, and placed in the tight coffin Mercier had prepared. Bean, in the meantime, acted as if the whole matter of his wife's death were of no concern to him. "For a while," writes Mercier, "we strongly suspected [him] . . . of having been guilty of the crime, so strange was his behavior. . . ." Without so much as thanking the other traders, Bean departed downriver with his son and his dead wife. He planned to reach St. Michael, but the imminent freeze-up led him to stop at Nulato instead. Here he interred her, it is said, nine feet deep in the ground and enshrouded in a double layer of thick canvas. In all probability she lies there unchanged to this day, preserved by the permafrost just like the mammoths and saber-toothed tigers trapped by the last Ice Age. To her left, not ten paces away, lies Lieutenant John Bernard of the Royal Navy, and just to her right, Vasili Deriabin of the Russian-American Company—a cosmopolitan graveyard for such a little place as Nulato.

At the time of Mrs. Bean's murder there were no sheriffs, marshals, policemen, soldiers, courts, judges or jails within hundreds of miles of the Yukon. Indeed, there were only a dozen white men on all the river in 1878, and after Mrs. Bean's death, no white women at all. The murderers freely acknowledged their guilt; according to McQuesten ". . . they used to come down to the [Nukluroyit] Station every spring, but there would only be two or three traders and they didn't think it was safe to arrest them as the Indians had always threatened to rob the Station most every spring." Mrs. Bean's murderers did not rob her husband's post, however. Their crime had apparently been an impetuous reaction to a minor slight; they explained to the traders that they had expected the bullet that killed Mrs. Bean to pass through her and kill Bean as well.

The commercial rivalry and price war at the Tanana-Yukon confluence, which had prompted Bean to strike out up the

Tanana, induced McQuesten to attempt reopening Fort Reliance, then abandoned. Because of Indian hostility following the stolen tobacco incident he was not sure this would be possible. However, when he nosed the *Yukon* in toward the high bank in front of the post, an amicable fusillade of shots greeted him; "being received so friendly" calmed his fears. The Indians obviously wanted the trader and his wares in their midst, and their chief now presented McQuesten with furs to compensate for the stolen goods. Another matter of compensation remained to be settled, however, before McQuesten felt safe to unload his goods. During his absence three women had died from eating flour that had been poisoned with arsenic. Though the flour had been stolen from the post, the Indians demanded compensation for the deaths it had caused. McQuesten negotiated a settlement in the following manner:

I told them that the poison was put in the store to destroy mice and it was out of the way of children and the old people ought to know better and [as for] the people that died it was their own fault for breaking into the store and taking things that didn't belong to them. There was one blind girl about sixteen years old that got poisoned— her father said she was a great deal of help to her mother and he had taken one of our dogs to replace the girl, but if I would pay for the girl he would return the dog. I told him I would think the matter over and let them know later on. Finally I told them the girl's Mother could keep the dog, so that settled the matter and that was the last I ever heard about the poison.

Next day McQuesten unloaded his trade goods and reopened Fort Reliance. He had no more trouble with the Indians that year.

There was nothing happened during the winter of any note [he writes]. We always had plenty of meat in store, and done very well in the fur line. In March I fell out of the loft of the store—I struck on a nest of Camp Kettles on my back. I broke one of my short ribs. It was two weeks before I could move and I was in great pain unless I was in a certain position. There were three bands of Indians within

[a] day's travel. . . . they would send in a messenger every day to hear how I was getting along and the Shoman [shaman] were making medicine for me to get well. . . . They thought if I should die that they might be blamed for killing me as there was no other white man in this part of the country.

During the summer of 1879, as in past summers, McQuesten spent much of his time freighting supplies to Fort Reliance and other ACC⁰. posts aboard the *Yukon*. For a decade now this little steamer which had seemed a child's toy puffing around San Francisco Bay had had the river all to herself. That year, however, she was joined by the *St. Michael* owned by the competing Western Trading and Fur Company, and she would not long survive being outclassed by her larger and swifter rival. In her voyages above the Tanana, McQuesten was the *Yukon's* captain, fireman, engineer, mechanic, pilot and often her only white passenger. "It is a wonder to me," he observes, "that we didn't blow her up or sink her as I didn't know anything about steam boating. Often we would get a moose in the water and all hands would grab the guns and let the steamer take care of herself. . . ." That fall the *Yukon*, now "very old and liable to blow up at any time," was hauled up into a slough near Fort Yukon to be protected from the crushing river ice of the breakup. The following spring brought a flood, however, and the high water sent huge ice floes into her slough. She was demolished. By then, the ACC⁰. had ordered a new vessel which lay awaiting assembly when McQuesten arrived at St. Michael the same spring.

During the summer of 1880 Arthur Harper and a man named Bates set out on foot to prospect the country between present-day Eagle, Alaska, and the upper Tanana. Reaching this river, they fashioned a boat from the skin of a moose and descended all the way to the Tanana's confluence with the Yukon at Nukluroyit. Until then, almost the entire five-hundred-mile course of the Tanana was unknown to white men. Dall, who passed its mouth in 1867, tried to find out about it from the Russians and Indians, but he apparently had little success: on his map the Tanana is merely guessed at, and poorly, by a vague dotted line. Since then

a few fur traders, McQuesten and James Bean among them, had
ascended it from the Yukon, but only for a few score miles.

Near the beginning of their trip, as Harper and Bates were
crossing the North Fork of the Fortymile River, Bates got swept
off his feet and nearly drowned. While he was recuperating and
drying out, Harper's eye was drawn to the sand at the edge of the
stream. He scooped up a sample and took it away with him. The
assayor in San Francisco to whom it was sent determined that a
ton of the material would contain twenty thousand dollars worth
of gold. Harper returned to the spot the following year only to
find that the ice had carried away the entire deposit. Such, as
usual, was the luck of this Irishman.

Fort Reliance was usually a lonely place at Christmastime. Mc-
Questen's neighbors celebrated the Feast for the Dead about this
time of the year, and no passing missionary had yet told them of
the Savior's birth. The nearest white man, and the nearest human
McQuesten could converse with, was hundreds of miles downriver. Besides, when Christmas falls at the latitude of Fort Reliance, day is but a twilight intermission in a night of twenty-two
hours, a meaningless reprieve in the cold darkness.

Christmas 1882 was different. There were white men at Fort
Reliance, a dozen of them, and McQuesten was host to their noisy
celebrations. There was a foot race and a snow-shoveling contest
in which the loser had to stand on his head. There was a banquet,
and there was story telling and card playing. On New Year's
Day there was even a brand new sport, which McQuesten describes as follows:

The Indians got a large moose skin and as many as could get
around it would take hold of the edge and then some young Indian
would get on top of the skin and they would toss him up. The white
men thought it great sport and they joined in the game. After a while
the men began to throw the women in the Moose skin and tossing
[sic] them up. After the women had been tossed they turned to and
caught the white men and they had to take their turn to be thrown up
in the air—it was great sport for those not in the Moose skin as a man

is perfectly helpless when he is thrown ten up. Some time he will come down on his head but they never got hurt.

The Christmas of 1882 was decidedly different from past Christmases at Fort Reliance. The change was a sign of the times: McQuesten's twelve guests were prospectors, and every year now more of them were coming into the Yukon.

9   *Half the Time You Find It Where It Aren't*

Now AND THEN the Yukon rives off great slices of its banks and rampages over its flood plains in an obliterating fury. In general, though, its destruction of the landscape is less dramatic; the units of demolition are ions, molecules and minute fragments. Time, after all, is on the side of the river, and spectacular achievements are unnecessary. Without fanfare, usually, and without cease, the river has abraded its way deep into the layered archives of the earth's past. One after another it has lain bare the geological records of former epochs, and one after another it has eroded them away. Several million years ago the slow rasping of the river's water reached the gold-bearing igneous rock of the Rocky Mountain foothills. This rock, upthrust from deep in the earth long before, had cooled and crystallized into quartz; the gold heaved up with it had been precipitated in its interstices—little metallic bits trapped and unglittering in the parent mineral. Flowing water unburied the rock, disintegrated it, and carried the detritus off toward the sea. The gold liberated in the process, being 19.3 times denser than water, and six or seven times denser than the rock itself, was too heavy to be transported far from its source. Instead, it was trapped nearby in the crevices and catch basins of creeks and river beds.

Such a gold deposit is called a "placer," a term thought to have come from the identical Spanish word which means "pleasure." Correct or not, the etymology is logical enough, for placer gold was relatively easy to locate and extract. It was never very deep in the ground, and rarely overlaid with rock; and since gold is one of the most inert of metallic elements, it does not form compounds that necessitate complex refining and smelting techniques. What a placer miner takes from a creek bed is very nearly the pure, finished product.

Relatively little of the world's gold has come from placer deposits. Much more has come from hard-rock mines, mines in which the metal has not been eroded out of its parent mineral. Yet the discovery of placer fields has set off most of the world's gold rushes. The reason is that placer gold is the small man's gold, the poor man's gold. While hard-rock mining requires capital, complex machinery and hundreds of men, placer mining required but one man with a few simple tools and a strong back. The technique could be learned in a day, and it had not changed much since an Egyptian artist depicted it on a tomb in 2900 B.C. Since placer deposits were relatively easy to find and exploit, they were quickly exhausted in civilized areas. For this reason, placer mining was an activity of the fringes of settlement, and the great gold rushes of the last century, in California, Australia, British Columbia, and the Yukon, were part of the conquest of the frontier. There are few frontiers left in the world today, and few placer mines.

If moving water will cause gold, because of its great density, to sink to the bedrock of a creek, it will also cause it to settle on the bottom of a vessel or sluice; what lies above can then be discarded. The miner's technique was thus an imitation of the natural process whereby the metal was deposited in the first place. Before the turn of the century three basic devices were used in placer mining. The simplest was the gold pan, a rounded sheet metal dish about eighteen inches in diameter. The miner dumped two shovelfuls of gravel into it, then, squatting down, he added water, and, holding the pan between his knees with both hands, agitated the mixture with a circular swirling motion. In the process the gold would be gradually sifted to the bottom and he

Panning

would then carefully pour off the material above it with the water. If the gold was in the form of nuggets, he could simply pick them up like acorns from under an oak. But if, as was more common, the gold was fine—the size, say, of particles of flour—and heavy sands remained mixed with it, he would add mercury. This element forms an amalgam with gold on contact, but has no affinity for the main impurities associated with it. Later, to separate the gold from the mercury, the amalgam was poured into a little bag of closely woven cloth and the mercury squeezed out, ready to be used again. What remained was heated and the small amount of mercury left with the gold was vaporized.

Only slightly more elaborate than the gold pan was the rocker, a box mounted on a base like that of a cradle. Atop the base sat a perforated metal screen (the "hopper") that prevented stones bigger than half an inch or so in diameter from entering. The miner shoveled gravel onto this screen, and as he rocked the rocker, he dipped water on it to wash the gravel down through the box. Below the screen was a piece of wool or felt (the "apron") stretched at a slant across the box from one side nearly to the other. As the gravel was washed down, the gold and the heaviest sands lodged on the "apron" and the rest was flushed out below. Periodically the apron was removed and washed, and its contents carefully panned out. A rocker was especially useful in dry places, as the water run through it could be used over and over.

Where sufficient water was available, however, sluice boxes were much more efficient. These were nothing more than long, narrow wooden troughs, with "riffles," wooden ribs perpendicular to the direction of flow, set at regular intervals along their bottoms. The gravel was placed at the top of the sluice box, and the water then introduced carried it down the sloping sluiceway. The gold sank as it was washed down and was trapped behind the riffles. The riffles were periodically removed, and the gold carefully washed down the sluice to an awaiting receptacle. Small particles of gold do not sink as rapidly as larger ones, and longer, more gently sloping sluices were needed to work fine gold.

Geologists are still not certain why gold occurs where it does. The early prospectors thought up all sorts of ingenious explanations, the general purport of which is perhaps best summed up in their dictum: "It ain't easy to find the stuff. Why, half the time you run across it where it aren't." It had been discovered in California in 1848, and later in South Dakota, Idaho, Colorado and other western states. In the 1850s and '60s it was found along the valley of the Fraser River in British Columbia, and then in the Cassiar District farther north in the same province. In 1880 a huge hard-rock deposit was discovered at Juneau, Alaska. In each case men rushed in, and a very few got rich overnight. The major-

Rocking

ity returned discouraged to the farms and factories they had left
in such haste. But each rush produced a few men, luckless and
hopeful like Arthur Harper, who headed for the unprospected
wilderness to seek a new chance at a new Eldorado. One of them
might eventually discover a virgin gold field and the cycle would
begin again. Juneau is less than a hundred miles from the headwaters of the Yukon, and it was inevitable that the flood of gold
seekers which poured into it in the early 1880s would overflow
onto the river.

The influx was initially blocked by the barrier of the Coast
Mountains and the people who lived there. The Chilkat Indians,
who had driven Robert Campbell from Fort Selkirk, shared their
trade monopoly over the interior tribes with their cousins the
Chilkoots. Since prehistoric times the Chilkoot traders had
packed their skin sacks of fish oil and berries from the coast up
over the mountains along the path they called the "High Grease
Trail." On the other side they bartered them for the furs of the
"Stick" Indians, so called by them because the trees in their interior homeland were so puny compared to the magnificent fir and
hemlock of Chilkoot country. When Russian, British and Yankee
traders appeared along the coast, it was natural for the Chilkoots
to become the middlemen between them and the "Sticks." By
jealously guarding their route to the interior, the only one in the
region then known to pierce the jagged barrier of the Coast
Mountains, the Chilkoots preserved this lucrative monopoly for
decades.

What white man first succeeded in traversing the High Grease
—later known as the Chilkoot—Trail is a matter of doubt. A lone
prospector named George Holt somehow managed to dodge or
bribe its Indian sentinels and reach the headwaters of the Yukon
in 1878. François Mercier relates, however, that back in 1874
when he was getting McQuesten established at Fort Reliance, he
was told by the Indians that a white man "surnommé Slim Jeams"
(Slim Jim?) had been seen prospecting near the headwaters of
the Yukon the preceding summer. Even at that time local tradition preserved the story of a Scot, employed by the Hudson's Bay
Company, who had crossed the trail in the 1860s. He was cap-

tured by the Chilkoots, but was well treated because his bushy red hair and beard were clear evidence to them that he was a powerful shaman. He was later ransomed, the story goes, by the captain of a company ship that put in to trade with his captors.

Whatever the case, crossing the Coast Mountains via the Chilkoot Trail, a hazardous enterprise even without the Indians was difficult in the extreme until 1880. That year Captain L. A. Beardslee of the U.S. Reserve Cutter Service, accompanied by twenty armed men, went over from Juneau to have a talk with the chiefs of the Chilkoots. A score of prospectors, headed by one Edmund Bean (not to be confused with James Bean whose wife was murdered on the Tanana), wished to cross the mountains to the Yukon that spring, and Beardslee planned to clear the way for them. He explained to the Chilkoots that the prospectors would in no way interfere with their trade, and that they must be allowed to pass. He had brought along a Gatling gun, something they had never seen before, and he showed them how it worked. They decided to let the prospectors pass.

Exactly where Bean and his party prospected is uncertain. All of them went back to Juneau in the fall, apparently without having found any paying concentrations of gold. Few, if any, of them returned, but each subsequent year others followed their route.

In the summer of 1883 a party of four, Richard Poplin, Charles McConkey, Benjamin Beach, and C. Marks, crossed the Chilkoot, built boats at Lindeman Lake, and drifted down the Yukon to the Stewart River. They ascended the Stewart, prospecting the bars and creeks along it as they went. By September they had taken from its gravels an average of ten dollars worth of fine gold per man per day of work, just enough, given the shortness of the mining season and the difficulty of bringing in supplies from Juneau, to justify their labor. Though their take was "just wages," it was the fruit of the first real mining ever done in the Yukon basin.

The Poplin party went down to Fort Reliance in the early fall to get additional provisions; the summer's mining was encouraging and they wished to stay in the region. McQuesten, however, had no supplies for them; the engine of his *New Racket* had blown a cylinder head, and though he fashioned a substitute of wood and sheet metal, he could get up only fifty pounds of steam, not enough to push the boat back up to Fort Reliance. Poplin and the three others therefore drifted down to Tanana Station where they wintered. Two of them, Poplin himself and McConkey, returned next spring to Fort Reliance with McQuesten in his stern-wheeler, now repaired, and continued on from there to the Stewart. There seems to be no record of how they did that season, but they were content enough to come back again the following year. In the fall, as they were making their way out toward Juneau, they passed two men, Boswell and Frazer, who were working the bars of the Yukon itself with a rocker. Poplin and McConkey told them of their success on the Stewart, and Boswell and Frazer decided to try their luck there next season. They wintered at Fort Reliance with McQuesten, and the following April dragged their sleds over the ice to the mouth of the Stewart. As they worked their way up it, they stopped at the gravel bars that looked most promising, built fires to thaw the ground, and tested what they thawed with their gold pans. They marked the richest bars, planning to return after the ice had gone out. About ninety miles above the Stewart's mouth they examined the gravel on what was later called Chapman Bar. They went no farther that season, for the gravel held "fifty cent prospects"; that is, a standard miner's pan, filled with two shovelfuls of the stuff and washed, yielded fifty cents' worth of gold dust. At this rate, Boswell and Frazer were able, with the rocker they set up, to take out ten or twelve ounces a day, worth about two hundred dollars. Though this would be a paltry sum indeed by the standards of a few years later, no deposit yet found on the Yukon had approached such richness.

As Boswell and Frazer were beginning their mining operations on Chapman Bar, Poplin returned with three new partners. They set to work on what became known as Steamboat Bar, seven miles above Chapman, and they too did very well. The six men apparently coalesced into a single party, for Boswell was delegated to get provisions for them all. McQuesten saw him at this time.

We had about fifty tons of miners [sic] supplies landed at Fort Reliance on 10 August. T. Boswell was there when we came coming [sic] up the river, we had taken aboard J. Ladue, Franklin, Thomas Williams, H. Madison, [and] Mike Hess who were prospecting along the river. They had not found anything to speak of. When Boswell left his party it was understood that he was not to tell anyone what they were making, so he said they had found nothing; that they were going to trap that winter—he bought supplies for six men for one year. . . .

After unloading his consignment of miners' supplies McQuesten piloted his stern-wheeler upriver from Reliance to Fort Selkirk to barter furs. The Stewart empties into the Yukon about halfway between the two places, and he left Boswell at its mouth to await his return. The others debarked farther upriver.

Franklin and Harry Madison got off at White River and went up it to prospect and they remained there all winter and found nothing to pay. T. Williams, J. Ladue, [and] Mike Hess went on to Selkirk— there they built a boat and went on up the river to some bars that had been worked the summer before. . . . I done my trading with the Indians and returned to Stewart River as I had made arrangements to take Boswell up [it] . . . as far as I could go. Boswell then told me for the first time what they had found and how much they had made before he had left. I thought it was very wrong in his not telling the other boys as there was only five of them and they were all prospectors. . . . the river was so low we could not go any further [than 27 miles up] with the steamer. . . . Boswell and myself went on in a canoe, we found the boys working near Steam Boat Bar. . . . I worked five days with them and made $250.00. . . . There were fifteen men in the country that winter and they were all expecting to strike it big. . . . [It] was the coldest winter on record . . . on the 4th of January it was 80 degrees below; the month average was 56 degrees below. Steve Custer froze his foot so he had to go down to St. Michael and have several of his toes amputated.

Some of the men who had worked the Stewart bars during the summer of 1885 avoided this bitter winter by going back over the Chilkoot Trail to Juneau. They carried with them the account of what had been found there, and a little fine gold to substantiate their story. When they recrossed the Chilkoot next spring they were joined by about a hundred other prospectors heading for the new diggings on the Stewart. Not all of them found bars as rich as Steamboat or Chapman, but it has been estimated that by the following September they had taken out an average of eight hundred dollars in fine gold per man.

That summer, 1886, McQuesten and Arthur Harper abandoned Fort Reliance and established a new post at the mouth of the Stewart. From now on their stock in trade would consist mainly of shovels, gold pans, beans and bacon rather than glass beads, powder and shot. They would be paid in raw placer gold poured out of a miner's moosehide poke* and no longer in stiff round beaver and soft, sleeve-shaped marten pelts. It was just half a century since Glazunov had initiated the era of the fur trade on the river with his speech to the naked men in Anvik's urine-fetid kashim. This era was now drawing rapidly to a close.

10 Forty Mile

A FEW years ago an old French Canadian named Bill Couture lay dying in his sod-roofed cabin in the town of Forty Mile, Yukon Territory. He had come into the country years before as a prospector and miner, but as one creek after another was staked, mined and exhausted, he turned to chopping cord wood for the river boats. A stern-wheeler had not passed Forty Mile in several seasons, so now woodchopping had failed him too. He tried trapping, but even without the worn-out heart that was presently killing him, he was getting too old for the rigors of life out on the trap line. He was an old man stranded in the wilderness and near giving up the ghost.

One morning Bill Couture summoned up all his remaining strength, went down to the river's edge and fashioned a little raft of scrap wood. Aboard it he placed an SOS note scrawled in his untutored hand. Then he shoved the raft into the current of the Yukon, crossed himself, most likely—for he was a very devout Roman Catholic—and struggled back to his bunk. Somebody downriver at Eagle, Alaska, recovered the note and radioed Dawson City. Couture was quickly brought to the ramshackle old gold town, but despite the ministrations of the good Sisters of Saint Anne who ran the hospital there, he died a few weeks later.

In this manner, in 1958, Forty Mile, the oldest town on the Upper Yukon, lost its last inhabitant.

Harry Madison and Howard Franklin were its first inhabitants, and they, like Couture, had come to the Fortymile River to prospect. They arrived in 1886. The fall before McQuesten's *New Racket* had deposited them at the mouth of the White River as it steamed upriver to Fort Selkirk. Boswell was aboard, but he wasn't telling anyone about the rich strike he had made on the Stewart that summer. The two men went ahead with their plans for winter prospecting on the White. They found nothing of consequence, so in the spring they went to the Stewart anyhow. The prospects they found there were encouraging by most standards, but Franklin, who seems to have been the leader of the two, was not impressed. It was bad enough that the wrong kinds of trees grew there, but, even worse, wild chives luxuriated along the Stewart and he knew that such plants could not possibly grow atop a real gold field.

Franklin and Madison therefore left the Stewart in disgust early in the summer of 1886. They drifted down the Yukon to Fortymile River, a large stream of brown-stained water so called because its mouth was approximately forty miles below Fort Reliance. Arthur Harper, who advised them to try their luck there, had once started to prospect the stream, but turned back after the Indians described to him a "terribly dangerous cañon" that blocked all passage. Franklin and Madison had no easy time lining their boat up rapids that would later receive such names as "Hell's Gate" and "Deadman's Riffles," but they found no impassable canyon. Twenty-three miles up they sunk a prospect hole down through the muck and gravel to the schist bedrock. They struck gold.

For ages a placer banquet table lay set under the frozen muck of the Fortymile, and now the delicacies glimmered in the dim light of the candles Franklin and Madison held shakily in their hands. The feast was of nuggets the size of a rice grain, of a miner's blackened thumbnail, of a corn kernel—flat ones, round ones, oblong ones, amoeboid ones with distended pseudopodia worth ten dollars apiece. The Stewart with its wild chives had only gold dust, while the road to the placer miner's paradise is paved with chunks like these that clank and jangle in the pan.

In those days the prospectors on the Yukon belonged to a fraternity that, though nameless and without written laws, had a definite code which most of them strictly obeyed. The code, among other things, obliged a prospector who had made a strike to proclaim the fact to his fellows. Boswell had not done this, and he is the only man of whom McQuesten speaks harshly in his journal. In October, Franklin and Madison went up from the Fortymile to the miners' camp that had grown up at the mouth of the Stewart that summer. The hundred or so prospectors who worked the bars in the vicinity had done reasonably well that year, better, probably, than most of them had ever done before. The average take was about $800 per man. At the news of the Fortymile strike, however, most of them left their diggings and decamped without second thoughts. They might in fact find better prospects there, but as they left the Stewart, they all *knew* they would: a footloose credulity was as much a part of the Yukon prospector's outfit as a gold pan or a pot of sourdough. Again and again he would stampede off to new boom camps in the wilderness, leaving behind him a trail of crumbling ghost towns to mark his erratic passage.

In the fall of the Fortymile strike, Arthur Harper was alone at the new store at Stewart River because McQuesten had gone out to San Francisco to order a new supply of provisions. As he watched his customers hastily departing down the Yukon toward the Fortymile, Harper anticipated that the discovery would draw scores of new prospectors in over the Chilkoot when the news reached the Outside. McQuesten, of course, knew nothing of the strike, and it became essential for Harper to get word to him so he could greatly augment his orders. Otherwise starvation was likely to threaten beginning the next summer.

George Williams, who volunteered to carry the message, was pilot on the ACCº.'s stern-wheeler. He had come in over the Chilkoot during the summer of 1882, and was one of the men initiated into the moosehide toss by the squaws of Fort Reliance the following New Year's day. While there exists no first-hand account of Williams' trip to the coast, the version that is preserved does not appear to have suffered too much from the pronounced regional vice of turning fact to folklore. Williams left Arthur Harper's store in January accompanied by a young Indian. By March, the story goes, all the dogs of their team had starved or frozen to death, and their own condition was hardly better.

For three days they lay huddled in a snowbank as a ferocious blizzard swept Chilkoot Summit. Each day the numb blackness of frostbite worked its way farther up Williams' limbs. On the third day of the siege the two men consumed their last handful of dry flour. When the storm abated, Williams could no longer walk, but the Indian, who had not been so badly frostbitten, managed to carry him down to timber line on his back. They then encountered some Chilkoots who sledded Williams down to his destination, John G. Healy's trading post on Dyea Inlet. When they arrived, Williams was unconscious. The miners who were at Healy's gathered around his comatose form, hoping to learn what desperate mission could have prompted such a suicidal journey. But Williams expired without saying a word. They turned for a clue to his Indian trailmate, who knew almost no English. He thereupon grabbed up a handful of kidney beans from a sack on the store counter, held them up, and said, "Gold all same just like this."

. Or at least that's how the story goes. Apocryphal or not, it is certain that the news of the Fortymile strike did somehow reach the Outside by spring, and that it sent several hundred eager prospectors clambering up Williams' deadly route during the summer of 1887. Across the mountains, on Lake Lindeman, they whipsawed green logs into boat timber and started the drift downriver. They passed the camp at the mouth of the Stewart, all but deserted now, but as they rounded the first of the high-banked S-curves the Yukon makes as it prepares to leave Canada, they came upon dozens of men milling among the pitched tents and rising cabins of Forty Mile. Most of the camp's inhabitants had done very well that summer for the Forty Mile country had yielded up $200,000 in coarse gold. Lean-to's and tents dotted the upstream tributaries—Mosquito Fork, Steele Creek, Walker Fork and Chicken Creek (so called because its gold particles were the size of cracked corn). Some of the bars along the Fortymile proper were so crowded by men and rockers that the miners decided among themselves to limit each claim to the size of a circle two shovel lengths in diameter.

All the rich deposits along the Fortymile were a distance

upstream and supplies were freighted up to them by men who earned five dollars a day plus beans, the staple of the gold camp diet. At first, boats were lined up against the swift current, but later horses were used, and their trails are still visible, switching back and forth over the high bald ridges that separate one creek valley from another.

During the first few years of its existence the town of Forty Mile was the center of supply, social life, amusement and government, such as these things were, for about three hundred miners. Two thirds of them were obliged to go back over the Chilkoot in winter, however, for the two or three stern-wheelers then on the river could not freight in enough supplies to provide for all of them during the short navigation season. For those who stayed, the winter was a time of enforced idleness, "cabin fever" and sometimes scurvy. For six months they huddled in dark, fetid cabins next to sheet metal stoves kept red-hot. They lived on hardtack, sourdough pancakes and beans. As the author, Rex Beach, who got to know this life well a few years later, commented, "The real *Call of the Wild* is not a wolf howl. It's the dyspeptic belch of a miner."

In 1889 the ACC⁰. launched the *Arctic*, large, fast, and sleek by the standards of the Yukon. She could make several round trips from St. Michael each season, and could thus bring in enough supplies for all the Forty Milers to stay the winter if they chose.

Most of them did, mainly because of the ingenuity of a man named Hutchinson. The miners who came to the Yukon had gained their experience farther south, and they had never before encountered permanently frozen ground. The permafrost that bedeviled them at Forty Mile underlies most of the Yukon basin, and, for that matter, any other place in the world where the mean annual temperature is more than a degree or two below freezing. Permafrost, as the name implies, is a layer of ground that never melts. Sometimes over a thousand feet thick, it is sandwiched between warmer, deeper strata, and an upper layer that thaws in summer. Over extended areas of the southern portions of the river basin it is absent altogether, and in favored locations elsewhere, such as south-facing slopes uninsulated by trees or moss, it may

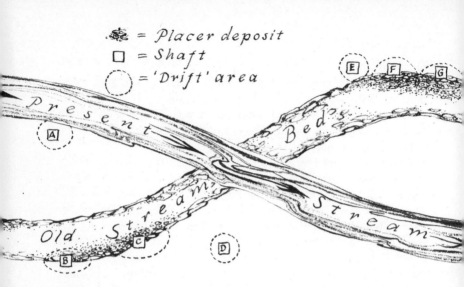

Present Beds

Old Stream *Stream*

A   E   F   G

C   D   B

begin at a depth of six or eight feet. On the Fortymile, however, the permafrost is much nearer the surface. On a hot August day when the sun beats down at 85°, a man's footfalls squash down through twelve or fourteen inches of muskeg and then thud to an abrupt halt. Beneath is the permafrost, muck and water frozen hard as rock.

Since virtually none of the water from melting snow or rain can percolate below the permafrost horizon, the Fortymile country and much of the rest of the Yukon valley is wet and boggy. This surface moisture provides a fine habitat for the mosquitoes as

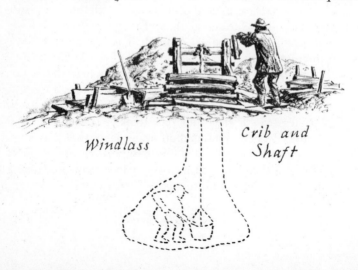

Windlass

Crib and Shaft

they evolve from egg to larva to human nemesis without parallel on the river, but without it most of the region would be semi-desert instead of forest. Precipitation is low, lower than in many parts of New Mexico. Yet what ground water there is is held by the permafrost at levels accessible to tree roots.

To sink their shafts to bedrock the miners at Forty Mile daily scraped away the thin layer of ground thawed by the sun. Progress was extremely slow and confined to the three summer months. It was Hutchinson, a miner on Franklin Gulch, who first tried "burning," as it came to be called. In the evening he would set a big log fire on the frozen bottom of his shaft, and the following day he would excavate what had been thawed. He was ridiculed for a season or two, but since burning was so much quicker than thawing by the sun's heat, he was soon universally imitated. From then on most mining at Forty Mile was done in winter when all ground water was frozen and there was no problem of flooded holes. Spring and summer were spent in washing the gold from the gravel thus excavated.

The first step in the mining operation was selection of the site at which to sink a hole. While a miner could plainly see the twistings and turnings of the present creek, chances were the gold, if any, had been deposited long before the creek occupied its present course. And even if he struck the old bed, there would be no assurance that he would hit the gold-bearing portions of it. The Forty Miler could do no better than sink a test shaft and hope for the best.

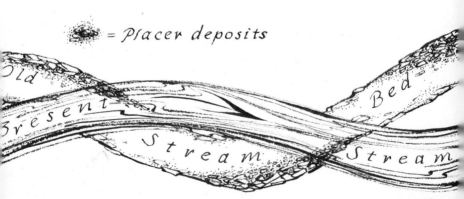

= Placer deposits

Old Bed

Present Stream

Stream

The shaft was square, usually about five feet on a side. Night after night the miner set his fire, and day after day he shoveled up what had been thawed. When the hole got too deep to shovel from, he mounted above it a windlass, a reellike device fashioned from a rounded spruce log. To the windlass was attached a rope, at the other end of which was a bucket. The miners of Forty Mile usually worked in pairs, and when one of the pair, down in the hole, had filled the bucket with thawed gravel, the other cranked it up with the windlass and dumped it out. As the "dump" grew around the entrance of the hole, a criblike cage was put in place to keep the gravel from falling back in.

Bedrock is the level below which gold does not readily penetrate; it can be of solid rock as the name implies, or of dense, tightly packed shales or gravels. On the Forty Mile, bedrock was generally shallow, seldom deeper than twenty feet. As the miner approached it, he carefully put aside samples of the day's diggings to pan out that evening in his cabin; in this way he could tell if and when he "hit the pay." Whether he encountered gold or not, when the miner came to bedrock he began "drifting," which meant that he placed his fires against the sides of the shaft and thus thawed out a subterranean chamber. The object of drifting was to test—or mine—as much of the gravel just above bedrock as possible from a single shaft. If the shaft hit the "pay streak" squarely, the miner drifted his way along it as it meandered in uneven richness along the ancient water course. Needless to say, most holes and drifts at Forty Mile ended in "skunks"—holes with no "colors" (no gold)—or in "prospects" (the average amount of gold in a panful of bedrock gravel) too unrewarding to exploit. But once a miner struck the pay streak, he could usually get an idea of its orientation, and sink another shaft directly to it—that is, if the streak didn't "pinch out."

In the previous diagram, Shafts A and D were "skunks," and E very nearly was, but it led to pay on F and G. Such a technique was not very thorough, and later, when the Fortymile was dredged, untouched deposits such as the one on the left were recovered.

If the gravel being cranked up on the windlass was found to

contain gold, it was piled in a separate part of the dump. As soon as it was exposed to the winter air it refroze and didn't thaw till spring. Then, when there was plenty of flowing water around, it was shoveled into sluice boxes and the gold was washed out. This was the time of fat pokes and prolonged sprees in the saloons of Forty Mile.

The town had six saloons by the early '90s, but the first, a part of Jack McQuesten's new store, was always the most popular. It was, in fact, the social, juridical and financial heart of the backwoods community, and the reason for this was to be found in the personality of its proprietor. Everybody liked McQuesten, for he was amiable, fair and intelligent, and everybody respected what he had to say about the Yukon for the only man on earth who knew it better was Arthur Harper, and he was now up at Selkirk operating a new store. McQuesten was also generous. The credit he extended to miners down on their luck was nearly endless, and such was his way with people that virtually nobody thought of defaulting. William Ogilvie, the future commissioner of the Yukon Territory, came to know him well when he made his survey of the U.S.-Canadian boundary in 1887–88. He relates this example of McQuesten's credit practices: A miner entered his store and asked how much he owed. McQuesten checked his records and told him the bill came to $700.

"Seven hundred! H–l, Jack, I've only got five hundred, how'm I goin' to pay seven hundred with five?"

"Oh, that's all right, give us your five hundred, and we'll credit you and let the rest stand till next clean-up."

"But, Jack, I want some more stuff. How'm I goin' to get that?"

"Why, we'll let you have it as we did before."

"But, d—n it, Jack, I haven't had a spree yet."

"Well, go and have your little spree, come back with what is left, and we'll credit you with it and go on as before."

The man had his spree and it wasn't so little; he spent the entire $500. He came back to the store. McQuesten gave him another outfit and put his debt at $1,200.

By 1893 McQuesten was faced with competition in the form of

a rival store over on the north bank of the Fortymile River. John G. Healy, the man who ran it, had operated the trading post at Dyea where Williams had arrived, frozen and comatose, a few years before. He thus knew as soon as anybody on the Outside about the strike of Madison and Franklin, but he headed first for Chicago, not Forty Mile. There he interested a meat packing millionaire named Cudahy in backing a new company, to be called the North American Trading and Transportation Company, that would challenge the ACC⁰. monopoly on the Yukon. In 1893 Healy arrived at Forty Mile aboard the new stern-wheeler *Portus B. Weare,* at four hundred tons the biggest boat yet to ply the Yukon. He built a store which he called Fort Cudahy, and began selling gumboots, gold pans and grub to the miners. Healy was a cantankerous man with a tough-looking Irish face and a tightfisted Scotch method of doing business. He did not endear himself to the miners at Forty Mile, accustomed as they were to McQuesten's largess, nor did they endear themselves to him.

In the early Yukon gold camps, where there were neither legal officials nor written laws, the miners made and enforced their own code; the justice they dispensed was swift, summary, and, at least at the beginning, generally fair. The court of law was the miners' meeting, and anybody with a grievance could call one by simply posting up a few notices. All miners who possibly could were obliged to attend. They convened, usually at McQuesten's, and at each meeting they elected a chairman to preside and a secretary to keep the minutes. The defendant and plaintiff were heard, and when their testimony was done, one of the miners would rise and suggest a verdict and possibly a punishment. If the others concurred, they stood and shouted their approval. If not, other suggestions were heard. When they reached a consensus the trial ended. In this way divorces were granted, hangings decreed, banishments ordered, quarrels settled, and a reasonable degree of law and order maintained. The meetings also decided on such important aspects of mining law as claim sizes, recording procedures and water rights, and they ruled on disputed claims.

As time went on the institution of the miners' meeting suffered a decline. The trouble seemed to be that they were usually held in saloons where the increasing population of nonminers and barflies could take full part in them.

The proceedings against John G. Healy, McQuesten's unpopular commercial rival, are a case in point. Healy had brought his wife to Forty Mile, and, to ease her burdens, a girl servant. The girl, according to William Ogilvie, didn't take to the social isolation that good behavior in a subarctic mining camp would have involved, and she began staying out later and later at nights. After a while she wouldn't show up at Healy's house till dawn, and then hardly fit for a day of cooking and scrubbing. Healy warned her, but she persisted, and he fired her. The girl, well known to the miners by then, tearfully spread the word of her sad plight. The miners responded by calling a meeting. One after another, grandiloquent speeches of sympathy and indignation echoed against the log walls of the saloon. One man in particular waxed eloquent as he described the heinousness of Healy's throwing a poor innocent girl out into the cold wilderness where womenless miners stalked like timber wolves. Amidst shouts of outrage a unanimous verdict was decided on whereby Healy would have to pay her a year's salary and give her a boat ticket back home. Healy had no alternative but to accede, but he was bitter, especially when he learned that the man who had raged most eloquently against him during the meeting was the object of the servant girl's nocturnal wanderings. At the time he wrote one of two letters requesting the presence of a detachment of North West Mounted Police.

The other letter was written by William Carpenter Bompas, Bishop of the Anglican Diocese of Selkirk. He too had complaints about the miners, but of a different sort.

A number of years before, Bompas had made a missionary journey west over the Rockies to the upper Yukon. He preached, baptized and catechized, but had to leave after a short while to take care of other matters at Fort Simpson, the Mackenzie River headquarters of his immense diocese. A few years later, during another brief visit, he stopped at an Indian fish camp whose occupants he had known the time before. One of them, pointing at the dying campfire, said to the bishop in Takudh: "That is how you have left us. You kindled the fire of the Gospel among us, and you left it untended to die out again. Why have you done this?" Bompas returned to Fort Simpson, split his diocese in two, keeping the western half, and returned to the Yukon a year later as the first Bishop of Selkirk. En route to his new diocese he was joined by his wife whom he had not seen since she left for England five years before to recuperate from the effects of life in northern Canada. The reunited couple made their headquarters at Forty Mile where they arrived in August, 1892.

Bishop Bompas was not quite sixty when he began his ministry at Forty Mile, but the rigors of an extremely arduous life had by now plucked the last hairs from his pate and whitened his bushy beard. His frame was still erect and his muscles strong, however, and he could still stop an Indian knife fight or break twenty miles of trail a day in front of his dog team. He was a tall craggy man, just gaunt enough to suggest an El Greco saint; he looked every bit the ascetic that he was. He drank sugarless tea from an iron cup, and while his wife was away ate off a tin plate with the back of a knife. On his nomadic missionary journeys he had slept as often as not on spruce boughs laid crossways on the snow, in igloos and huts, and under upturned canoes. He had become so inured to his hard, lonely life that the thought of departure, even temporary, caused him to write: "I feel so long dead and buried that I cannot think a short visit home, as if from the grave, would be of much use."

William Bompas was not, however, a joyless man. He took great delight in children and was continually bringing home wretched little orphans whom the childless couple would adopt. Mrs. Bompas, in her Victorian way, would give them lessons in hygiene, English, and Christianity, in that order, and her husband would delight and frighten them as they perched for rides atop his high shoulders. Bompas, a graduate of Cambridge, was deeply interested in ancient languages and biblical scholarship, and he took joy in studying them. "I feel thankful," wrote his wife from Forty Mile, "when for a short time in the evening he retires to his study and takes up his beloved Syriac."

Bishop Bompas conducted several services each week in Takudh, a language he had by now thoroughly mastered. On Sunday nights he held an English service for the miners, and usually about twenty attended. He also taught school in his cabin, and traveled by canoe and dogsled to the distant camps of the Indians.

Forty Mile was a new experience for the Yukon, and also for Bishop Bompas, for never before had there been a white man's town in his diocese. Like other missionaries who worked long and hard among primitive people, he developed a profound paternalistic attachment for his spiritual charges, an attachment that allowed him to persevere in the face of innumerable irritations and disappointments they caused him. Of the Takudh-speaking Indians, he wrote, ". . . indeed, I think I may say that, had I ever found at home such a warm attachment of the people to their ministêr, and so zealous a desire for instruction, I should not have been a missionary."

There were no white women at Forty Mile until Mrs. Bompas arrived—for being the first, the miners presented her with a fifty dollar nugget at Christmas, 1892—and there was a lot of whiskey. These two circumstances, womenless white men and abundant alcohol, would undo years of patient missionary toil. And they would be repeated every time a prospector's strike set off the spontaneous generation of a boom town, jerry-built of spruce logs and wild expectations, and no longer-lived—except in its effect on the Indians—than either. Wrote Mrs. Bompas from Forty Mile:

Thus our Indians, being brought into contact with the white man, fall in only too easily with his taste for luxury, love of gambling, coarse, vile language, and for the miserable and ruthless degradation of women.

And again:

The sweet, oval face and laughing eyes of our Indian girl please him [the white miner]. . . . She is sadly, deplorably vain, poor child, and a gay shawl or two, a pair of gold earrings, will sorely tempt her, as the bag of flour has tempted her father to wink at the transaction.

In both the letters cited above Mrs. Bompas speaks of "our Indians"; the paternalism implied, shared by all the early missionaries, caused them a deep feeling of personal hurt and futility at the spectacle of miners debauching their flocks.

Before long, the Diocese of Selkirk would be invaded by such and influx of womanless whites and inundated by such a flood of whiskey that the Bompases' experiences at Forty Mile would seem to have occurred before the Fall. The bishop would do what he could to preserve his flock, and this would be a good deal, but he would be hopelessly outnumbered.

In the early days at Forty Mile little whiskey seems to have got to the Indians, for the miners had decreed that the crime of selling it to them be punished by banishment. But later on, both in Forty Mile itself and in other impermanent towns along the river, there was no such interdiction. Just after the turn of the century Father Jetté, S.J., wrote apropos of a later gold stampede on another part of the Yukon:

The dirty whites are flooding us from all parts. A gasoline boat went up the Nowi [Nowitna River] after the Indians with a good load of hootch. Moral conditions are distressing. Venereal diseases are becoming an ordinary occurrence, a pretty safe mark that the women are being corrupted. . . . The blessed martyr Ignatius had only ten leopards, in the shape of soldiers, and I have hundreds of ravening wolves, in the shape of miners, saloon keepers, bums & C. & C. . . .

Bishop Bompas appealed for a detachment of police to be sent to Forty Mile partly for the same reason that John G. Healy did: the miners' meetings were becoming a farce. His main reason, though, was the hope that the establishment of formal law and order would lessen the impact of the miners on "his" Indians. In his appeal he stated, among other things, that the Forty Milers "were teaching the Indians to make whiskey with demoralizing effect both to the whites and Indians . . ."

In 1894 Inspector Charles Constantine of the North West Mounted Police, a humorless man of Prussian bearing and utter incorruptibility, came to Forty Mile to determine if the petitions of Bompas and Healy were justified. He decided they were, in fact to the extent of twenty constables, with whom he returned the following year. He set his men to cutting logs for Fort Constantine, as the miners quickly baptized it, to be constructed next to Healy's store, and in a few months the northernmost Union Jack in the British Empire fluttered atop a substantial police post. Meantime, Inspector Constantine set about replacing the miners' capricious unwritten laws with the Code of Canada, outlawing the bloomers the troop of San Francisco dance hall girls had been wont to wear, creating a strictly bureaucratic mining recorder's office and levying a tax on the local manufacture of hooch.

By 1895, the year that the police arrived, Forty Mile consisted of eighty or ninety log cabins strung out in an uncertain row along the Yukon. Empty coal-oil cans and wood chips littered the quagmire between them, and the stumps still poking up all around were a reminder both of the town's youth and of the hundreds of miles of spruce forest that separated it from the nearest outpost of civilization. That year Mrs. Bompas compiled a list of the town's businesses for a friend in England, and it included six saloons, two blacksmiths' shops, two stores (stocked with items ranging "from a flour-bag to a wedding ring"), several restaurants and hotels, a dressmaker's shop and a watchmaker's shop, the lending library she had helped to establish, and a few stills. A proper Victorian, she neglected to mention the "Opera House" where the girls from San Francisco, though no longer in bloomers, still provided lively entertainment for the miners with vaudeville numbers, dances, and other recreations.

She does not mention the squaw dances either, but then these did not really belong on a list of businesses anyhow. They had a large appeal, though, especially to miners whose pokes were too slim for the fancy prices at the Opera House. Josiah Spurr of the United States Geological Survey, sent to make a reconnaissance of the upper Yukon during the summer of 1895, happened upon one of these dances the evening he arrived at Forty Mile:

. . . we were attracted by observing a row of miners, who were lined up in front of the saloon engaged in watching the door of a large log

cabin opposite. . . . On being questioned, they said there was going to
be a dance, but when or how they did not seem to know: all seemed to
take only a languid looker-on interest, speaking of the affair lightly
and flippantly. Presently more men, however, joined the group and
eyed the cabin expectantly. In spite of their disclaimers they evidently
expected to take part, but where were the fair partners for the mazy
waltz?

The evening wore on until ten o'clock, when in the dusk a stolid
Indian woman, with a baby in the blanket on her back, came cautiously around the corner, and with the peculiar long slouchy step of
her kind, made for the cabin door, looking neither to the right nor to
the left. She had no fan, nor yet an opera cloak; she was not even
décolleté; she wore large mocassins on her feet—number twelve, I
think, according to the white man's system of measurement—and
she had a bright colored handkerchief on her head. She was followed by a dozen others, one far behind the other, each silent and
unconcerned, and each with a baby upon her back. They sidled into
the log cabin and sat down on the benches, where they also deposited
their babies in a row. . . . The mothers sat awhile looking at the
ground in some one spot and then slowly lifted their heads to look at
the miners who had slouched into the cabin after them—men fresh
from the diggings, spoiling for excitement of any kind. Then a man
with a dilapidated fiddle struck up a swinging, sawing melody, and in
the intoxication of the moment some of the most reckless of the miners
grabbed an Indian woman and began furiously swinging her around in
a sort of waltz, while the others crowded around and looked on.

Little by little the dusk grew deeper, but candles were scarce and
could not be afforded. The figures of the dancing couples grew more
and more indistinct and their faces became lost to view, while the
sawing of the fiddle grew more and more rapid, and the dancing more
excited. There was no noise, however; scarcely a sound save the fiddle
and the shuffling of the feet over the floor of rough hewn logs; for . . .
the miners could not speak the language of their partners. Even the
lookers-on said nothing, so that these silent dancing figures in the dusk
made an almost weird effect.

One by one, however, the women dropped out, tired, picked up
their babies and slouched off home, and the men slipped over to the
saloon to have a drink before going to their cabins. Surely this squaw-
dance, as they called it, was one of the most peculiar balls ever seen.

11 The Paris of the North

BISHOP BOMPAS was not the first Anglican missionary on the Yukon. In the 1860s, while the Hudson's Bay Company was still trespassing on Russian territory at Fort Yukon, Reverend Robert McDonald used that place as a base for his missionary work. In 1863, the year after his arrival at Fort Yukon, a band of Indians from the south reported strange sounds emanating from a hilltop. McDonald, anxious to combat superstition, went to investigate.

The Indian [he recounts] said no one could shoot to the top of the hill where the sounds were and his companions made a bow and arrow for him and he did not shoot half-way up. . . . Just below that bank I found gold. . . . There were no nuggets, only gold dust. I could take it up with my hand. . . . I sent samples to a young man at Norway House [in Manitoba] and he tested it and found it gold.

The Reverend Robert McDonald was preoccupied with spreading the light of Christianity in a dark and heathen land, and with making the Takudh Gospel translations which are still used in the region; he did not exploit his discovery. He told others about it, though, and a clerk at Fort Yukon speaks the following year of "a small river not far from here that the minister, the Rev. McDonald, saw so much gold . . . on that he could have gathered it with a spoon." The clerk complained that he had no time off in which to go to the river, but he was hardly the prospecting sort anyhow, for he viewed gold digging as "merely a last resort when I can do no better." At the time he received an annual salary of about $200 from the Hudson's Bay Company; McDonald's "little river" was eventually to yield over $1,000,000 in gold.

The legend of a "Preacher's Creek" persisted on the Yukon long after Hudson's Bay and Robert McDonald had gone back up the Porcupine to Canadian soil. When Arthur Harper arrived at Fort Yukon in the spring of 1873 he was told about it, but by then the memory of its location had been lost. During the next thirty years "Preacher's Creek" was lined with solid bullion by the fertile imaginations of dozens of prospectors, but though they scoured the ground from the Teslin to the Koyukuk, they could not find it.

In 1893 Jack McQuesten grubstaked* two Indians, Syroska and Pitka, to prospect in the Yukon Flats. Either that fall, or the following spring, they discovered rich placer deposits on Birch Creek, a little serpentine river that parallels the Yukon for a hundred miles before finally meandering into it. When the news reached Forty Mile, a few score of miners dropped their shovels and tramped off hurriedly to the new strike. During the summer of 1894 they slogged and prospected over the waterlogged flats and discovered several rich tributaries of Birch Creek. As hitherto unknown streams, given such names as Deadwood, Greenhorn, Yankee, and Mastodon, began yielding up their treasure, it became evident that the new placer field was even richer than Forty Mile. Before the fall's ice floes congealed into a solid, deepening sheet, nearly a hundred miners were at work putting up cabins on the flat, muddy bank of the Yukon. McQuesten, too, had come down from Forty Mile, and his two-story store, to be the most imposing structure in the settlement, was taking shape. The site of the new mining town was a point on the river about eight miles from one of the loops of Birch Creek. It was called Circle City, though it neither lay on the Arctic Circle (but fifty miles below it) nor ever would become what could possibly be called a city in any other part of the world.

From 1894 to 1896 the population of Circle City swelled to over a thousand, and the production of its creeks to over $1,000,000 worth of gold annually. It was, boasted its residents,

---

* That is, he gave them food and supplies in return for an interest in any gold they might discover.

the biggest log city in the world, the Paris of the North. Circle City was one hundred and seventy miles downriver from Forty Mile, well to the west of the 141st Meridian which is the Alaska-Canada border. There were no red-coated mounties here, nor Anglican bishops, and the miners again ran things as they saw fit; their meetings, though, generally avoided the capricious decisions of the sort to which Inspector Constantine and his deputies had put a quick end just before in Forty Mile. It was a closed community, hermetically sealed in by the frozen Yukon for eight months of the year, not the sort of place where a man would lightly risk the ire of the citizenry by some low act. Tacked up on the wall of McQuesten's new store was this warning:

NOTICE
TO WHOM IT MAY CONCERN

At a general meeting of miners held in Circle City it was the unanimous Verdict that all thieving and stealing shall be punished by WHIPPING AT THE POST AND BAN-ISHMENT FROM THE COUNTRY, the severity of the whipping and the guilt of the accused to be determined by the Jury.

SO ALL THIEVES BEWARE!

On the same wall where this was posted, McQuesten had mounted a tall flagstaff. Below the flag of the United States and the red burgee of the ACC⁰. was a yardarm for hangings.

The yardarm was never used, and the whip seldom, because dishonesty was uncommon in Circle. Men often left fat pokes of gold in their cabins, but the only ones who bothered to lock their doors posted instructions explaining how to open them: the Indians were illiterate as well as lousy. The code of the place dictated that a miner could use any other miner's cabin providing he replaced the kindling and logs he used. Not to do so was a serious offense, as the next occupant might arrive so frozen and exhausted that only an instant fire would save his life. Since there were few violent incidents at Circle, the miners' meetings were most often called to consider claim disputes and such personal entanglements as that of the unfaithful fiddler and the promiscuous maiden. The fiddler, it seems, had gotten the girl pregnant, gaining the opportunity to do so by a promise of marriage. When he showed his intention of breaking the promise, the girl had him hauled before a miners' meeting. It was held in one of Circle's many saloons, an American flag, as usual, being draped over the bar for the occasion. After listening first to the girl, then to the fiddler, a miner rose in the back of the room and suggested a verdict: the fiddler could marry the girl and pay her $500, or not marry her, pay her $5,000, and spend a year in jail. Others voiced agreement, and since there was no jail in Circle, the talk turned to plans for constructing one if the fiddler's choice made it necessary. The fiddler was given until five o'clock that afternoon to decide between the two alternatives. When the miners reassembled, the judge elected to preside that day reported that the fiddler had shown satisfaction, both monetary and matrimonial, and that his wedding to the girl was scheduled for later in the evening. The case was closed, and the miners trooped off to the saloon where the newlyweds were celebrating, and spent a night of toasting and revelry with them.

A few years later James Wickersham, the first judge on the American part of the Yukon, arrived in Circle with the brand new Alaska Code in his suitcase. He heard about the fiddler case, and was prompted to remark that "It would have taken my court two years, with many pleadings, hearings and arguments, instead of two hours, to give judgement, which in all probability would have been reversed on some technicality!" Wickersham's presence in Circle, after so many years of home rule, caused some consternation among the miners. One winter day he stopped his sled at a cabin along the river and introduced himself to its occupant. He explained that he was the district judge, Third Judicial District, Territory of Alaska, to which the old sourdough replied, "Oh, the hell you are!" By 1900, the year Wickersham arrived at Circle, the miners had finally got around to building a jail, but of a type the judge had never before seen. On its door he read: "Notice; All prisoners must report by 9 o'clock P.M., or they will be locked out for the night."

To Circle City came a number of people who concluded, correctly in most cases, that it was easier to mine gold from miners than from mines. Harry de Windt, an aristocratic British wanderer who passed through town during the summer of 1895, noted that "there was certainly more gaiety, or life, of a tawdry, disreputable description than at Forty Mile, for every tenth house was either a gambling or drinking saloon, or a den of an even worse description." Circle, he concluded, was a sort of Arctic Babylon peopled by "mud-stained men and painted women."

Working conditions in the Circle Mining District were not good. Aboveground the miners breathed the stagnant air of tiny cabins, and below, the lingering fumes of the last night's thawing fires. They lived on beans, flapjacks and dreams of future wealth. To get their supplies out to the creeks from Circle, a distance of up to a hundred miles, they had to backpack them across a morass of swampy muskeg and dead-water sloughs, while swarms of mosquitoes pierced their skins and sometimes punctured their sanity. Arthur Walden reports that the horses used to freight supplies were often covered with canvas sheets to protect them from the mosquitoes; it was important, he adds, to clear the insects from their nostrils to prevent suffocation.

Walden himself was a dog driver, so he did his work mainly in winter. There were no mosquitoes then, of course, but the winter brought the deep cold that had its own perils and inflicted its own suffering. There was no thermometer in Circle until Mc-questen fashioned one by placing four liquid-filled vials in a rack. One contained mercury, the next a good, unwatered rye whiskey, the next kerosene, and the last Perry Davis' Pain-Killer. They congealed in that order, the mercury solidifying at —38.4° F., the whiskey at —55°, the kerosene at —63°, and the painkiller at —70° F. Walden made a careful check of the vials before beginning his outbound trips. "A man starting on a journey started with a smile at frozen quicksilver," he recounts, "still went at whiskey, hesitated at the kerosene, and dived back into his cabin when the Pain-Killer lay down."

When the miners of Circle came into town from the creeks, they came to forget the mosquitoes and the cold, the fetid cabins and smoky shafts, the backbreaking toil and the loneliness. Mc-

Questen had appealed to the San Francisco office of ACC⁰. to
make a donation toward a library, and the company had sent a
morocco-bound quarto Bible, the Encyclopedia Britannica, and
tomes of Macaulay, Hume, Carlyle and Darwin. Some of the men
undoubtedly found diversion and self-improvement in these volumes. But to expect the average miner to climb up out of a fume-
filled hole in the frozen ground only to plunge into the malarial
swamps of "England in 1685," or start slogging down the high-
road from Aardvark to Zygote, was a bit too much. For most of
them de Windt's "life of a tawdry, disreputable description" was
a more accessible balm.

In 1896 there were twenty-seven saloons and eight dance halls
in Circle, not to mention the Tivoli Theatre. The whiskey sold at
the bars was watered to twice its original volume and, at fifty
cents a shot, sold at many times its original price. The hoochinoo*
was cheaper. A concoction made by distilling fermented sugar,
molasses, flour, berries or any other fermentable substance, potable or not, it was, according to one Circle City man, "so hefty that
after a few drinks you could sit on a glacier all day."

In the dance halls a miner could dance with one of the girls for
a dollar per three minutes. If she didn't know him she might ask
his name and go over to the check list of rich claim owners kept
in the corner before accepting. Bathing in the subarctic requires a
stoicism such as that of Robert Campbell, and few of the miners
possessed it. When the fiddlers warmed up with the waltzes and
quadrilles, and the gyrations of the dance became rapid, the
miners, becoming uncomfortably warm, would shed their rubber
boots. What resulted, one of them said, was "a smell that would
offend the nostrils of a Chinese wooden god."

Most of the Circle girls were in no position to protest against
their unhygienic clients. They were, in general, a faded lot,
underneath their paint, and they would never have come to this
cold, remote place if they could still have commanded a decent

---

* "Hoochinoo" or "hooch" for short, is an Alaskan contribution to American slang. It appears to be derived from the name of a small coastal town,
Hootznahoo, where a soldier named Doyle, discharged from the Sitka
garrison for drunkenness supposedly taught the Indians to brew the stuff.

price on the flesh markets of Seattle, Vancouver, and San Francisco. An exception was a girl of sixteen, whose real name no one knew. She was called "The Virgin" because, according to one of the miners, "Possibly they thought she had seen one." She was the great favorite of all and made love while fighting off mosquitoes by the broad Yukon. Ella the Glacier, on the other hand, was ungenerous with her favors, for she was saving them up for a curly-haired bartender with whom she became infatuated. This man paid her no heed, however, so she decided to demonstrate the depth of her affection by an *attempted* suicide using wolf poison. According to plan, the doctor arrived promptly, but he was unable to unfreeze his stomach pump in time. Thus did Ella the Glacier melt from this world. One of Ella's colleagues was Lottie. All that is known about her is that

> Lottie went to the diggings;
> With Lottie we must be just.
> If she didn't shovel tailings—
> Where did Lottie get her dust?

Despite the high life, the silence of Circle's still, chill air was seldom much disturbed. Pack trains and men shuffled noiselessly out toward the creeks over the summer's dust and the winter's snow. There were no church or school bells to ring out their obligations. As a door opened, a shaft of dim light momentarily punctured the night, and half a bar of scraped violin notes spilled out, but the door slammed tight in an instant and the dark silence was restored. A pall of smoke shrouded the settlement; in winter it came from a hundred red-hot sheet iron stoves, and in summer from scores of moss smudge pots set out to deter the mosquitoes —a spectral place where the men spent themselves in permafrost holes and the women in vice.

12 The Place That Vanished

WILLIAM B. HASKELL was nobody special, either in the chronicle of the Yukon or that of any other place. His parents, God-fearing Vermont dairy farmers, scrimped and saved in order to send him to a private school down in Massachusetts to enhance his chances of entering the ministry. Their investment was unsound, for young Haskell spent most of his time reading exotic adventure tales and daydreaming about faraway places; his textbooks of Greek and geometry remained unlearned, his marks were low, and at graduation he was not found to be worthy seminary material. Since the chief thing about farming that had impressed him was its scanty rewards, he did not return to Vermont, but went instead to Boston where he obtained employment as a dry-goods clerk. A robust young man, imbued with wanderlust and great expectations, he found skulking behind the counter an utter bore. One day during the spring of 1889 he read a newspaper account of a new gold strike in southern California, and, as he says, "the temptation became too great for me to resist." He quit his job, bought a ticket for Chicago and boarded the train at South Station with thirty dollars in his pocket. From Chicago he worked his way west as a laborer on the railroads. At that time the Cripple Creek Mining District of Colorado was booming, and he joined the excitement as a mine laborer. He later did some prospecting and participated in several local stampedes, but in neither of these was he notably successful. In 1895 he joined forces with another miner-prospector, a man considerably older than he named Joseph Meeker. Meeker was a North Carolinian by birth, but for many years now he had been a wandering and temporary citizen of a dozen different western mining camps. A few years before he met Haskell he had gone to the Yukon country and he was full of stories about the rich ground of Forty Mile. Eighteen ninety-five had been a year of dimming prospects in Colorado, so the two men decided to venture the Yukon. Within the next four years thousands of others would make the same decision, and since they would be faced with similar problems and like circumstances, and would take the same route, it is worthwhile following the experiences of Haskell and Meeker in some detail.

Their first step was to pool their money (the total came to $1,500) and go to San Francisco to purchase an outfit and steamship tickets. At this time there was no assurance that supplies would be available at the few trading posts on the river, and in any case prices there were often more than double those in San Francisco. The outfit they bought cost them about $400—big money in those days of depression—and weighed 3,200 pounds. Both Meeker and Haskell were experienced prospectors and wilderness travelers, and what they chose to bring reflected this. They carefully calculated how much food they would consume each day, and bought enough to last them a year and a half: eight hundred pounds of flour, three hundred of bacon, two hundred of beans, one hundred and fifty of sugar, fifty each of dried apples, peaches and apricots, fifty of pilot crackers, fifty of evaporated milk, twenty-five of tea, twenty of baking soda and even two pounds of ground mustard. They bought eighty pounds of candles, thirty of tobacco and fifteen of laundry soap. Since they would have to build boats, cabins and sluices, they brought a nearly complete set of light carpenter's tools. Their prospecting and mining equipment included gold pans and scales, mercury, picks, shovels, buckets and rope. They bought a tent, sleeping bags, three suits each of heavy woolen underwear, Mackinaws, rubber boots, rain gear, sweaters, "long German-knit socks" and "leopard seal waterproof mittens."

On March 15, 1896, Haskell and Meeker steamed out of San
Francisco Bay bound for Alaska. After a few days' wait at Juneau
they took a smaller steamer into Lynn Canal, a finger of the
Pacific that points at the Yukon's headwaters just across the Coast
Mountains. Dyea, where they landed, would mushroom into a
sizable town two years later, but for now it was only a debarkation point, and a poor one at that. The cove on which it was
situated is so shallow and mudbottomed that all cargo had to be
lightered in from ship to shore by shallow-draft scows. Haskell,
Meeker and the several dozen other prospectors who debarked
from the Juneau ship had their outfits carried in to the mucky
beach where ten inches of wet spring snow had just fallen. They
spent that afternoon sorting out their mountainous piles of provisions, while clusters of Chilkoot packers, "some of the dirtiest
looking Indians on the face of the earth," according to Haskell,
"hovered around like evil spirits." During the last decade or so the
Chilkoots, seeing that they could no longer block off their High
Grease Trail to outsiders, concluded to profit from the traffic as
porters. Haskell wanted to hire some of them to help pack his
outfit across the mountains, and he arranged a deal with a one-
eyed chief and his men to do this for seventeen cents per pound.
But the porters procrastinated and haggled so much that the two
men decided to do the job themselves. "I would rather pack our
stores over a dozen Chilkoot passes," comments Haskell, "than
fool with heathen like these."

The Chilkoot Trail winds up from Dyea Inlet, traverses the
crest of the Coast Mountains, and then drops down to Lindeman,
one of the headwater lakes of the Yukon. The Chilkoot Trail is
only twenty-seven miles long, but in crossing it one must climb
3,739 feet, then descend another 1,550. It would not be so bad if
the ascent were better distributed, but in places the trail is so
steep that a man crawling up it on his hands and knees is forced
into a vertical position. De Windt, the Englishman who took such
a dim view of the recreations the Circle miners enjoyed, ascended
the Chilkoot the summer before Haskell and Meeker. "I have
roughed it," he states, "in most parts of the world—among others,
Borneo, Siberia, and Chinese Tartary—but I can safely describe

that climb over the Chilkoot as the severest physical experience of my life."

At its beginning, though, the trail was easy enough, for it led gently up the valley of the Dyea River. The day after landing Meeker and Haskell managed to relay their entire one and a half ton outfit five miles up this section of the trail. Each of them would haul four hundred pounds on a sled, returning several times to the beach at Dyea for a new load. Along the way they passed a few other parties, and occasional heaps of cached provisions, but in general they had the trail to themselves. At the end of a long day they pitched their tent and warmed up around a roaring fire in their sheet metal stove. After an immense meal of beans and bacon, they sat puffing on their pipes and congratulating each other on the good progress of the day. At their present rate, they would be on the shores of Lindeman Lake within the week.

The next seven miles were a lot tougher. Haskell and Meeker were forced to cut their loads to one hundred and fifty pounds each, and the stretch took them four arduous days. Midway they entered the cleft of Dyea Canyon which funneled the trail to the boulder-strewn amphitheater called Sheep Camp. Here the trail crossed the timber line, and Sheep Camp was thus the last source of firewood until well down the other side of the divide. The difficult part of the Chilkoot began there, and even before Haskell and Meeker reached Sheep Camp, they "met more than one man who had turned back, not caring to brave the pass for all the gold that might be on the other side." Others faltered but somehow kept going.

Haskell and Meeker no sooner reached Sheep Camp than a blizzard began. It did not let up for two solid weeks. The hundred or so people encamped there huddled in their tents, emerging only to fetch wood and hurl invective at the swirling opaque sky. "There was no laughter there," says Haskell. "Cut off from the world, a man feels himself dwindling into a mere atom amid the silent, everlasting hills. He feels almost like speaking in whispers. . . ." A thundering roar would punctuate the gloom now and then as the bottle-green glacier that hung above Sheep Camp hurled great ice masses down into the valley floor. As the blizzard finally abated, Chilkoot Summit jutted into visibility, its granite mass still buffeted by high winds and shredded storm clouds. It was only four miles away, but the last mile alone required an ascent of 1,250 feet.

From Sheep Camp, Haskell and Meeker sledded their outfit through the deep new snow to the foot of Chilkoot Summit. From there to the top their sleds were of no use because of the steep grades. They divided their outfit into fifty pound parcels for backpacking, and during the next days hauled load after load slowly up the icy 30–40 degree inclines. The trail, such as it was, followed a running notch between two smooth flanks of rock.

In the steeper places steps were cut in the ice and snow, and in taking a pack up one was compelled to lean forward and use his hands on the icy steps. Occasionally a tired man would make a misstep, or his foothold caved off, and down the precipice he rolled, landing in the soft snow, from which he had to extricate himself and again attempt the tiresome climb.

To get back down after depositing a load on the summit the prospector would simply sit down in a well-worn chute in the snow, give himself a slight shove, hold his breath and close his eyes till he arrived at the bottom hundreds of feet below. "It took less time to slide down than it takes to tell of it . . ." relates Haskell. "After awhile the experience began to have the flavor of true sport, and the more we tried it the better we liked it."

Over a score of women debarked at Dyea with Haskell and Meeker. A few of them, very few, were the bona fide wives of miners, but most were bound for the fleshpots of Circle City. When they reached Chilkoot Summit they were at first a little apprehensive about the snow chute, but sliding down was so much easier than descending via the ice steps that one of them finally tried it.

We could see her fidgeting a little at the top; then she wrapped her coat about her, dropped into the trench, and down she came like a flash. She picked herself up out of the snow rosy and smiling. Then this method of descent became general. They seemed to enjoy it as much as the men, but most of those whom I saw going down were of the dance-hall variety. It appeared to be a little too much for the staider matrons, even in men's clothes.

Day after day Haskell and Meeker toiled up the Chilkoot Pass. Each made forty trips. At last they reached the summit with the last two fifty-pound packs. They had gone fifteen miles since leaving the mud beach of Dyea twenty-three days before, but they had hauled a ton and a half of supplies up more than 3,700 feet above sea level. Below them now, to the northwest, lay Lindeman Lake and the Yukon. After three days they pitched their tent on the lake's frozen shores.

Haskell and Meeker planned to build a boat on Lindeman while waiting for open water, but they found little usable timber in the vicinity. Though it was nearly May, the lake ice was still firm, so they dragged their sleds down Lindeman to Bennett Lake, and then to Tagish Lake. By the time they reached Tagish, where there was plenty of good timber, the ice was beginning to get soft and dangerous, so they stopped to build a boat. The white spruce of the Yukon Plateau are generally stunted, but they found several that would yield eight or nine inch planks. They built a sawpit, a crude platform on which to place the logs so that one of them could stand beneath with one end of the long whipsaw and the other above with the other end. It was trying labor especially for the man below who was showered by a continual rain of sawdust, and before the first plank was sliced off they were both in foul humors. They accused each other of deviating from the chalk guideline, of not pulling hard enough, of purposely trying to throw each other off balance, and finally of being dirty sons of bitches and other things. Before they had mastered the art of whipsawing green timber into planks they nearly came to blows, nearly severed their partnership. "It was more trying than the Chilkoot Pass," comments Haskell. Within a week, however, they had enough lumber, and a few days later they had hammered it into a twenty-six-foot boat. They caulked her with the oakum they had brought for the purpose, baptized her the *Tar Stater* in honor of Meeker's home state, and packed their outfit into her. Haskell thought the boat a little small to carry such a heavy load through rough water, but Meeker, her architect, insisted she was just right; he, after all, had been down the river once before. Haskell deferred to the older man's judgment. "I was a fair swimmer," he reflected, "and I knew that I could get out of any place that he could." On a beautiful spring morning the two men launched the *Tar Stater* out among the ice floes of Tagish Lake. By alternate sailing and rowing, they traversed Tagish to Marsh Lake and descended to its foot.

Here the Yukon begins, and it begins with a grand display of boiling water and raw strength. It is as though the river stages a violent temper tantrum at being exiled from the indolent Eden of currentless pure-green lakes. Or perhaps it celebrates its coming of age, or suddenly becomes aware of its pressing appointment with the Bering Sea eighteen hundred miles away. Miles Canyon begins twenty miles below Marsh Lake. Within this narrow trench cut into sheer walls of black basalt, the river is compressed to a width of fifty feet. The green water, sunless in the gorge, plunges downward with the speed of a millrace and the roar of a freight train. It pounds down against the dark walls, is heaved back by them into a seething ridge of turbulence that runs down the center of the canyon from start almost to finish.* Midway the canyon widens into a swirling whirlpool, a fine place to catch grayling from the bank, but a trap for boats.

When Haskell and Meeker heard the low swishing roar of Miles Canyon they knew what it meant, and pulled the *Tar Stater* up on the bank a safe distance above. Several other boats were beached there, and their crews were portaging their outfits via a trail that led to calmer water four miles below. As they stood on the shore, they watched a boat shoot down and disappear into the canyon "at the speed of a race horse." They debated whether to run the *Tar Stater* through, but decided she was too unsea-

---

* The hydroelectric dam at Whitehorse, completed a decade ago, has since drowned out the swift water.

worthy a craft with too heavy a load. So they hoisted a gun, some clothing, a sack of beans and a hundred pounds of sugar on their backs and started down the portage trail. It was a hot day, and the cumbersomeness of their heavy loads made it difficult to fend off the swarms of mosquitoes. At the far end of the trail, just below Whitehorse Rapids, they left their burdens and walked back for others. They had moved one hundred and fifty pounds, which left three thousand to go. On the way back they watched another boat, fully loaded, dart in apparent safety through the roiling froth "in less time than it took us to fix a single pack on our shoulders." "I know the *Tar Stater* will ride as well as that coffin did," said Meeker. Before starting a second trip they met a couple of men who said they had piloted seven boats through that day; they offered to take the *Tar Stater* for five dollars, and their offer was readily accepted. Meeker took a spectator's position on the rim of Miles Canyon, but Haskell, younger and more adventurous, went aboard with the two pilots.

We pushed off [writes Haskell] and in two minutes my heart failed me, and I would have given all the gold I ever expected to get in these regions had I staid out. . . .

The two men started in to manage the boat cleverly enough. Not far from the entrance the boat seemed to take a fall of several feet, while all the waters in creation seemed to have fallen into a space seventy-five feet wide. The moment we struck the first high wave we shipped some water, at the second we shipped more, at the third it poured in around the whole outfit, and at the next we were full, and over we went into the ice-cold water with the worst part of the cañon before us. The boat turned toward the side I was occupying, and I sprang out so as to avoid being covered up. The moment I struck the water all fear was gone. It was easy swimming, for the current took one along whether he would or not.

When the boat came up she was about ten feet from me, and it was not easy to reach her, for struggling against the current was another matter. Finally I caught hold of the stern and climbed up. As I was swept by one of the other fellows, I got hold of him and pulled him in so that he could climb up, and a little afterwards the other man was able to reach us. There the three of us were riding on the bottom of

the boat, which was whirling about in the wildest manner. As straight as a crow flies runs the cañon for an eighth of a mile. The roar was like a cannonade. On the top of the bluffs which fled by us grew dense forests of spruce which shut out the sun, and a weird darkness pervaded the deep and angry channel. The boat shot forward with lightning speed, leaping like a racer or bucking like a mustang, now buried out of sight in the foam, and now plunged beneath a terrific wave. We clung desperately to the bottom as helpless as flies.

A moment later we came to the worst place in the current, where there are three heavy swells, and where those who are steering boats through incline a little to the left to avoid the roughest part. But the current was steering us, and into the swells we dived. The waters swept us from the slippery keel as if we had been so many leaves. Again we struggled in the current, and again we caught on to the whirling boat, for after the swells the water became smoother, and in a twinkling we shot out of the cañon like a rocket, amid the reefs of boulders and bars thickly studded with drifts of timber. Two men were waiting at the foot of the bluffs in a boat, and when they saw us come out they rowed after us and took us in. Thus we left the *Tar Stater*.

. . . We had had a little over four minutes of experience. Some of the boats go through in three minutes.

Wet and shivering, I sat down on a rock on the bank and felt very blue. Ten minutes before we had boasted the best outfit that any two men we had seen were bringing in; everything we would need for the next eighteen months. It was worth over $800, according to the way things sold in Alaska, and we had lost very many things which could not be bought on the Yukon. All we had left was the sack of sugar and a few beans; nothing to cook them in. We had no tent to sleep in, and we were 250 miles from Juneau and five hundred miles from the nearest trading post down the river.

Meeker had watched the *Tar Stater* go under from the bank. He now came down to Haskell and said, "Well, the milk is spilt," and gave the bean sack a despondent kick. They were not so unlucky as some, however; next day two men were drowned. Each season the canyon and the rapids had sluiced miners' corpses down to calmer water below, and their toll grew with each new discovery of gold downriver.

Meeker and Haskell were lucky in that they managed to recover the scarred and battered *Tar Stater* when she lodged against the bank just below Miles Canyon. They recaulked the boat, and were able to beg, borrow and buy a few essential provisions from acquaintances of the trail. Nearly empty, the *Tar Stater* made it through the spume and foam of Whitehorse Rapids without mishap. From there to the Bering Sea nearly 1,800 miles away there is no serious impediment to navigation if one is cautious, and they had no trouble drifting down to Forty Mile. Others did, however, especially on Lake Laberge and along what was then called the Thirty Mile River.

Lake Laberge, the only lake on the Yukon proper, is thirty miles long and at least two miles wide in most places. Its green, crystal-clear water is never many degrees warmer than the ice that stays upon it for a full two weeks after the river is free. To swim twenty yards in such cold water is a feat. The shores are steep rock cliffs of yellows, browns and duns, alternating with splendid beaches of nut-sized pebbles washed clean and bleached by the sun. A strong wind from north or south can spring up without warning and whip the lake surface to a sudden frenzy of choppy five-foot waves. Many boats have been caught in the middle, or next to the cliffs in such circumstances, and gone down with all hands.

The Thirty Mile River is that section of the Yukon between Lake Laberge and the confluence with the Teslin, a major tributary coming in from the Rocky Mountain foothills to the southeast. Just above this confluence, and usually just below the water level, is Casey's Rock. It got its name, the story goes, from a miner of that name, an old-timer who preferred to travel alone. He was headed for the gravel bars of the Stewart in the days before Forty Mile, and he packed in his outfit over the Chilkoot, built his boat on Lindeman, skirted Miles Canyon and Whitehorse Rapids, and drifted down the Thirty Mile and head on into Casey's Rock. He lost his boat and his outfit but somehow managed to save himself and trudge all the way back over the Chilkoot to Healy's store in Dyea. There he bought a new outfit and again set out for the bars of the Stewart. Again he crossed the Chilkoot, built a boat and drifted down the Thirty Mile. And once again Casey's Rock tore the boat bottom from under him and sent his outfit on ahead in the current. Casey saved himself this time too. He crawled dripping onto the flat bank where the long-abandoned Mounted Police post now rots away. Some prospectors were camped there, but at the moment they were off hunting. Casey went into their tent, rummaged around for a while, and found what he was looking for. When the prospectors returned they discovered him lying on the ground, a small bullet hole in his left temple.

At Fort Selkirk, Haskell and Meeker stopped at the trading post—the first they had come to since Dyea on the coast—that Arthur Harper ran there then. They bought a tent and a few other supplies to replace what they had lost, and continued on. A few days later they hauled the *Tar Stater* up on the bank at Forty Mile. Back in Colorado Meeker had decided, on the basis of what he had seen on his first trip, that the best prospects lay on Mosquito Fork, a tributary on the Alaskan portion of the Fortymile River. His hunch was sound, but he had come too late. When he and Haskell went up to Mosquito Fork they found it was staked from end to end with claims that were proving to be exceptionally rich. There were still plenty of the insects for which the creek was named, however:

. . . apparently no larger than the ordinary mosquito of lower latitudes, [writes Haskell, they] are several times as venomous. . . . They seem to thrive on any ordinary smoke. They revel in fire unless it consumes a whole forest. One may hurl a blanket through a cloud of them, but ranks are closed up and the cloud is again intact before the blanket has hit the ground. All day long, and of course in July that means for about twenty-four hours, they are on the alert, always after anything that has blood in its veins. . . .

They rise in vast clouds from the peculiar moss along the banks and creeks, and their rapaciousness knows no limits. They have been known to drive men to suicide, and the sting of a few dozen will make a man miserable for days. I have seen tough miners sit and cry, and it is a common sight to see them so worn out and nervous that they can not sleep even after they are protected from them.

Mosquitoes were, and are, so numerous in the Forty Mile country, and in fact nearly everywhere in the Yukon basin, because the impervious barrier of permafrost blocks seepage of ground water to lower levels. The boggy surface is a splendid breeding ground and the mosquitoes swarm up from it like morning mist rising off the landscape. Like that of all creatures, the mosquito's reproductive drive is inexorable, but unlike most others, the drive cannot end in success without the warm blood of mammals. Although mosquitoes are sustained by plant juices, the female of the species must have blood in order to lay fertile eggs. (The male has no need for it, and never bites.) Man, soft-skinned and hairless, is as good a source as any.

The advance guard of Yukon mosquitoes hatches out among the river's spring ice floes, and the stragglers contend against the flakes of the first fall snow flurries. In between times, the main force of countless millions hovers thick as smoke, probing mammalian flesh with marvelously agile proboscides, and buzzing endlessly. It is this buzzing that is the most enervating, perhaps because the anticipation of being bitten is worse than the bite itself. It is like a doctor's telling a child of an injection two weeks before the event.

Many a man on the Yukon has been driven to conjuring up the fantasy of a single giant mosquito that he might either kill or be killed by, but the insects are like a Medusa with an infinite multiplicity of tiny self-regenerating heads. And many a harassed victim has vainly wished that mosquitoes were a little educable, or at least less suicidal, as he slapped a good dozen or two with a single swat only to find that before he even lifted his hand to slap again it was covered with as many new mosquitoes ready to repeat the sacrifice. The mosquitoes of the Yukon don't even provide the sadistic pleasure some derive from tearing insects limb from limb, for one can be sure that while his hands are thus occupied the allies of his victim will cause him more misery than he can possibly cause by his vivisection; and, if he prolongs his operation to eke out the last quantum of pain, so will they prolong theirs, at ten times the intensity.

The gentle and long-suffering Bishop Seghers was moved to write of the Yukon mosquitoes in these terms:

What a plague they are! One is involuntarily reminded of the third plague of Egypt, the celebrated *sciniphes*. They unceremoniously drop into your cup of tea, they are uncouth enough to fill your spoon before you take it to your lips, you open your mouth either to speak or breathe and half a dozen of mosquitoes sail into your throat and give you a fit of coughing. We wrapped ourselves in our blankets and having covered every inch of our bodies, we victoriously bade defiance to the bloodthirsty insects and enjoyed a sound sleep until 3 o'clock the following morning.

Frederick Schwatka, the U.S. army lieutenant who made a military reconnaissance of the river in 1883, found that the mosquitoes caused more distress than Miles Canyon and Whitehorse Rapids together. Concerning the Thirty Mile River section of the Yukon, Schwatka reports that

. . . not a sign of any game was seen except a few old tracks; and the tracks of an animal are about the only part of it that could exist here in the mosquito season. . . . Had there been any game, and had I obtained a fair shot, I honestly doubt if I could have secured it . . . for the reason that they were absolutely so dense that it was impossible to see clearly through the mass in taking aim. . . . I know that the native dogs are killed by the mosquitoes under certain circumstances, and I heard reports, which I believe to be well founded . . . that the great brown bear . . . of these regions is at times compelled to succumb to these insects.

Jack London, who came to the Yukon a year after Haskell and Meeker, entered these mosquito observations in his diary:

One night badly bitten under netting—couldn't vouch for it but Jim watched them & said they rushed the netting in a body, one gang holding up the edge, while a second gang crawled under. Charley swore that he has seen several of the largest ones pull the mesh apart & let a small one through. I have seen them with their proboscis bent and twisted after an assault on [a] sheet iron stove. Bite me through overalls & heavy underwear.

And, finally, a nameless prospector describes the mosquito agonies he suffered during a summer's search for a lost miner in the Chandalar country north of Fort Yukon:

It was the rainiest summer ever I seen, and the mosquitoes was a
terror. I had a veil and I honestly believe them mosquitoes eat it up,
for it went to pieces all at once. I honestly believe they eat it up they
was that thick and that venomous. The only chance to sleep was to
travel so long and so hard that I fell asleep as soon as I stopped.

The mosquito figures in the Yukon's folklore as importantly as
the kangaroo in Australia's or the baboon in South Africa's,
though much less benignly. He can snatch the catch from a trapper's snare or a prospector from the face of the earth; he has been
taught to sink shafts to bedrock with one deft thrust of the proboscis; it is he who drove the sabre-toothed tiger and the mastodon to extinction. George Edward Lewis, the doggerel poet,
catalogues four types of Yukon mosquitoes, each more horrific
than the other.

> The fourth is Alaska's most noble defender,
> His victims all call him "The big double-ender,"
> When ravenous mad, like bees in the attic,
> Their little twin pumps, they run automatic,
> Tho hard to believe, this mystical kind,
> Bore into their victim both ends at one time.

Finding nothing unclaimed on Mosquito Fork save the mosquitoes, Haskell and Meeker staked two claims on an unproven creek
nearby, but had so little hope for them that they decided to leave
the Forty Mile country altogether and go to Circle City. There,
they heard, good wages could be had even if good claims could
not. They recorded the unpromising ground they had staked with
Inspector Constantine who, aside from being, as he put it, the
"chief magistrate, commander-in-chief and home and foreign secretary" of Forty Mile, was also its mining recorder. They then got
back into the *Tar Stater* and drifted the one hundred and seventy
miles down to Circle City.

They reached Circle one evening in July. To celebrate their
arrival they wandered up and took a tour of this Paris of the
North, stopping in at a few of its twenty-seven saloons and the

dance halls. In one of the latter their erstwhile trailmates, the girls who slid down Chilkoot Summit in reinforced bloomers, were at work swinging in the arms of grizzled miners. When they returned to the *Tar Stater*, they discovered that the town's famished dogs had eaten a dish rag, a flour sack and forty pounds of food. "But they were too precious to shoot," Haskell complained.

Since the two were nearly out of money and supplies, one of them had to stay in town and work for wages. This Haskell elected to do, while Meeker went off to the flats around Birch Creek to prospect. Haskell was handy with an axe and saw, and he soon found himself earning fifteen dollars a day as a cabin builder. This was five times what he would have made at similar work back home in Vermont, for there was a shortage of workers in Circle—and an abundance of gold, the currency in which he, and all others, were paid. The creeks of the Circle Mining District produced over a million dollars' worth of gold that year, and the town itself was in the midst of a real estate boom; some of the building lots where Haskell worked were selling for $5,000. The atmosphere was one of excitement and great expectations. "People talked glibly of the coming metropolis of the Yukon," says Haskell. "No one could have imagined a livelier place of its size. . . . Most of the gulches were then running, miners were working on double shifts . . . and large profits were reported. On Mastodon Creek, which seemed to be the best producer and which was thoroughly staked, over three hundred miners were at work."

Toward the end of that summer of 1896 Haskell had the opportunity to make a round trip to St. Michael on one of the five sternwheelers then plying the river. On the Yukon, where even craft of four foot draught often ran aground, it was advisable to draw the least water possible. This was done by loading the main weight of the cargo in wide-bottomed barges pushed ahead, while the sternwheeler itself carried little more than its crew and the wood it burned. The early steamers on the Yukon had little in common with the later "floating palaces," with their mahogany railings and gingerbread fretwork. The craft Haskell took looked to him "like a small barn on a scow." He and the other passengers had quarters in a barge that had been topped over with canvas. Crude bunks had been installed, and any bedding desired was up to the passenger to supply.

Haskell returned to Circle City about a month after his departure. When he arrived Meeker happened to be in town for supplies. He had found good prospects, he said. After talking over the matter they decided that Meeker should continue working where he was, while Haskell would return to Forty Mile and start work on the unpromising claims they had staked there back in June. Haskell therefore continued upriver aboard the sternwheeler that had brought him up from St. Michael.

When we reached Forty Mile it was at once apparent that something had happened to that lively little settlement with which we had become acquainted. . . . A great change had come over it, and we were not long in discovering the reason. The greater part of the place had vanished, moved bag and baggage to the "Throndiuck," the moose valley forty miles above. . . . Boatload after boatload of men went up from Forty Mile. They went up any how and any way, starting at all times of day and night. Men who had been drunk for weeks and weeks, in fact, were tumbled into the boats and taken up without any knowledge that they were travelers. One man, it was related, was so drunk that he did not realize that he had left Forty Mile until he was more than two-thirds of the way. . . .

In less than three days every boat had gone from Fort Cudahy and the town of Forty Mile, and only enough people were left to watch the business houses and the police barracks, while a few who could not obtain boats were acting in the most distracted manner. No one knew anything about the richness of the new discoveries; they only knew that a man had been there and had come away with a few gold nuggets.

Haskell was at first skeptical. Most of the good ground around Forty Mile had long since been staked, and the town was full of claimless men who would believe anything, tramp off anywhere. A few days after his arrival the first of the stampeders drifted back down to Forty Mile to record their claims. Obviously they had not had time to prospect these claims thoroughly, but they were excitedly optimistic. "It's a big thing," they told Haskell;

"Everybody is finding big pans." Haskell's skepticism succumbed. He threw a tent, a stove and a month's provisions into the bottom of his boat, joined up with three other prospectors, and started laboriously poling and tracking upriver in the cold September drizzle. Stampeders headed down for the Recorder's Office passed him, shouting, "Hurry up boys. It's a great thing. Five dollars to the pan!" At this his party ceased stopping to cook meals on the bank and munched pilot crackers on board instead.

On the evening of the third day they reached their destination and camped in a growing cluster of tents. All night long other boats arrived and were hauled with a crunch up the gravelly beach. Men gathered, huddled, whispered. A man came down from the hills and announced: "Ten dollars to the pan, right in the bank of the creek on No. 11." Everyone cheered and shouted and the newcomers swarmed around him like mosquitoes to hear the details. "The gold is coarse. $12 nugget. $4,000 from two lengths of sluice box. $75 in four hours." Gradually one after another of the newcomers would unobtrusively detach himself from the excited throng, slide a pack on his shoulders and slip out of camp. A short distance away the trail he took contoured across the steep bank of the Klondike River, and the inevitable minor avalanche of small stones his passage caused told all below that he was off to Bonanza Creek.

13 A Sort of Siwash Hula-Hula

THOUGH he read destiny in the stars, and even in the scales of fish, the man who led the gold seekers forth out of the wilderness of Forty Mile had not been known to them as a prophet, nor even as a prospector. To them he was Siwash George the squawman, and aside from occasional ridicule or contempt they paid him little heed. Jowly and round-faced, he had a pendent Manchu mustache and a reputation for embellishing the truth even after inventing it. They called him a squawman not because of his Indian wife and half-breed children—McQuesten and Harper both had these and no one would have thought of calling them squawmen —but because with each passing year the Caucasian in him seemed to recede further behind a mien of placid native indolence, a mane of oily black hair, and an odor of rancid salmon.

It was the salmon that attracted him to the Klondike River. Each year these magnificent anadromous fish swim up from the Bering Sea, the kings first, then the chums, to spawn and die childless in almost the exact spot where they were spawned and born orphans six years before. In summer as they left the silted Yukon to ascend the deep blue water of the Klondike, Siwash George and his Indian in-laws lay in wait to intercept them. For years the Klondike had enjoyed local fame as a salmon stream. The river's name, a corruption of the Indian "Thron-diuk," means "hammer-water," and it was so called apparently because of the

148

numerous stakes hammered into the river bottom to anchor fish traps and act as wiers.*

George Washington Carmack had come into the Yukon in the 1880s. He was born in California where his father had sought gold in the stampede of 1849. In his teens he had worked on the ferries in San Francisco Bay, and later he signed on as a dishwasher on a Juneau-bound steamer. Once in Alaska he stayed. By 1887 he had been around Dyea and on the upper Yukon long enough to have acquired a passable fluency in the dialects of both the Chilkoot and Tagish Indians, and he had risen to a position of some influence among them. Carmack's straight-haired, pudgy Tagish wife was the daughter of the chief in a tribe where the chieftaincy was passed down matrilineally, and it is said that Carmack hoped to succeed his father-in-law to that position.

Carmack's closest companions were Skookum ("Strong") Jim, his brother-in-law, and another Indian, Tagish Charlie. Jim, hawk-nosed, high cheekboned and tall, was, according to Carmack, "straight as a gun barrel, powerfully built, with strong sloping shoulders, tapering . . . downward to the waist, like a keystone. He was known as the best hunter and trapper on the river; in fact, he was a super-specimen of the Northern Indian." William Moore, who founded Skagway, recounts that Jim once killed a brown bear with his empty gun barrel and a few stones, though when he returned from the hunt nearly all his clothes had been ripped off. Carmack, Jim and Charlie were in Dyea in 1887 when William Ogilvie landed there en route to the interior for his boundary survey. He engaged all three of them to pack his supplies over the Chilkoot Trail, and watched in astonishment as Jim strode up to the summit under a load of one hundred and fifty-six pounds of bacon. Jim was also intelligent, reliable and truthful, as Ogilvie and others attest. Tagish Charlie was less of a "super-specimen" but he was "lithe as a panther . . . alert as a weasel."

Between 1887 and 1896 Carmack and his Indian relatives wandered back and forth from the coast to the Yukon, packing occa-

* Mrs. Martha Taylor, who related the Beaver-Man tale at the beginning of this book, maintains however that it was called "hammer-water" because the oblong stones in its bed were especially well suited for making hammers.

sionally, doing odd jobs for John G. Healy at his trading post at
Dyea now and then, but mainly living off the land. At one point
Carmack established a little trading station near Five Finger
Rapids, and he made vague attempts at exploiting the seam of
bituminous coal that stuck out of a bluff there. The coal has since
been mined by United Keno Hill Mines, Ltd., and the town of
Carmacks, Y. T., has grown up in the vicinity, but Carmack
posted a note on his door there in 1895 saying "Gone to Forty
Mile for Grub", and he never returned.

Perhaps there is something about the way the Pelly sweeps
down into the Yukon, or about the high crumbling bluffs at the
confluence that makes the place conducive to portents. Here Robert Campbell had seen the magpie that tried to warn him of Fort
Selkirk's impending doom. And Carmack, as he sat among Campbell's blackened chimneys one May morning in 1896, read a portent in the morning star; this one, however, was an omen of great
good fortune. "Right then and there," he later recalled, "I made
up my mind to take action on that hunch at once, so, taking a
silver dollar out of my pocket (that was all the cheechaco
money I had), I flipped it high into the air." It came down tails,
which meant that Fate intended him to go downriver, not up. So
without further ado, he got into his canoe and paddled down to
Forty Mile. The night of his arrival, a dream came to his aid by
adding details to the "hunch" suggested by the morning star:

I dreamed that I was sitting on the bank of a small stream of water,
watching the grayling shoot the rapids. Suddenly the grayling began to
scatter and two very large King salmon shot up the stream in a
flurry of foaming water and came to a dead stop in front of the bank
where I was sitting. They were two beautiful fish, but I noticed that
instead of having scales like salmon, they were covered with an
armour of bright gold nuggets, and $20 gold pieces for eyes. As I
reached out my hand to grasp one of the fish, I awoke with a death
grip on my right ear. . . .

Because his imagination was now fired—and his right ear in
pain—he could sleep no more that night and lay pondering the

meaning of his dream. One thing was clear: he must go salmon fishing. But on which Yukon tributary the dream gave no clue. He decided on the Klondike because he knew it to be a good salmon stream. That morning he bought twine from a store in Forty Mile and set to work making a gill net.

On the first of July he left Forty Mile for the Klondike. He was joined there, it appears, by his wife Kate, at least one of his children (a girl the miners called "Graphic Gracey" because they found her real name unpronounceable), and Jim and Charlie. The men set the nets and hauled out a few king salmon, beautifully purple and rich in oil, while Kate split their deep orange flesh down the middle and hung them on racks to dry. But that year the racks remained nearly empty, for the run was poor, the poorest Carmack had ever seen. Since the fishing was proving to be a failure, Jim, Charlie and Carmack decided to cut timber instead. There were good stands of spruce in the valley of the Klondike, and the sawmill at Forty Mile would pay twenty-five dollars per thousand board feet of it.

In July Jim went up the Klondike to search out the best timber. About a mile up he turned to the south and followed a brook named Rabbit Creek until he came to a stand of trees such as he was looking for. He then began his way back down Rabbit Creek carefully examining its course to see if logs could be floated down it. In the process he sighted flecks of gold, but since he had neither pan nor shovel, all he could do was report the news to Carmack and Charlie when he returned to the camp at the mouth of the Klondike. Neither of them showed much interest, and the subject was soon forgotten.

Toward the end of July a lone man named Robert Henderson, a Nova Scotian who had wandered the earth from the Rocky Mountains to New Zealand searching for gold, beached his boat at Carmack's camp. According to Carmack, Henderson told him that he had found "surface prospects" high up on one of the little creeks that, he thought, drained into the Klondike about fifteen miles up from Carmack's camp.

"What are the chances to locate up there?" Carmack asked.

Henderson directed a look of contempt toward Jim and Charlie, and replied, "Well, there's a chance for you George, but I don't want any damn Siwashes staking on that creek."

With this, he shoved his boat off the rocky beach and began poling up the Klondike River.

A few weeks later Carmack and, despite Henderson's injunction, the two Indians decided to have a look at the new diggings. They followed the Klondike and then Rabbit Creek, and several miles up the latter they paused to rest. During the halt, Jim and Charlie panned out a little of the creek's gravel, and washed out about ten cents' worth of gold per pan, not a bad "prospect." On the basis of this, they decided to return and stake this portion of Rabbit Creek if Henderson's stream didn't look promising. A few days more of trekking through muskeg swamps and spruce jungles brought them to Henderson's camp where, because of the presence of Jim and Charlie, they were coldly received. Henderson had named his little stream Gold Bottom because, he explained, "I had a daydream that when I got my shaft down to bedrock it might be like the streets of the New Jerusalem," but Carmack, Jim and Charlie were not impressed by it, and they started back toward the Klondike. Before leaving, however, Carmack pledged that he would let Henderson know if he struck anything exciting on the way.

A few days after leaving, they consumed the last of their dried salmon and had to stop and hunt for other food. Jim shot at a moose but missed—the first time in his life this had happened, he assured William Ogilvie, who carefully took down his and Charlie's accounts of the trip. He was more lucky with the second moose, which he got while hunting alone. Before Carmack and Charlie arrived on the scene, he had butchered the animal and cooked part of it. With a chunk in his hands, he went to Rabbit Creek to get a drink of water. And there, in the sand of the creek bed, he saw more raw gold than he ever had before. When the others arrived, famished, he let them have a big feed before showing them.

Throwing off my pack [Carmack recollected], I walked down to the rim, and as soon as I reached it I stopped and looked down. My heart skipped a beat. After rubbing my eyes with the back of my hand to wipe away a misty film that enveloped the pupils, I reached down and picked up a nugget about the size of a dime. I put it between my teeth and bit at it like a newsboy who had found a quarter in the street. . . . Charley grabbed the pan and the shovel, started down on the run, tripped and fell, and would have rolled into the creek if I had not caught him. I took the shovel and dug up some of the loose bedrock . . . I could see the raw gold laying thick between the flaky slabs, like cheese sandwiches.

I walked back to the rim and set the gold-pan on the ground. Then as near as I can remember, three full grown men tried to see how big damn fools they could make of themselves. We did a war dance around that gold pan. It was a combination war dance, composed of a Scotch hornpipe, Indian fox trot, syncopated Irish jig and a sort of a Siwash Hula-Hula.

When they stopped dancing, the three men panned out a few grains and nuggets and filled a spent cartridge of Jim's .44 Winchester with them.

That night, after Jim and Charlie were asleep in their blankets, Carmack had visions that, while hardly befitting a convinced squawman, would later be fulfilled in the main. He conjured up "a trip around the world with a congenial companion [Kate, his plump, straight-haired wife?]. A beautiful home with well kept lawns, shrubbery and flowers. A sum invested in government bonds, the income of which would be sufficient to enable me to enjoy the good things of life in a decent way and keep me comfortable for the balance of my life." Behind the frowzy exterior of Siwash George there lay hidden a middle-class soul waiting to be revealed by the gold of the Klondike.

Next morning Carmack made a blaze on a spruce tree with his axe. On it he penciled:

TO WHOM IT MAY CONCERN:

I do, this day, locate and claim, by right of discovery, five hundred feet, running up stream from this notice. Located this 17th day of August, 1896.

G. W. Carmack.

According to Canadian mining law at that time, a placer claim ran for five hundred feet along the course of a creek, and across the creek's valley from one rim to the other. A prospector was limited to a single claim on a given creek, except when his was the first to be staked there; in that event he could stake a "discovery claim" and in addition a second one. Claims were numbered, and named, for their distance up- or downstream from the discovery claim. Thus, for example, Number Ten Above would be ten claims—or five thousand feet—above the claim on which the discovery was made. In the case of Rabbit Creek, Carmack and Jim shared the discovery claim, Carmack claimed One Below, Jim One Above, and Charlie Two Below. The staking finished, Carmack slashed off a piece of birch bark, wrote on it, "I name this creek 'Bonanza'" and entered his name below. He then attached the bark to the stake driven in at the site of Jim's discovery.

The journey back to the mouth of the Klondike took them only five hours, despite the bogs and the "devil club thorns." En route they passed two parties of prospectors, one of which was on the way to Henderson's Gold Bottom, and Carmack advised them to try Bonanza. From their Klondike fishing camp, Carmack and Charlie boarded a raft of saw logs they had cut a few weeks before and drifted down to Forty Mile to record their claims. Meantime, Jim hiked back up to Bonanza to keep an eye on their ground, and begin sawing up lumber for sluice boxes. They made no attempt to apprise Henderson of their discovery, though they might have if Henderson had not insulted Jim and Charlie and, by implication, Carmack himself. As it turned out, Henderson reached Bonanza only after it had been staked, and though he was the first man to mine any of the Klondike's placer tributaries—for Gold Bottom did indeed prove to be one of them—he never got rich. In later years he roamed the Northwest in search of another Klondike; one wonders if his attitude toward "damn Siwashes" had changed by then.

Now Carmack was a man whose word inspired little confidence among the whites of Forty Mile, especially when he talked "prospects." For one thing, the fact that he had "gone native" made him an eccentric even by the standards of the eccentric confraternity of Yukon miners. For another thing, he spent his time fishing, hunting, backpacking and trading; he had done little prospecting, and the only substance he had mined was, of all things, coal. Finally, he was, as Officer Hayne of the Mounted Police detachment of Forty Mile put it, a man who "would never acknowledge himself beaten, and always endeavor to present his fortunes in the most advantageous light." Other Forty Milers put it more succinctly: McCormick, as they called him, was "the all-firedest liar of the Yukon."

When Carmack got to Forty Mile he went to the mining recorder's office, but on the way he stopped off at Bill McPhee's saloon. It was late in August, and a number of miners had come into town from the creeks to place their orders for winter supplies. The saloons were crowded. As he entered McPhee's, he felt "as if I had just dealt myself a royal flush in the game of life," and he wanted to deal in the men of Forty Mile as well. He was nervous, standing there at the bar, on the threshold, as he hoped, of fame, respect and admiration; no more would people address him with derisive comments about his regression into barbarism. To calm himself he gulped down a glass of hooch; it made him "feel like another man, so the other man had to have a drink" too. Thus doubly fortified, he turned his back to the bar and announced to the crowd of miners:

"Boys, I've got some good news to tell you. There's a big strike up the river."

"Strike, hell!" somebody shouted, and a chorus of similar reactions filled the barroom.

But Carmack was ready for this. He brought out the cartridge full of gold and dropped it on the bar. It did not contain very much (three quarters of an ounce, worth about thirteen dollars), nor was it very pure (being mixed with black metallic sand), but the gold of each creek is characteristic of that creek alone, and none of the miners in the saloon had seen any quite like what Carmack poured out on the bar. They crowded around, and their skepticism vanished; they had no idea how rich the creek this gold came from might be, but they were certain that an entirely new gold-bearing stream had been discovered.

One of Carmack's most vociferous detractors of a few minutes ago fingered the little heap and said to Lying George, as he was sometimes called, "I've known you since '88, and I've never known you to lie to a white man or a Siwash, and I can lick any hootch-guzzling, salmon-eating son-of-a-gun that says you lie now. But say, old man, if it ain't asking too much, where in hell did you get it?"

So George Washington Carmack, ex-Siwash George the squaw-man, dealt in the Forty Milers, of whom there were very few when Haskell arrived a couple of days later.

14 Klondike

By the beginning of September, Carmack, Jim and Charlie had neighbors all up and down Bonanza Creek. William Haskell was one of them. The night he reached the mouth of the Klondike he was thoroughly exhausted from three days of bucking the Yukon current; he pitched his tent and went to sleep, but was constantly awakened by new stampeders scraping their boats up on the rocky beach. Next morning he loaded a packsack with a few days' food and set out on the trail for Bonanza Creek with three other men from Forty Mile. It was raining and the two-week old path was churned to an ankle-deep ooze. Men up ahead of Haskell's party would pass acquaintances going down, stop briefly to exchange some arcane intelligence in whispers, and start off again with quickened, nervous strides. They were gaunt and gray with sleeplessness; gold had mined their health. Haskell and his companions slithered up to Carmack's claim where Jim was sluicing pay dirt that held five dollars of dust and nuggets to the pan; they had never seen anything like it before. All the ground along Bonanza they had passed so far was staked, and they continued on. A few hundred yards above Discovery Claim, Haskell noticed a small stream, or "pup," entering Bonanza from the east through a little valley between gentle, worn-down hills. "It certainly appeared more like a gold stream [than Bonanza]," he noted, "but, of course, like the rest at first, we rushed [past it] with the herd;" if they had stopped to prospect the pup they might all have been rich men. A few miles above this pup they stopped to ask a claim owner how much farther up Bonanza Creek was staked. He didn't know, he said, but his claim was Forty-three Above.

Haskell was discouraged. Perhaps there was no good ground left. He brewed some tea in the drizzle. It was getting dark. He and his three companions slept in the lee of a spruce tree and woke up drenched. They continued on next morning, crossing and re-crossing Bonanza to avoid the alder and willow thickets. They waded right through the stream for they were so wet by now that it made no difference. They hoped each claim they came to would be the last, but each time their expectations rose they would spot another set of stakes and blazes. Finally, in the Seventies Above, over six miles from Discovery, they came to un-claimed ground. No gold had been found this far up, and they were not optimistic, but they staked anyhow. There was nothing else for them to do, since they were fast running out of food and had to get back to their caches at the mouth of the Klondike as soon as possible.

A day or two after Haskell and his friends reached upper Bonanza, another party of four followed in their footsteps. On the way up they camped near the mouth of the pup that had seemed promising to Haskell. That night two men, Anton Stander, a swarthy Austrian immigrant of twenty-nine, and Frank Keller, an ex-railroad worker from California, stopped by at their camp and spent an hour and a half drinking tea and talking. Stander told one of the party, a William Johns, that he had found good pros-pects on upper Bonanza where, he indicated, his own camp was located. He advised Johns and the others to try their luck there, and next morning they set out to do so. They too ascended as far up as the Seventies, prospecting as they went, but they found nothing they thought justified staking. They returned to their camp of the night before, having decided to prospect the nearby pup next day. Just as they were breaking camp the following morning, Frank Keller again appeared. He was dressed in cor-duroys, a rifle slung over his shoulder; he was, he indicated, start-ing out on a hunt. Keller asked them how they had done on Bonanza, and when they told him, he reaffirmed his confidence in its richness; they must have looked in the wrong places. He then asked them where they were going that day.

"To prospect that 'pup,'" Johns replied. "Do you know any-thing about it?"

"Oh, I found a five-cent piece [i.e., five cents' worth of gold to the pan, a poor prospect] on rimrock, about a mile up," said Keller, as if to dismiss the possibility that the pup could amount to anything. With this, he went on his way.

Johns and his companions found Keller's report discouraging enough, but they were determined to have a look for themselves. They walked over to the little stream. The first one of them to reach it halted suddenly. He pointed down at it. "Some one is working," he said, "the water is muddy."

Like hunters who have scented game [Johns relates], we lapsed into silence, and, with eyes and ears alert, kept on. We had gone only a little way when suddenly we came upon four men. Three of them were standing around the fourth, who was holding a gold-pan. All were intently looking into the pan. The man with the .pan was Anton [Stander], and the other three were J. J. Clements, Frank Phiscater [sic], and old man Whipple. When they looked up and saw us, they acted like a cat caught in a cream-pitcher. Seeing that we had found them out, they loosened up and told us all they knew. They showed us then what they had in the pan. There was no less than 50 cents. While we were talking, along came Keller. He had taken off his corduroys and was in working-clothes. . . .

By that afternoon there were twelve claims staked along the pup. Jay Whipple had One, and Three, which was the discovery claim. Phiscator had Two, Clements had Four, Frank Keller, the would-be hunter, had Five, and Anton Stander Six. Others of the same group had Seven through Nine, and Johns and two of his partners tacked on Ten, Eleven and Twelve. In the evening the stakers gathered around a fire to decide on what to call the pup. Old Man Whipple wanted it named after him since he had staked the discovery claim, but he had irritated some of his partners that day and they refused to go along with him. One of Johns' group, a Norwegian who had perhaps read Voltaire, jokingly proposed the name "El Dorado," but the others took him seriously and it was adopted.

News of gold on the pup quickly spread through the little camps up and down Bonanza valley, and within a day or two Eldorado was staked nearly to its sources. None of the stakers had any real idea how rich the creek might turn out to be, however; surface showings were promising, but, to use a cliché then current, "On the Klondike, indicators don't indicate." One reason they didn't was that most of the first, surface gold found on both Bonanza and Eldorado was not indigenous to these creeks, a fact not realized until well into the summer of 1897. For thousands of years the level of these stream beds had been much higher in relation to the surrounding hillsides. Then, quite recently in geological terms, the terrain was upthrust five to seven hundred feet. Since the upthrusting was local, the streams, being forced to fall from this heightened elevation, became rapid and abrasive; they cut new, deeper beds for themselves, the beds approximating those of today. The gold eroded from the quartz lode before the uplifting was left in placers high on the hillsides, while that eroded after was deposited in or near the creeks' present beds. While the hillside deposits were still to some extent intact—they would be a subject of astonishment when discovered—some of the gold in them was washed down to Bonanza and Eldorado. This was the gold of the surface showings, the gold that Skookum Jim had found, the gold that Anton Stander was panning when Johns found him in the cream pitcher. Such samplings of the metal naturally told little about what might be found on bedrock.

Fifteen to twenty feet of frozen muck and gravel, and weeks of unremitting toil still separated the stakers of Eldorado from bedrock where the big pay would or would not be. Johns for one was not optimistic, and he was glad to get five hundred dollars for the half of Twelve he sold within a week of staking. Frank Phiscator sold half his claim, Two, for eight hundred dollars and accounted himself a lucky man. Thirty-One went for one hundred dollars, eighty in gold dust, twenty in beans. Twenty-Nine was staked jointly by Alfred Thayer and Winfield Oler, and almost their first thought was to get rid of it; an oft-told story relates how they did so.

Back in Forty Mile, after recording their claim with Inspector Constantine, Thayer and Oler met a Swede named Charlie Anderson. He had just returned from a summer on a remote creek in the Sixty Mile country; he labored there hard and alone, and brought out eight hundred dollars in dust and nuggets. It was the sum total of his worldly wealth. Thayer and Oler found him drinking in a saloon, the story goes, and they generously saw to it that he continued. At that time no one had reached bedrock on Bonanza or Eldorado, and there was a lot of talk in Forty Mile that the Klondike was a "bilk," a "bunco," a promotional stunt on the part of Joseph Ladue and Arthur Harper who had just bought from the Crown a 178-acre townsite where Dawson City would soon mushroom. Once the enthusiasm of the August stampede waned, Thayer and Oler were as skeptical as anyone in Forty Mile, but the gilded picture of Eldorado they painted for Anderson, now fairly well drunk, led him to inquire if by any chance there was any ground left to stake there. No, they replied, not a foot of it, but it just so happened that they themselves had a claim they might consider selling. Anderson asked the price, and they allowed as how the gold Anderson had right there in his poke just might be enough. So the deal was concluded and duly signed. Anderson staggered back to his cabin with an empty poke and a deed to Eldorado Twenty-Nine. The light of dawn found him, hungover and furious, appealing to Inspector Constantine for help in recovering his gold; he had been defrauded, he said, and he demanded justice. "I'm sorry, Anderson," the gruff officer is reported to have told him, "but there's nothing I can do about it. You have no witnesses to show it was a robbery. The money's gone, but you have the deed, and that's genuine. The only advice I can give you is to work the claim for what you can get out of it."

So Anderson got some beans and bacon on credit and hauled them up to the middle reaches of the little brook now called Eldorado. He had no cabin to live in, no firewood cut, and the first snow already dusted the desolate landscape, but he set to work burning and scraping his way to bedrock, and, as we shall see, to a radical change of fortunes.

The only other active digging on Eldorado that fall was down on Six, Anton Stander's claim. In September, Stander had gone down to Forty Mile to get supplies for the winter. He was broke, but counted on getting liberal credit at the ACC⁰. store. The manager would not extend him credit, however, unless he got someone to guarantee it. Stander did not know where to turn. He was lamenting his predicament in Bill McPhee's Saloon when the bartender, Clarence Berry, came forth and offered him the needed guarantee. Berry had already staked on Bonanza late that summer, but he thought little of his claim. To put his Klondike eggs, if there were to be any, in more than one basket, he got Stander to agree to an arrangement whereby each would have a half interest in the other's claim.

Clarence Berry had been a fruit farmer in the Imperial Valley of California, and would still have been, most likely, if the Panic of 1893 had not ruined him. He had come to Forty Mile in 1894, and though he was a strong, sober, hardworking man, he had found no gold. He returned to California the next year to get married and brought his young wife back to Forty Mile. To support her and himself he was obliged to tend bar, but he had not lost sight of his main aim, finding gold. By the time of his chance encounter with Anton Stander he had sufficient resources to outfit himself, and so, with a half-interest in Eldorado Six, he and the Austrian left Forty Mile for a winter's mining.

Night after night they burned the frozen ground, and day after day they shoveled up what had been thawed. During the first week in October they received some encouraging news: over on Bonanza, on Twenty-One Above, Louis Rhodes had reached bedrock, apparently the first man to do so in the Klondike region. At the bottom of his shaft the gold-studded gravel fairly glittered in the candlelight; the bedrock of Bonanza, at any rate, was rich indeed. By November first Berry and Stander were down sixteen feet. A few days later they were at eighteen, and at that level their shovels and picks struck into the bedrock of the richest placer creek ever discovered anywhere.

There were some forty-odd claims on the first four miles of Eldorado; each was five hundred feet long, and the average amount of gold in each foot of each one of them was worth $1,200. An average claim held $600,000, but several held more than twice this. During the winter of 1896–1897 no one knew this, of course, but Berry and Stander quickly grasped the fact that they were working the richest ground either of them had ever seen or heard of. They began hiring men to work for them; within a month they had a daily payroll of $150 to meet, and this Berry did by panning out a tiny portion of the day's diggings; he did it every evening, and it took only a few minutes. By Christmas Clarence and Ethel Berry were showing visitors at their cabin three preserve jars, each of which held the gold washed from a single pan (that is, two shovelfuls) of bedrock gravel. The first contained $175, the next $230, and the last $560. These were not average pans, of course, but twenty-five-dollar ones were routine.

As the richness of the Berry-Stander claim, and of Rhodes's Twenty-One Above on Bonanza, and a little later, of Charlie Anderson's Eldorado Twenty-Nine, became known, other stakers began to sink shafts. Men who had been poor all their lives became suddenly, magically rich. But in this subarctic muskeg valley, seventy miles distant from the nearest ramshackle town and a thousand from the nearest city, there was scant opportunity for them to manifest the miraculous transformation by their mode of living. Never did such rich men live so poorly as on the creeks of the Klondike during the winter of 1896–1897.

Their dwellings were huts, lean-to's, tents, and ten by twelve cabins of unbarked green logs. They slept on spruce twig mattresses over dirt floors. They peered out on the twilight landscape of winter through tiny windows made of serried vinegar bottles chinked with clay. They toiled on all fours in smoke-filled holes in the ground, and after a few hours of this, they clambered sweating out of the earth into the −40° air to crank up their windlasses. They did not bathe from fall to spring, and "graybacks" (lice) thrived in their bedding. They lived on starch and a number of them got scurvy; they had almost nothing fresh to eat until the little hothouse gardens they planted on the dirt roofs of their cabins began to produce lettuce and radishes in May.

William Haskell hadn't reached Bonanza until September, and he had time only to put up a hut backed up into a crevice in the side hill before the cold weather set in. Like others, he lived hardly better than a caveman, but it was not so much the primitiveness that oppressed him as the solitude; he was a naturally gregarious man, and to work, eat, and sit smoking his pipe after supper all alone were hard on his morale. He was much happier after Joseph Meeker came up from Circle City to join him in January. At first they tried living in Haskell's hut, but the unventilated air became so foul with two men breathing it that they moved into their tent. The tent could be kept warm as long as the stove was hot, but at night the fire went out and the interior became as cold as the outdoors. It took Haskell a while to get used to crawling out of his sleeping robe in the −50° dark to start the morning fire, but in general he was comfortable enough.

The deep cold was dangerous for anyone who ventured far from shelter. It has a pleasantly soporific effect on the psyche, making the snow seem like an infinite bed of eider down; those who lie down don't get up again. Frozen bodies were found that winter along the trail from Bonanza to what was becoming Dawson, and Haskell came dangerously close to being one of them. This was his first winter in the subarctic, and he probably took risks that old-timers would not have. One day in January, he writes:

. . . I started out from Dawson to pull a sled load of provisions up to the camp. When I had gone a few miles I became so cold that I could not pull the sled. It was too far to go on, so I left the sled there and walked back to Dawson. . . . My eyelids kept freezing together, but I had to be very careful about pulling off my gloves to thaw them apart. I did it as quickly as I could, but several times my hands nearly froze before I could get them back into the big mittens. When I reached Dawson City the thermometers registered fifty-eight degrees below.

The miners that winter lived on a nearly unvaried diet of "Yukon strawberries" (beans), sourdough bread ("about as dense as the gold we panned"), and flapjacks. It is peculiar how depressing a bland monotonous diet can be, even if it is adequate and well balanced; the diaries of Arctic explorers contain more complaints about the never-changing meals of pemmican than about the cold. Haskell says he would gladly have given a hun-

dred dollars in nuggets for a slice of beefsteak, and some of the
Klondike miners did actually buy salt, which was very scarce, for
its weight in gold.

Diversion was as hard to come by as decent food. One could
trek down to Dawson, but that winter the nascent boomtown had
but a single bar, Joe Ladue's, and the whiskey was watered and
bad. Ever since he had wasted his private school education on
adventure stories and books of exotic travel, Haskell counted
reading as one of his favorite pastimes, but that winter he could
obtain scarcely any reading matter save the labels on provision
boxes.

If one wishes to realize how interesting they can be, let him camp in
a gulch somewhere in latitude sixty-four, North America. A trademark
on a pick handle becomes fairly eloquent in that solitude.

Haskell was fortunate in getting to know Charlie Myers and Dick
Butler, two old-time prospectors working on Eldorado Thirty, for
they had the Klondike's only library. It consisted of a packet of
old Seattle newspapers sent them by a friend. Nightly miners
from neighboring claims would congregate in their cabin to
quench their thirst for the written word by the light of a "bitch,"
a bacon grease lantern used in lieu of the candles that were not to
be had. One night when Haskell was there Butler announced,
"Boys, I don't mind your reading the papers, but I think you
ought to remember the fellow who sent them. I'm going to put up
a little collection box." That spring, says Haskell, he sent his
Seattle friend the $400 in dust that had by then accumulated.

As at Forty Mile and Circle City before, the thawed gravel of
Bonanza and Eldorado was hauled up by windlasses and emptied
into dumps at the top of the holes. Since this was a wintertime
operation, the material immediately refroze, and the dump was a
solid block until spring. The rich winter pans, such as those of the
Berrys, were washed out only to sample the dirt being mined,
and to pay wages. The real clean-up had to wait till May, when
the dumps thawed and there was flowing water for sluicing. Only
then did the incredible richness of the Klondike placers become

evident to their astounded owners. During that month Berry and
Stander washed out roughly $130,000 worth of gold dust and
nuggets—just short of a quarter of a ton—from Eldorado Six.
Charlie Anderson, the "buncoed" Swede, took about $100,000
from Eldorado Twenty-Nine, Frank Phiscator $50,000 from Two,
Keller the would-be hunter, $35,000 from Five, Thomas Lippy
$108,000 from Sixteen. Over on Bonanza Twenty-One Above,
Louis Rhodes took $60,000 from the claim he had tried to sell
for $250 eight months before. And so it went, on every claim that
was worked on Eldorado from One to Forty-Three or -Four, and
on most of those on the central portion of Bonanza. Not everybody did so well, of course, for there were "skunks" on the top of
both Eldorado and Bonanza, and whole creeks that were prospected that winter were devoid of gold. There were old-timers,
seasoned prospectors, who found nothing of consequence and
totally green men who struck it rich. Robert Henderson, who had
mined the first Klondike gold of anyone, on Gold Bottom, was
one of the former. Another was Arthur Harper, the father of all
Yukon prospecting; he was now preparing to leave the region
after a quarter of a century, and he would go with fatally tuber-
cular lungs and not an ounce of gold. And McQuesten, who came
up from Circle toward the end of the winter, had a claim worth
only $10,000. On the other hand there was the young ex-dry-
goods clerk from Buffalo, New York, who sluiced on Bonanza
that spring. He had tramped into the Yukon two years before,
he told Haskell, and never found a grain of gold. He had lived for
months on nothing but dried salmon and in the fall of 1896 he
was too poor even to return home. He found the prospect of
another winter on the Yukon so grim that he considered suicide.
A friend, trying to cheer him, convinced him to make one last
effort at reversing his misfortunes, and he came to Bonanza in
September. Now, in the spring of 1897, he had $35,000 in gold.

Of all the fortunate cheechakos the Klondike placers produced
that year, the most extraordinary was an ex-slave named Atherton, who had come into the Yukon with a freighting outfit. He
had never had the slightest intention of mining gold. Joseph
Meeker visited him one day on his claim, and that evening told
Haskell:

Well, you may believe it or not, but the old rascal has cleaned up thirty thousand dollars in gold dust. You ought to hear him talk about what he is going to do with it. His name, he says, is St. John Atherton, and he comes from down in Georgia, "just a piece out of Atlanta." The daughter of the man who owned him during the war is living there yet, he says, on the old plantation, but very poor. The old fellow says he is going back to buy that plantation, and then he is going to have that woman do nothing but live like a lady all the rest of her days. I believe he means just what he says. He's a queer old darky, but he seems to have a good heart.

To the nascent magnates and potential princes the spring clean-up seemed like a dream. Could it all be for real? Could it be happening to them? They wandered aimlessly about according to the whims of their happy stupefaction. Said one of them, "If we get any worse we'll all be crazy." Officer Hayne, who had left the police post at Forty Mile to stake on Bonanza, reported that:

Some men were literally so intoxicated with their good fortune that they were utterly unable to settle down to steady work, and just went around from one claim to the other showing what they had found. The gold was so abundant that when a miner went down into his prospecting hole with a lighted candle, the bystanders could see the gold glittering in the gravel. . . . The oldest Californian "boys" were speechless with amazement, and affirmed it was the richest strike they had ever known by a very long way . . . men were afraid to speak of it in its full richness. It seemed too marvellous to be true.

The first two stern-wheelers to reach Dawson that spring were the ACC⁰.'s *Alice* and the North American Trading and Transportation Company's *Portus B. Weare*. Officer Hayne took passage aboard the latter, along with a few dozen miners and a ton and a half of gold. He describes the trove, some of it lying about on deck in suitcases, sacks, and blankets, some stored in the ship's safe which had to be specially buttressed to support the weight, some tucked away in the passengers' cabins in canisters and pickle jars, moosehide pokes and Royal Baking Powder tins. It was worth just under a million dollars. Clarence Berry owned over a tenth of it, but forty-five others had enough to call them-

selves rich. And every last one of them, no doubt, had more than
all but his wildest dreams of affluence or avarice could have
conjured up six months before.

The *Portus B. Weare* reached the old Russian port of St. Michael on June 27, a day after the *Alice*. Most of her passengers
transferred to the steamship *Portland,* bound for Seattle, while
most of the *Alice*'s passengers boarded the ACC⁰.'s *Excelsior,*
headed for San Francisco. The *Portland*'s journey across the
Bering Sea and the North Pacific was rough and slow. Officer
Hayne commiserated with more than one new gold prince as they
heaved with seasickness on their bunks, wondering—though possibly not too seriously—if hauling gold by the satchelful was
really worth it after all.

When, a month out of St. Michael, the *Portland* nosed into
Schwabacher's Wharf in Seattle, she was fully expected. For one
thing the *Excelsior* had arrived at San Francisco the day before;
she brought a cargo that made headlines, and also the news that
the *Portland* carried an even richer freight. For another, the
Seattle *Post-Intelligencer* had dispatched a tugload of reporters to
intercept the *Portland* as she steamed into Puget Sound. The
reporters boarded her, photographed her bullion and her passengers, hurriedly collected a few facts about both, then returned to
Port Townsend to telegraph their story. This was on Friday, July
16. Next day, when the *Portland* docked, the *Post-Intelligencer*'s
report appeared under these banner headlines:

GOLD! GOLD! GOLD! GOLD!
Sixty-Eight Rich Men on
the Steamer *Portland*

STACKS OF YELLOW METAL
Some Have $5,000, Many Have More, and
a Few Bring Out $100,000 Each

A day later similar headlines appeared all over the nation.

The *Portland* was greeted by an excited throng, and by a con-
tingent of Wells Fargo guards who formed a double line through

it from the gangplank to their waiting wagons. Amidst cheers from the crowd, leather-faced miners heaved their bags and canisters and boxes of gold onto their shoulders and trudged down the gangplank with bent backs. Officer Hayne noted that men with $20,000 or under carried their own gold, men with around $50,000 teamed up and made two trips, while men with over $50,000 had to hire porters. Handles were pulled out of suitcases, straps snapped, ropes broke and the throng shouted out, "Hurrah for Klondike!"

As the *Portland*'s passengers descended into the city, they were repeatedly encircled and besieged by reporters. Officer Hayne, an Englishman, was prompted to shout as a knot of them closed in upon him, "Look here, I have been for two years in a country where the only drink is poison. Let me at least have a thimbleful of good Scotch whisky before I suffer the torment of an interview." Mr. and Mrs. Berry managed to escape only by dropping out of sight in rural California, and Jacob Wiseman, on returning to Walla Walla, Washington, his home town, was so badgered that he slipped secretly away to Tacoma one night and stayed there under an assumed name.

The reporters did succeed in getting their interviews, however, and what they wrote imbued the word "Klondike" with magic and introduced it into the everyday vocabulary of millions of households. The magic derived from the metal itself, to be sure, but even more it stemmed from the biographies of the men who mined it. For it quickly became obvious from countless interviews and articles that these men were, in fact, nothing more nor less than the American Everyman. When, for example, reporters talked to Clarence Berry, they learned not only that he brought $130,000 in gold with him to Seattle, but that he was an ex-fruit farmer ruined by the Panic of 1893, that as a stopgap he had been a bartender, that he had had no special skills, no capital when he went to the Klondike. His wife Ethel showed the journalists $10,000 in nuggets and explained how she had collected them from her husband's dump to bring home as souvenirs for her friends. What had she done before going to the Klondike and becoming a millionairess? they inquired. She had been a waitress in a small California town, she said. William Stanley displayed his dust and nuggets to the press, and stated that "the Klondike is no doubt the best place to make money that there is in the world." And he went on to relate that he had been a bookseller in Seattle, that his shop had failed and his wife had been compelled to take in laundry to help feed their four children. He had gone north on borrowed money in a last desperate attempt to recoup his fortunes. He was no young man; he limped and his hair was greying, but he got to the Klondike and struck it rich, and there were the bagfuls of gold to prove it. There was James McMahon who had been a longshoreman on the Tacoma docks; he had $65,000 and he implied to reporters that anyone else could have done, could still do, as well. "All you need is a pan and plenty of water," he said.

Clearly, Everyman was getting rich in the Klondike, while back home he was languishing in one of the nation's worst depressions. So from all across the land, about a hundred thousand strong, he rushed north toward McQuesten's old Trundeck River. He was a farmboy from Iowa, a clerk from Cincinnati, a cowboy from the Oklahoma Territory, a streetcar conductor from Tacoma; he was doctor, lawyer, merchant, thief, and if not actually an Indian chief, at least a turbaned Hindu and a Maori from New Zealand who would build wattle teepees on the Chilkoot Trail. He was a millhand, a schoolteacher, a butcher, a baker, a lantern maker, a cardsharp, and a preacher straying into the Arctic in hot pursuit of Mammon. He was you and I, and if we were to become rich by kicking over stones and plucking out fistfuls of nuggets from underneath each one of them (as we were certain we would do), what matter that we knew nothing about placer mining, or packing, or cabin building, or boat making, or muddling through at fifty below?

15 Letter Carrier Beckwith ET AL.

Toward the end of July 1897, about two weeks after the *Portland* landed in Seattle, the editors of *Harper's Weekly* dispatched correspondent Tappan Adney to report from the Klondike. Adney took the Canadian Pacific west from Montreal, and stopped at Winnipeg to buy his winter clothing at the big Hudson's Bay Store there. There was none to be had; "the town," he reports, "was already cleaned out, not a fur robe nor skin coat to be had." Already, weeks before, the Klondike fever had taken its toll in the heart of the Canadian prairie. Adney went on to Victoria B. C., his debarkation point. Here, fifteen hundred miles closer to the Klondike, the fever was several degrees higher.

The streets of leisurely Victoria are thronged with strange men. . . . The crowd is cosmopolitan. It has gathered from remote points. There are Scotch and Irish, French and German, together with plain American. Klondike!—magic word, that is possessing men so that they think and talk of nothing else. . . . Even in the singsong of the Chinaman the ear will catch the sound "Klondike." Boys who at other times might be impudent, now, with a look of wonder, point and say, "He's going to Klondike!"

All up and down the Pacific coast the atmosphere was the same. "Seattle," the New York *Herald* reported, "is going stark, staring mad on gold." Within weeks of the *Portland's* landing, the city had lost a dozen police officers, the Seattle *Times* half of its

171

reporters, the city government its mayor, and the state militia a brigadier general. Crowds jammed the waterfront, the hotels, the outfitting stores. Business boomed. Noted the *Post-Intelligencer*, "Prosperity is here. So far as Seattle is concerned the depression is at an end." Up at Tacoma the streetcar operators deserted en masse, and down the coast the University of California lost its football captain and its star sprinter; the mines at Sonora and Angel's Camp had to be shut down for lack of miners.

The extent of the madness of that otherwise dull time (it was the summer after Bryan's cross of gold campaign, and the one before the Spanish-American War; and the deadening shadow of the Panic of 1893 still lay across the land) is revealed in these New York City newspaper reports:

GOLD-LIKE SAND DUG IN CITY

——

Williamsburg Italians Think They Have a Klondyke at Their Doors

——

LOCATION KEPT SECRET

——

Policeman O'Malley Knows, but He Doesn't Want Prospectors to Swarm In

——

JEWELER TESTING A SPECIMEN

——

JULY 27—A number of Italian laborers in Williamsburg have the gold craze in a severe form and believe they have found a new Klon-

dyke at their very doors. They have sand with rich-looking yellow
streaks in it, and are sure it is gold. If the craze spreads it may be hard
to restrain them from digging up the cobblestones and starting placer
mines in the gutters.

Policeman James O'Malley, of the Bedford avenue station, says the
gold field is in the vicinity of Roebling and North Eighth streets . . .

From the *Journal*, July 23, 1897:

William Miller is being watched by a policeman to-day to prevent him
from harming his wife and child. He lost his reason from brooding
over his inability to get to the Klondyke gold fields. . . .

He refused to go to work this week and spent his time in an attempt
to raise $500 among his friends to enable him to reach the gold
regions. He failed, and the fact of his inability to procure the funds
unbalanced his mind.

From the Brooklyn *Daily Eagle*, August 6, 1897:

OFF FOR THE KLONDYKE

——

Letter Carrier Beckwith Leaves His
Home Suddenly

——

GOES WITH THREE COMPANIONS

——

Gives His Wife an Hour and a Half's
Notice—Resigned From the Post
Office, Taking Advantage of His
Leave of Absence—Said to be Grub-
staked by Montague Street Capitalists.

And finally, this report, again from the *Journal:*

SEPT 27—Three youthful argonauts are weeping silently in their
homes in Jersey City. They were caught by the police in the wilds of

the Hackensack meadows, where the first stop on the way to the Klondike was made.

The youngsters [aged six to ten] have been reading about the glittering metal on the Yukon and decided to start just as soon as the Fall school term began.

They disappeared on Saturday, and their parents, alarmed, notified the policy. . . . their "grubstake" consisted of three pounds of potted ham, one dozen sandwiches, fifty-one cookies and two bowls of raspberry jam.

During 1897 and 1898 perhaps one hundred thousand people swarmed to San Francisco, Portland, Seattle, Vancouver and Victoria to debark for "Klondyke." From these ports most of them took passage for Lynn Canal, the fiord just across the Coast Mountains from the Yukon headwaters, carried by dozens of steamers diverted from other routes, and a picturesque flotilla of whalers, fishing boats, sloops and schooners snatched from every boneyard of the Pacific Northwest. Many of these craft were commanded by freshwater captains and manned by landlubber crews, and they were invariably overcrowded, dangerous, and absurdly expensive.

As Tappan Adney steamed out of Victoria on the *Islander* in mid-August, a great dockside crowd shouted out, "Three cheers for Klondike!"; it was the closest they could come to participating in the voyage. There were one hundred and sixty passengers bunked among the hay bales on the upper deck, and below scores of horses so tightly packed in they could not lie down during the whole voyage. Frightened by the ship's whistle they reared and bit and within a day each bore the tooth- and hoofmarks of its neighbors. For these poor beasts, though, it was but an innocuous initiation to later terrors. Adney's fellow human passengers included a housebuilder from Brooklyn, a contractor from Boston, a newspaper business manager from New York, and a hunter fresh from the Black Hills who clad himself in buckskins and shot ducks from the railing. Most of them, no doubt, had a better idea of what lay ahead than the Minnesotan who wrote to the Seattle Chamber of Commerce: "as to hardships I fully understand what to expect. . . . Does the Ship land you right into Dalson City

[sic]?" But just how much better is uncertain. Two things were true of every passenger Adney talked to: none had had any experience either with placer mining or with the rigors of subarctic life; and every last one of them expected to be a rich man before the year was out. Now Haskell and Meeker, not to mention McQuesten and Arthur Harper, knew a great deal about mining and roughing it; they were a stone's throw from the Klondike when Carmack made his discovery. And gold made none of them rich.

The *Islander* landed at Skagway on August 20, or rather it anchored a mile off shore while its cargo was tumbled helterskelter into scows for lightering to the mud flats, and the horses aboard were shoved into the water to swim ashore. Six weeks before, Skagway hadn't existed; Mooresville, it is true, had been on the site for years, but Mooresville was only the pretentious title a cantankerous old captain named Billy Moore had given his homestead. Back in the late '80s Moore had found another pass across the mountains to the Yukon headwaters, an alternative to the Chilkoot, and he hoped that, if "something big" happened along the river, Mooresville would boom as the starting point for the traffic across his White Pass. The Klondike had happened and Mooresville was now booming, but the old captain was dispossessed of his homestead by the stampeders, and robbed of his immortality when they changed the name of the place to Skagway, after the river that falls down the mountains and into Lynn Canal there.

Moore's route to the Yukon was longer than the Chilkoot Trail, forty-five miles compared to twenty-seven, but it was less steep and pack animals could be used along its entire length. The two trails, roughly parallel, were five to six miles apart. The promoters of each competed—and misrepresented—fiercely for traffic until the White Pass Railway, roughly following Moore's route, put the Chilkoot Trail out of business in 1899.

Though there were hundreds of people in Skagway when Adney debarked from the *Islander*, it had not yet become the roaring, evil town it was a year later. By then—early 1898—it had a floating population of over ten thousand and was run by a coalition of gangsters and corrupt government officials. The stampeding sheep who poured out of the ocean-going vessels en route to the Klondike were fleeced, and sometimes butchered, between the mud flats called Skagway Beach and the summit of White Pass. Beyond the pass they were safe from this sort of trouble, for the North West Mounted Police did a remarkably effective and humane job of law enforcement. But in Skagway shootings were routine, robberies common and dishonesty banal.

When Adney arrived Skagway was not an evil town, even considering its four tent saloons and its handful of whores; in fact, it wasn't really a town at all yet, but an overgrown campsite full of confusion and white canvas tents. These were Adney's first impressions:

. . . such a scene as meets the eye! It is simply bewildering, it is all so strange. There are great crowds of men rowing in boats to the beach, then clambering out in rubber boots and packing the stuff, and setting it down in little piles out of reach of the tide. . . . Tents there are of every size and kind, and men cooking over large sheet-iron stoves set up outside. Behind these are more tents and men, and piles of merchandise and hay, bacon smoking, men loading bags and bales of hay upon horses and starting off, leading from one to three animals along a sort of lane . . . in the direction of a grove of small cottonwoods, beyond which lies the trail towards White Pass.

Outfits, hundreds of them, lay all about in heaps, defying segregation or classification; it was as though all the bins, shelves and racks in a huge department store had suddenly been removed, and the sum total of goods dumped at random on the tidal ooze of Skagway Beach.

Haskell and Meeker, it will be recalled, had had a hard time on the Chilkoot Trail, and they would not have found the White Pass Trail much easier. But what about the booksellers and bank tellers, the ex-mayor of Seattle, the Tacoma streetcar operators? The inexperience of most of the men who scurried nervously about at Skagway made a strong impression on the few old-timers among them. Adney asked a veteran mining engineer from

California for his opinion of the milling men. He replied that he had

> . . . never seen men behave as they do here. They have no more idea of what they are going to than that horse has. There was one fellow in the tent alongside of mine—I saw him greasing his rubber boots. I said to him, "What are you doing that for?" "Why, isn't that all right?" he asked. Another man came along and asked a fellow where his mining-pan was. The fellow said, "I haven't seen any mining-pan." Just then the man saw the pan lying alongside the tent, and said, "Here it is! Is that a mining-pan? I didn't know that was a mining-pan."

Nor were these men in any frame of mind to instruct themselves, save when lessons were literally thrust upon them.

> Every one seems to have lost his head [says Adney], and cannot observe or state facts. The very horses and animals partake of the fever and are restless. All is strange and unaccustomed to both men and animals. Accidents and runaways are occurring every few moments. Suddenly there is a commotion; a horse starts off with a half-packed load or a cart and cuts a swath over tents up through the town, scattering the people right and left. . . . This sort of thing is getting so common that a fellow only looks to see that the horse is not coming in the direction of his own tent, and then goes on with his work. One man was asleep in his tent, 10' by 14', when a horse galloped through it and carried it off bodily. No one gets hurt, which is amazing. The horses are green; the men are green.

The White Pass Trail, like the Chilkoot, began with deceptive gentleness. For the first ten miles or so horse-drawn wagons could be used; after that freight was packed up to and over "The Hill" on the animals' backs. The upper reaches of the "trail" (for in 1897 there was nothing deserving of the name) wound up and down the steep gorges of the Skagway River, and across the smooth flanks of granite that sloped at forty-five-degree angles. It was strewn with slippery, fragmented boulders and between them were little holes and crevices ideally sized to trap a horse's hoof. Where the trail was not of rock it was of muck. The following year it was considerably improved, but in the summer of 1897 it was a graduated horror for the green men who crossed it, or started to.

It was the pack animals, though, and not the men, who suffered worst. They were of no value on the other side of the mountains, where the journey to Dawson was continued by boat, and where hay cost as much as $240 a ton. In most cases it was enough for a stampeder if his beast got him to Bennett Lake before dropping dead from starvation, exhaustion, or wounds. Beyond the logistics and economics, there was the willful brutality. One man, when his oxen could pull no more, lit fires under them and finished by burning them alive. Mules and horses, grossly overloaded, would fall in exhaustion in the muck, rise again as a ferocious beating squeezed out a last drop of adrenalin, then flop down dead in the next bog. Such scenes were so common that bypassers on the trail hardly took notice. A man named Graves tells of a horse on the trail that had broken a leg. Its load was removed, and it was mercifully killed with an axe blow. The carcass lay across the trail, and the stampeders and their animals stomped right over it. When Graves returned to the spot a few hours later, the head and tail lay just as they had been; the rest had been minced and carried off on the hoofs and boots of those who had passed.

At Log Cabin, a stopping place on the far side of White Pass, a couple named Hartshorn ran a blacksmith shop.

The trail passed in front of our cabin [Mrs. Hartshorn recalled years later]. . . . The packer would bring his horse to be shod. I will never forget the look of a horse as I fed it a few scraps of bread or a dish of water. I have seen skinned hip sores as large as my two hands, where the bone showed through. The packers always kept these sores covered with blankets. I wondered why until I found out that the Mounted Police were ordered to shoot on sight any horse so crippled.

Mrs. Hartshorn gives this account of a trip across the White Pass Trail during July:

Before long I knew why I should not drink from the streams, for on all sides were dead horses. Not a few, but hundreds. My pony would stop, look down, then step carefully over her comrade of the trail.

Once my pony stopped to drink at a sparkling mountain stream. How I wanted just one sip! Glancing up, I saw two dead horses not five feet away, and one was lying in the clear water.

Out of our train of twenty-five horses, five lost their lives on that one trip. Their loads were added to the already heavy loads of the other pack animals.*

It has been estimated that three thousand beasts of burden perished on the White Pass Trail in 1897 and 1898. Most of them either broke legs and were shot, or plunged to their deaths from the precipices along the way. In winter the trail ran atop frozen flesh. In summer the flesh turned to carrion and one could determine the trail's course in the distance by the clouds of ravens that hovered. "There is nothing more revolting," observed one stampeder, "than stepping through a bloated wormy hide." The stench finally got so bad that the merchants of Skagway, fearing that men would be driven to the competing Chilkoot Trail, came up and buried many of the carcasses.

Tappan Adney ascended only part of the White Pass Trail, and he did so only for journalistic reasons. He reached the Yukon headwaters via the Chilkoot, which, in 1897 at least, was a better trail. Not that it provided any sylvan idyll through the grandiose scenery of the Coast Mountains; just that its misery was less prolonged. The men packing up it in a solid black line seemed to be going against their will; the famous photographs of them are less suggestive of high-spirited argonauts on a golden quest than of the remnants of a defeated army, or a vast coffle of the pharoah's slaves lost in the wrong latitude and mistakenly hunched under sacks of flour instead of pyramid stones. A hope, a wild hope, drew them forward from sump hole to precipice to muckbog, and the impossible humiliation of quitting goaded

---

* In recent years a bronze plaque has been placed along the railroad that follows the old trail; it commemorates the animals who died in Dead Horse Gulch, visible hundreds of feet below. Mrs. Hartshorn, more than anyone else, is responsible for its being there.

them from behind. Some perished; they were frozen to death or buried by avalanches.* Others gave up hope and with it the will to survive; they were buried by strangers in shallow graves, victims of a weird pilgrimage through a forbidding land. Among the broken carts, and rusty picks, the abandoned fold boats and white bones that litter the old trail still, are crude plank slabs where these casualties of accident or despair lie buried. Seventy years of wind and weather have effaced the names painted on them with boatbuilding tar, but it is unlikely anyone bothered to stop and read them even when they were fresh.

For the men on the Chilkoot and White Pass trails in 1897 and 1898 were in a hurry. Was it not true that with every passing day more claims were staked? Would the man ten yards ahead on the trail stake the very last good ground on the Klondike? Would there be anything left?

When Haskell and Meeker crossed the Chilkoot in March 1896, they occasionally passed other parties; just below the summit, at

---

* During the first few days of April 1898, sliding snow just above Sheep Camp killed at least sixty-seven men, while dozens of others who had been buried alive were dug out and saved.

Sheep Camp, Haskell estimated that about a hundred people accumulated during the two weeks that a blizzard completely blocked the pass. When he finally reached the summit Haskell, who was quite sensitive to natural beauty, was impressed by the grandeur of the unpeopled white landscape that fell away on all sides. He even wrote a poem about it and the poem's theme was that nature here showed no evidence of man's presence. Two years later a Norwegian stood on the same spot and wrote:

The top of Chilkoot Pass is a peculiar place. When you are up on the highest point, you can see far down toward Lake Lindeman on one side and down the valley toward Dyea on the other; in both directions extends an unending line of people as far as the eye can reach.

This was during the spring of 1898, the climax of the Gold Rush, but thousands crossed the Chilkoot the year before and the traffic was nearly as heavy. There was still no cable tram up to the summit then, and Adney watched from below as the stampeders trudged up the glowering brow of Chilkoot Pass.

They walk to the base of the cliff, with a stout alpenstock in hand. They start to climb a narrow foot-trail that goes up, up, up. The rock and earth are gray. The packers and packs have disappeared. There is nothing but the gray wall of rock and earth. But stop! Look more closely. The eye catches movement. The mountain is alive. There is a continuous moving train; they are perceptible only by their movement, just as ants are. The moving train is zigzagging across the towering face of the precipice, up, up, into the sky.

Other men are coming back empty, as if dropping back to earth. "The Scales," as the foot of the precipice is called, is one of the most wretched spots on the trail; there is no wood nearer than four miles, and that is poor.

Fred Thompson, a young Californian, crossed the Chilkoot just a month before Adney. He camped at The Scales on August 30, 1897, and his diary entry for that day, like so many of the entries in so many diaries of the experience, speaks of the undramatic unpleasantness of life on the Chilkoot.

Rain and wind Summit very bad made 2 trips and moved our Camp to foot of Summit where we camped on the cold rocks with ice water running underneath then gathered what brush and moss we could find spread it on our rocky floor in tent, ate our scanty supper and we had barely wood enough to get breakfast with as we had to pack it 2 miles, spread our blankets and tried to get some sleep laying on the soft side of many sharp stones.

The Chilkoot was a place of aching muscles, bruises, broken ankles, dislocated joints, diarrhea (from a steady diet of half-cooked pancakes and beans), snow blindness, frostbite, and above all fatigue. Tempers frayed, psyches listed dangerously out of balance; fights broke out, animals were insanely beaten, partnerships split. A man named Ver Mehr wrote in his diary one day on the Chilkoot:

Nobody speaking on the trail. We move forward like dead men. Not even a howl out of the dogs. The Chilkoot [Summit] is in front of us. The dogs are only [sic] decent uncomplaining members of this party.

R. pulled his knife on me yesterday. Maybe I deserved it. This would be a hell of a place to be left. Would H. bury me? I wonder.

Short tempers and endless frustrations would magnify mishaps into catastrophes:

Sometimes [recalled a young Canadian] you would think that a man had gone crazy when his sled had upset off the trail. They would throw their caps in the snow, shake their fists, throw their heads back and ask Jesus Christ to come down there on the trail so that they could tell Him what they thought of Him for playing a trick like that on them.

From the summits of Chilkoot and White Pass the stampeders descended with relative ease to Bennett and Lindeman lakes on the headwaters of the Yukon. At the head of each a transient town sprang up. The awesome silence of these grand lakes, a nature-silence of the unpunctuated sounds of wind and moving water, which, like Hindu music, have no definite beginning or end, this silence, old beyond age, was broken now; and the sheer walls that cradle the lakes, cold, grey, granite walls thrust almost straight up from invisibility below the emerald water to conceal-ment under perpetual snow fields two thousand feet above, these walls echoed for a few brief seasons with the bang of hammers and the rasp of whipsaws slicing green spruce timber into boat planks.

The temporary inhabitants of Bennett and Lindeman were happy men. They sang as they sawed, Adney noted, and their launching bees were celebrated with fusillades of revolver shots and comradely shouts of good luck. The pilgrims had surmounted the chief obstacle in their path, and the rest of the way to the Promised Land, some six hundred miles along the Yukon and its headwaters, was all downhill. The only impediments still separat-ing them from the Klondike and great wealth were the stretch of treacherous water that began with Miles Canyon, some protrud-ing rocks in the reach between Lake Laberge and the Teslin, and, especially in 1898, the fact that most of the good placer ground of the Klondike had been staked long since. The rapidly published guidebooks distributed by chambers of commerce in the west coast ports told them of the first two difficulties, but made no reference to the third.

They were a heterogeneous crowd, what with the party of Scots who had a bagpiper and a dog team composed of setters, poodles, and sheepdogs; the woman who was bringing in the equipment for a laundry on a sled pulled by six angora goats; the Englishman who had come "just for a jolly good time, you know," and brought along thirty-two pairs of moccasins, one case of shoes, one bulldog puppy and a lawn tennis set; the Chilkoot Indian packers with one hundred and twenty pigs, live and squealing, in burlap sacks on their backs; the men hauling in a branch office of the Canadian Bank of Commerce; those carrying the pieces of small stern-wheelers that would ply the river above Miles Canyon; those with the presses of the Klondike *Nugget* and the Dawson *Midnight Sun.*

And the boats they turned out at Bennett and Lindeman were as heterogeneous as they were. They ranged from tear-shaped tubs through dories, wherries and skiffs of every conceivable size and shape, to rafts and scows that could carry ten tons. The better craft reflected the erstwhile occupations of their designers, whether fishermen, voyageurs, rivermen or sailors. Mostly, though, they showed plainly enough that their builders had had nothing to do with boats before.

As the boats were finished and caulked with oakum and tar, their crews, three or four men usually, unfurled makeshift sails and moved down out of Bennett and Lindeman to Tagish Lake. Here they had to pause at a hovel topped by a Union Jack that served as the North West Mounted Police customs post. They paid their duties—sometimes, when they lacked funds, by chopping wood for the Mounties—and continued on through Marsh Lake to the beginning of the Yukon proper. These lakes claimed a number of boats and men during 1897 and 1898; they are large bodies of water, and the wind whipping down out of the Coast Mountains can raise a heavy sea on them in the space of a few minutes. Then, too, the boats were usually leaky and lacking in sufficient freeboard, and of course their crews were generally inexperienced.

Curiously, Miles Canyon and Whitehorse Rapids did not add any names to their list of victims in 1897, at least as far as Tappan Adney was able to learn. He and his partner Brown managed to swirl through with nothing worse than a drenching of spray. Even a water spaniel shot the rapids successfully that year, and so did the kegs of whiskey, bound for Dawson City's saloons, that were unceremoniously dumped in at the top of the rough water and retrieved below.

According to the computations of the old steamboat captains, it is 460 miles from Whitehorse to Dawson City. On this entire stretch of the Yukon there are less than three hundred people today, and of them all but two families live in Carmacks, the sole inhabited village. Few people make the trip downriver now, though it is difficult to imagine a more appealing meander through the wilderness. And because the river is so silent and untraveled, it is difficult to conjure up a picture of what it was like during the Gold Rush. Here and there the signs of a busier era are still visible, however: rotting cabins with rampant vegetation poking up from swaybacked roofs of sod; and pilothouses of abandoned stern-wheelers that gaze forlornly at the deserted waterway from behind stands of young poplars. The old North West Mounted Police post still stands at Hootalinqua across from the mouth of the Teslin. It has not been used for years, but the flagstaff still rises tall and straight out of the encroaching brush. From this post and about a dozen others strung out all along the route from the passes to Dawson City, the mounties kept their highly competent vigil over the stampeders of 1898. Farther upriver, on the eastern rim of Miles Canyon, the remains of the logs that once served as rails are still visible. They are all that is left of the horse-drawn tramway that skirted the rapids in 1897 and '98; they were laid down by one Norman Macaulay who did very well for himself at a freight tariff of five cents a pound.

In 1897, when Adney passed down the river, innumerable campsites blossomed with white canvas tents. Hundreds of men at a time were engaged in getting their outfits around Miles

Canyon and Whitehorse Rapids. On Lake Laberge, just below, odd boats with sails of Mackinaw coats and Hudson's Bay blankets were constantly in view, and at night the dark shoreline was punctuated with the bright dots of campfires.

Just how many people descended the Yukon in 1897 is uncertain, and there is wide divergence between the estimates. At Fort Selkirk, the trader who was running Arthur Harper's post (Harper himself had left the Yukon in August and was now in Arizona suffering the advanced stages of consumption) kept a register which all who stopped were requested to sign. Fred Thompson, a Californian who stopped at the post on October 6, says in his diary that he was the 4,845th person to sign in the past two months, and further, that the trader indicated to him that "several thousand" had gone past the post without signing. This would mean that over seven thousand entered the Yukon that year. Tappan Adney, who signed on October 22, reports on the other hand that "it appears that about 3600 persons have passed in." Adney was a careful observer, and his figure is probably nearer the truth. The statistics for the following year, when the Gold Rush reached its peak, are much more reliable because by then the Mounted Police were equipped to keep careful records.

On October 31, 1897, Adney and his partner Brown were gingerly nudging their ice-encrusted boat through the running floes of the Yukon. The navigation season was fast drawing to a close and in a day or two the river would be frozen solid. Some miles below the mouth of the Stewart they spotted numerous beached boats and pitched tents on the shore. "How far is it to Dawson?" Adney shouted to a parka-clad figure.

"This is Dawson!" he yelled.

16 Winter

ACTUALLY it wasn't Dawson at all, but the satellite settlement on the south bank of the Klondike River generally known as Lousetown. A year before there had been no such place as Dawson itself, only a lone cabin, a sawmill and a few dozen tents set up haphazardly on a mud flat and called "the Ladue townsite." Now Dawson even had suburbs.

It was an odd sort of place, this New Jerusalem, and full of incongruities. It was a town dedicated exclusively to the unburying of bullion that would soon be reburied in treasury vaults, to the production of gold, hardly a useful element, and valuable because of the mistrust people have for the promises and promissory notes of their governments. It was a town of Americans living under the Union Jack. It was a town sprouting at an unhealthy rate out of the subarctic permafrost miles from anywhere anyone had ever heard of, where the climate was atrocious, the mosquitoes worse, the whiskey watered, the women wanton, the prices absurd, and the chances of finding good unstaked placer mining ground getting poorer each day. And yet it was the shrine toward which fifty thousand pilgrims were trudging their weary way; it was the Promised Land of the Tacoma streetcar conductors and the Wheeling millhands. A boom town, it should have been wide-open and evil like Skagway or Cripple Creek and Angel's Camp in the old days, but in Dawson men didn't tote handguns, nor shoot each other up; they seldom stole, and the gold-laden pack trains coming down from the creeks were never once hijacked, though escorted only by a couple of muleskinners and worth several hundred thousand dollars. True, Dawson had

187

its gambling joints and its whorehouses, but even they were
closed up tight on Sundays in accordance with Canadian blue
laws.

The town had grown from nothing in no time at all, and one
would have expected a city planner's nightmare of sprawling
improvisation. Yet Dawson was laid out in uniform rectangular
blocks with avenues, from First to Ninth, each exactly sixty-six
feet wide. This was the work of William Ogilvie, the government
surveyor, and the man who named the town in honor of his chief,
George Mercer Dawson, head of the Geological Survey of Canada. The site itself had not been chosen by Ogilvie, but by Joe
Ladue, once of Schuyler Falls, New York. Ladue had been on the
Yukon ever since 1882, the year he spent Christmas with Mc-
Questen of Fort Reliance, six miles downriver from his present
townsite. He had prospected scores of creeks and rushed hither
and yon on a dozen stampedes, but as of the fall of 1896 he was
none the richer for his efforts. So when he heard about Carmack's
discovery he was determined to exploit it as a real estate operator, not as a miner. In late August or early September of that year
he came down from the Sixty Mile River, where he ran a trading
post and a sawmill, and staked a townsite patent covering 178

Front Street - Dawson

acres of Crown lands on the north bank of the Klondike. By the end of September he had rafted down his sawmill (boards for sluice boxes were in great demand), and soon thereafter he had put up Dawson's first building, a one-room saloon. His townsite occupied a flat, muddy plain between the Yukon on the west, the Klondike on the south, and the scarred ridge of Midnight Dome on the east and north. It was not a good site, for aside from the primordial ooze that lay atop the permafrost like a loose reptilian skin, there was a yearly risk of inundation. The Yukon is narrow and swift here, and during the spring breakup its ice floes are apt to form an instant dam, behind which rises an instant lake, under which Ladue's site could be, and was, periodically drowned. The same ice-dam phenomenon can occur on the Klondike, and in fact has done so in every decade from the 1890s to the 1960s. The stampeders were not fastidious, however, and at last Ladue was being handsomely recompensed for his long and goldless years on the Yukon. Building lots in prime locations were going for five and ten thousand dollars.

In the fall of 1897, when Tappan Adney arrived, a number of Ogilvie's neat blocks remained to be filled in; in fact, Front Street, parallel to the Yukon, was the only street as yet solidly

hedged with buildings. It was the heart of town. The two big store-warehouses of the trading companies there supplied most of Dawson's material necessities, at least when they chanced to have them in stock, and a dozen saloon–dance-hall–gambling houses saw to the town's social needs. Law, order and government were provided by Inspector Constantine, up from Forty Mile that summer, and a police detachment with headquarters just then being finished on the south end of Front Street; their compound was equipped with barracks, offices, a messhall, a jail, and an immense stack of wood where offenders did penance with a bucksaw. The spaces between the big two-storied log buildings —the ACC⁰. store, the M & M Saloon, the Pioneer, the Palace, the North American Trading and Transportation Company store, the Opera House, and the police post itself—were filled with the tents of barbers and restaurateurs, the scantling shacks of mining brokers and moneylenders, and the sod-roofed cabins of residents. Across the street, on the bank of the Yukon, more tents sat atop beached boats, the dwellings of new arrivals. Joe Ladue's original saloon, at one year Dawson's most venerable structure, occupied part of Front Street itself. Ladue had put it up before Ogilvie's survey, and that fall it had to be torn down.

The human traffic along Front Street in October 1897 could be visually divided into two categories. There were the newcomers, the cheechakos,* bearded mostly, and dressed in Mackinaw coats and high leather or rubber boots; their gait was apt to be hurried and impatient, their faces taut and eager. And there were the veterans of mining and life on the Yukon, the sourdoughs,** generally clean-shaven (a beard is bad in cold weather because the moisture in one's breath freezes on it), clad in twill parkas,

* The term is derived from a word in the Chinook dialect that denotes an innocent, a tenderfoot, a greenhorn.

** They were called this because of the pots of fermenting dough they used in place of fresh yeast. The definition of a sourdough was a matter of dispute. Some maintained that a cheechako became a sourdough as soon as he had wintered on the Yukon and witnessed the spring breakup. Others claimed that this was not enough, that one had to have shot a bear and slept with a squaw as well. Still others objected to this, averring that the true sourdough would have slept with the bear and shot the squaw.

coiffed in lynx or marten fur caps, and shod in mukluks; their gait was slow and deliberate, reflecting, perhaps, the fatalism the harsh land had taught them.

That fall both old-timers and newcomers betrayed an evident anxiety as they clustered in knots along Front Street to exchange alarming rumors. Of gold, to be sure, there was plenty; canvas sacks of the stuff were stacked up like cordwood in the ACC⁰. warehouse. But of food there was a dire shortage. On September 30 Inspector Constantine had posted a notice which stated, in part:

> The undersigned, officials of the Canadian government, having care-
> fully looked over the present distressing situation in regard to the
> supply of food for the winter, find that the stock on hand is not
> sufficient. . . . For those who have not laid in a winter's supply to
> remain here longer is to court death from starvation, or at least a
> certainty of sickness from scurvy and other troubles. Starvation now
> stares everyone in the face who is hoping and waiting for outside
> relief.

During the summer and fall eight hundred tons of supplies had been freighted up to Dawson from St. Michael on the half dozen stern-wheelers then plying the river. But the influx of new people over the passes had rendered this insufficient. All without enough food on hand to last them till spring were urged to flee for their lives—downriver to Fort Yukon where supplies were thought to be available, upriver and out to Skagway or Juneau, any place but Dawson. Hundreds left, but most did not. And though there was scurvy that winter there was no actual starvation.

What there was instead was inflation. An abundance of gold chased a very few goods, and prices (which in other places were roughly one fifth of what they are today) rose astronomically. Food was so expensive and uncertain of supply that Haskell and Meeker decided to go out to Juneau, and return in the spring with a large supply, on which they hoped to turn a huge profit. Just before they left, in November, they stopped in at one of the little restaurants on Front Street. This was its bill of fare:

Coffee, tea, or chocolate, .50   Ham & Eggs, 5.00
Sandwiches, .75   Porterhouse Steak, 5.00
Boston baked beans, 1.00   Cove oysters, fried, 9.00
                    Pie and Cake, 1.00

Wrote a miner to an associate later that winter:

I know you are wondering what the devil I mean by writing so fine
& making such a scrawl of it to the Everlasting injury of your Eyes—
I'll tell you—Paper is six sheets for a dollar—Envelopes 1.00 per doz.
. . . Coal oil [for lighting] is only 40.00 per gal & *rising*—same price
as whiskey only I hope not so profusely watered. . . . I paid Col.
Green the other day 1.50 for a pkge of toilet paper—& 5.50 for roll
of—well—he says its [sic] butter—the Cow was not in Evidence. . . .
Flour has ranged from *not to be had* down to 100.00—75—60 & c.
until now it is Even to be had, if you know how to get it, at 30.00 per
50 lb sack—sugar 1.25 per pound—Evap potatoes 2.50 & up . . .
Moose meat 1.50 per lb—Beef—(Ex pack ox)—1.25—sheep same. . . .
On the other hand, I disposed of my noble dog for the neat sum of
165.00—

Hay brought as much as $1,000 per ton, a circumstance that
drove the price of renting a horse and wagon up to $150 per day,
and with all the gold dust on earth one could not buy window
glass, safety pins, china or brooms.

Tappan Adney had brought in enough supplies so that the food
shortage caused him no great privation. After his arrival, on October 31, he spent a few days in Dawson gathering the material
for his first on-the-spot report to *Harper's*. He considered buying
a little cabin there, but in those days of illiberal expense accounts
he could not afford the thousand-dollar asking price. Instead he
joined up with a colleague, a New York *Times* reporter named
Pelletier, and they decided to build a cabin together near the
mouth of Bonanza Creek, a few miles from town. It was late in
the season to undertake such work, and the —39° November cold
snap made them so impatient to have a roof over their heads that
they roofed the structure before the walls had grown sufficiently,
and all winter long Adney had to stoop unless he was directly

under the ridgepole. The cabin was fourteen by sixteen and un-floored, a typical miner's cabin except for the windows Adney fashioned from his celluloid photographic plates; these, he says, became "the wonder of the gulch." Their cabin kept them warm and comfortable until the flood next spring, and since it was located just off the trail from Dawson to Bonanza and Eldorado, it gave the journalists a good chance to observe the passing traffic.

From dawn to dusk, a period of five or six twilit hours, men and dogs were seldom out of sight on the trail of polished ice. Stampeders trotted by en route to the site of some alleged new strike with a few days' grub in their backpacks; working miners trudged wearily past in harness to sleds piled high with provi-sions; express trains of malemutes, capable of sixty miles a day on a good trail, dashed past in front of seasoned dog punchers; and mixed teams of spaniels and Newfoundlands, incapable of ten, floundered by behind swearing cheechakos. One team in particu-lar stood out among all the rest. Its approach was heralded by the tinkle of little bells and it flew past in no time, the seven huge huskies racing together like parts of a single organism. On the sleigh behind rode a woman and a small child buried nearly out of sight beneath lynx robes—the family of one of the Kings of Eldorado being chauffeured to Dawson.

The night before Thanksgiving, 1897, Adney baked enough doughnuts to last a week, and next morning he and Pelletier set out on their first reportorial tour of the mines. It was a fairly cold day, below —38° F. at least, for the mercury of the miners they encountered was frozen solid. Their cabin was on claim Ninety-Seven Below Discovery, while the rich dirt did not begin until three miles farther up Bonanza, in the Sixties Below. From there on up for a dozen miles nearly every claim was being worked. The valley floor was splotched with conical heaps of gravel, the dumps, black against the snow, and in the middle of each was the shaft, still smoking from the thawing fire of the night before. It looked like a field of tiny volcanoes, a scene out of the earth's early history or final fate; and when blackened men emerged from the volcano cones, it was like a detail from Hieronymus

Bosch. Each cone was connected to the ones immediately upstream and downstream from it by the narrow dark line of Bonanza Trail.

Adney and Pelletier had got off early and when they reached
the first active mine the day's work had just started.

. . . sleepy men in Mackinaws and old cloth "parkies," canvas mittens,
with faces muffled and feet wrapped in sacking (the working miner
cares little about looks), had begun to turn creaking windlasses, hoist-
ing dirt out of the holes. Others were busy sawing wood with long,
single cross-cut saws. . . . The first early travellers were coming down
the trail. I shall not forget this first sight. A heavy bank of smoke from
the night's fires hung over the valley, and the air was laden with the
smell of burned wood. More cabins and smoking dumps; then strings
of cabins, first on one side, then on the other, the trail growing like the
street of a village. . . .
We hurried on, clambering over dumps, now shuffling along the
smooth, polished sled-trail, hardly comprehending the strange, weird
sight. . . . Three hours from camp we stood at the forks of Bonanza
and Eldorado. The sight was one never to be forgotten. . . . It was
hard to believe that this was the spot towards which all the world was
looking.

During the next two years this place, the junction of Eldorado
and Bonanza, grew into the town of Grand Forks with a population probably exceeding six thousand. By the end of 1898 the
gentle, worn hills were stripped of their last stick of usable wood,
and trails fanned out through a wasteland in all directions. Grand
Forks was long and narrow, and Bonanza Creek ran almost
through the middle of it; by then the creek's water was befouled
by sluicing, garbage and excrement and Grand Forks was supplied (by dogsled in winter and by dogcart in summer) from a
spring on Twenty-One Above. William Ogilvie's geometric sense
of order did not extend to Grand Forks. The settlement consisted
of two long dubious rows of shacks, cabins, warehouses, and tents
strung out at random along a twisting mud street cluttered with
cordwood, piled lumber, carts, sleds, dogs, horses, mules, men
and women. There is a splendid photograph of Grand Forks

amidst the bric-a-brac in the Dawson Museum; it was taken in 1898 or 1899, when the town was in its heyday, and a then resident appended a key identifying all the main structures. We learn, for example, that there was a Viennese confectionery, a Japanese eatery, and a German bakery, not to mention such ordinary establishments as blacksmith shops, stores, barbershops, hotels and rooming houses, livery stables and a NWMP post. There were also two churches, one Presbyterian, the other Anglican, and their pastors organized joint spelling bees, charity dinners and musicales on Friday nights. For those seeking other diversions there was the Gold Hill Hotel, Dance Hall and Card Room, and Dewey's Saloon.

Grand Forks, like Dawson itself, has been dying almost since birth, but Dawson grew to be much bigger in the first place and so it still has a few hundred decaying buildings and a few hundred people, while Grand Forks has only two people now and six buildings. Most of the original structures were burned for firewood just before the mining dredges ingested their sites, digested the gold that lay buried there, and excreted scalloped heaps of tailings where they had once been. A little way up Eldorado Creek from Grand Forks one of these dredges remains. It squats at an uncomfortable angle in a pond of its own making like some awkward dinosaur caught up short by evolution and sinking toward bedrock and immortality as a fossil. The dredge is five stories high, with a double row of bucket-shaped teeth, each one bigger than a man, attached to the great ingesting trunk. Since it has sunk some feet to the bottom of its pond, only four stories are actually above water. The flooded lower level, shaded from the sun, is full of ice summer as well as winter, and the top of a cast-iron gear housing protrudes from the crystalline mass like the finished part of an unfinished sculpture. It is an odd thing to behold, this great hunk of machinery (it is the biggest wooden-hulled gold dredge ever constructed anywhere), so expensive and complicated, and simply left for dead on the field of battle, never salvaged, burned or buried, never cannibalized nor even vandalized.

When Adney visited Grand Forks it still had a future, though as yet no past. It was not quite a town, but the first two hotels were already open for business. He and Pelletier stayed at one of them, Hotel Madden.

We were made welcome to the best in the house—namely, the use of a chair, a table, a stove for cooking, and a place on the floor to spread a blanket. The hotel was a two-storied log building, about 25 x 30 feet, a single room below, with a ladder to reach up-stairs. A large heating-stove stood in the middle of the floor, a cooking-stove and a long bare table at the other end. In one corner was what is even more essential than a dining-room to a Yukon hotel—the bar, a narrow counter of spruce boards, back of which on a shelf stood several long black bottles, one of which, it was announced gloomily, still contained a little rum, the house's entire stock of liquid refreshment.

From Hotel Madden, Adney and Pelletier went up to have a look at the Berry-Stander claims a half a mile away on Eldorado. Clarence Berry was still in California, and his brother Frank was living in his cabin on Number Five. Frank Berry supervised the winter's diggings not only on Five, but on Four and Six as well, two claims his brother had acquired the preceding spring. A bunkhouse and a mess hall had been erected, even a blacksmith's shop, and twenty-five men were at work. One of them did nothing but collect and pan samples from each hole a few times a day to make sure the miners stayed on the pay streak. Frank Berry invited the reporters in to supper (served directly from the cans), and Adney asked him for a quotable opinion about the richness of the Eldorado placers. He replied:

There is one dump I know on Eldorado where a man can take a rocker and rock out $10,000 in a day, or he can pan $1000 in four pans. Those who have high-grade dirt will not sell for less than from $50,000 to $150,000.

And, speaking of the Berry-Stander claims, he continued:

Twenty-five-dollar nuggets are *common*. We have a thousand dollars' worth, averaging $10, that came out of our first cut. Some men won't stay at work at any wages when they see the ground. One man came to me and said he wanted to quit. "Aren't you satisfied?" "Yes, I'm satisfied with you, but won't work for any man in a country where there is dirt like this," and he went up the hill-side and began sinking a hole.

By way of concrete demonstration, Berry went over to the neighboring cabin of Anton Stander and returned with a flat dull nugget recently unearthed. He put it on the scales and it weighed in at just short of a pound.

Further up Eldorado, on Number Seven, Adney met a lean, middle-aged Irishman in a martenskin cap, and he too talked about nuggets. A few days before he was in the hole while Young, his partner, was cranking the windlass.

Mike Young sees something bright like a pea in the bucket, and he brushed it off, and it kept gittin' bigger and bigger, and he pulled it out. You know Mike—nuthin' ever gits Mike excited. . . . He picked it up and come to the hole and hollered down, "I've found a nugget!" "How much?" I says. "It may be forty [i.e. worth forty dollars], and it may be fifty." "Gosh darn," says I, "it'll go a *hunder* and fifty." It went to two hundred and twelve. It was like a frog. I called it "The Frog."

What would Mike Young do with The Frog? Or Charlie Anderson with the $300,000 Eldorado Twenty-Nine had yielded him by spring? Or Clarence Berry with his million and a half? Doubtless there is a special inner genie in each one of us that can be liberated only by our sudden acquisition of substantial wealth. Once liberated this genie is apt to attain great influence over its owner. But of course it almost never has the opportunity to emerge from the lower recesses of the psyche where it lives, and where it stirs up a Walter Mitty daydream now and then but is otherwise quiescent. The gold of the Klondike liberated quite a number of these genies, at least more than are commonly seen at any one place at a given time. Some of them, it is true, led their human charges to sensible living and sound investments. Much more often they led them off on wild peregrinations, to palatial homes, private railroad cars, expensive women, London, Paris, the antipodes and, finally, the almshouse.

Take Charlie Anderson, for example. In the fall of 1896, when he trudged up to start working the claim he had been fooled into buying for $800, he was broke and didn't even have a cabin. Now, during the winter of 1897–98, he was worth several hundred thousand dollars and he threw big parties in his commodious steam-heated house on Eldorado Twenty-Nine. The dance hall girls trooped up from Dawson, and raucous music echoed up and down the gulch. He married one of these girls, Grace Drummond by name, after agreeing to endow her with $50,000. The new couple set off on a grand tour of Europe; nothing was too good: private railroad cars, the entire top floors of the best hotels, gems and furs for Grace Drummond. Soon and inevitably the gold ran out, and just as soon and inevitably Miss Drummond followed suit. Already before the First World War, Charlie Anderson was working at a sawmill in Washington for four dollars a day. "But he had no regrets," reported a friend of Klondike days who encountered him there, "and what a hell of a good time he had while the pay streak lasted." In 1939 he was still working in a sawmill, this time in Sapperton, British Columbia, and for $3.25 a day. He had vowed not to shave until he struck it rich again, and that year he wore his beard to the grave.

As one would expect, sudden wealth affected Clarence Berry in quite a different way. He was prudent, sober and happily married, and the winter Adney visited his claims he was Outside laying the foundations under a fortune that would grow for the rest of his life. He would take over a million and a half dollars out of Eldorado, invest some of it in Californian oil ventures, and make a second fortune.

Berry's partner Anton Stander, the indigent Austrian immigrant of the year before, spent the same winter acquiring the two habits that would ruin him: whiskey and Violet Raymond, late of the Juneau "opera," but more recently of a Dawson dance hall. Stander lured Violet Raymond away from a rival with the gift of $20,000, plus a lard bucket of nuggets, and he retained her at an additional $1,000 a month. Later he married her. They made a honeymoon voyage to China, and the San Francisco *Examiner* reported they took along a thousand pounds of gold as spending money. She spent it; he drank. Back in Seattle she continued to spend and he to drink. When drunk he sometimes became insanely jealous; once he tried to carve her up with a butcher's knife. She left him. Broke now, a reflex sent him back toward the land of his original fortune—or misfortune; he worked for his passage as a potato peeler in the galley, but he never got farther than the Pioneers' Home in Sitka, a refuge for destitute men. There he died.

The gold of Eldorado Thirteen permitted William Gates, alias Swiftwater Bill, to erase the discrepancy between his past and stature, on the one hand, and his grandiose pretentions on the other. An ex-dishwasher from Circle City, he was a short man, a scant five feet five, with a pinched, pallid face and a moth-eaten mustache. But he was rich now; he bathed in champagne and wore patent leather shoes and a Prince Albert coat, even on his claim. His stiff-collared white shirt, apparently the only one to be had in Dawson during the winter of 1897–98, became such a badge of his new rank that he reportedly stayed in bed when it was being laundered. The genie of sudden wealth guided him to the faro tables in town where he threw away thousands with an abandon that was marvelous to behold. And it guided him into the arms of ladies, for a homely, undersized fellow with a great deal of gold and very little prudence could be a most attractive specimen to the hussies of Dawson whose wont it was to stampede successful stampeders. He bought the promise of the hand of Gussie LaMore, it is said, for her weight in gold, and though only nineteen, she had gone to fat a bit and cost one hundred and thirty-four pounds of dust and nuggets. In 1898 Swiftwater Bill went down to San Francisco where he ensconced himself in a vast suite high in the Baldwin Hotel, and there he would slip nuggets to the bellhops to get them to point out the "King of the Klondike" to the other guests as he passed through the lobby. He had come to San Francisco to marry Gussie LaMore, but, alas, she reneged: not only did she now have his gold safely tucked away;

she had a husband as well. So he married her sister Grace instead. As a wedding present he bought her a big house in Oakland, from which she evicted him after the second week. After these initial hardships his luck improved and for a time he was married to two girls at once. What sort of deal Swiftwater Bill Gates and Fate finally worked out is unknown. After the Klondike he stampeded all over Alaska, then dropped out of sight for years. He seems to have surfaced again later, in Bolivia or thereabouts, where he was reportedly promoting a silver mining scheme of some sort. That is the last we hear of him.

George Carmack's gold sponsored his first trip outside in years. He, and Kate, Jim and Charlie, went down to Seattle to see what diversions civilized life might offer. They stayed in the Butler Hotel, one of the best in town. It was a big structure, and its many floors, halls and stairways were perplexing to Kate who had never left the Yukon before. To keep from losing her way on the trail from the Carmack suite to the dining room, she used her skinning knife to slash a series of blazes on doors and mahogany bannisters. From the suite itself she, Jim and Charlie—all three of them fond of champagne by now—flung bills and nuggets down into the street and watched in amusement as the crowds pushed and shoved and brought traffic to a standstill. In Carmack, as we have seen, a well-scrubbed, well-heeled bourgeois had always lurked behind the frowzy squawman exterior, and the genie of sudden wealth coaxed it into the open. In time he abandoned Kate and her people, along with his old ambition to become a chief among the Tagish Indians. According to one source he married a Marguerite Safteg, "an attractive and intelligent American woman," according to another he married Marguerite Laimee, the madam of a Dawson City brothel. The two accounts agree, however, that he lived quietly and respectably thereafter, invested in Seattle real estate, and died in 1922, a fairly wealthy man and a Mason in good standing.

If men such as Swiftwater Bill Gates and Charlie Anderson wished to cast their gold dust into the wind during the winter of 1897–98 they did not need to go as far as Seattle or San Francisco. By then separating miners from their gold was big business right in Dawson City. The town's fanciest, biggest and most crowded structures were devoted to it. In all there were about a dozen saloon-dance halls in operation by the end of 1897 (a year later there would be many more) and they occupied Joe Ladue's most valuable lots on the east side of Front Street. The M & M, usually referred to simply as "Pete's place," was the one Tappan Adney got to know best, and it was typical of them all. Adney was no barfly, but when he came down from his cabin on Bonanza he liked to stop in and warm himself by the big sheet metal stove, kept red-hot all winter, that glowed in the middle of the barroom. Pete served watered whiskey, the standard stock in trade of the Dawson saloons; it customarily sold for fifty cents a shot, and it generally became more and more watered until the stern-wheelers brought in a new stock in June. Hooch was also available and for the same price; one had a choice between Juice of the Snake, Kuprecof Dynamite and other distinguished brands. When it was time to pay, the customer poured gold dust from his poke into a little tray, called a "blower," which the bartender then weighed on his scales, taking out what was owed and returning the rest. Some bartenders are reported to have grown especially long fingernails and beards, which they panned out after each night's transactions, but Pete was known to be honest. Anyhow, he hardly needed to cheat because his establishment was doing very well, even for Dawson.

Pete had had serious competition from the Opera House until it burned to the ground on Thanksgiving morning.* Regarded as the best place in town, it had been equipped not only with a bar, a complete gambling layout and a dance hall, but a theater fitted out with blue denim curtains and candle footlights, and a troupe of Circle City vaudeville entertainers. Now that it was no more, Pete had much of its clientele and the better part of its female employees. To have dancing partners for the miners was of great importance because when a miner bought the right to a two or three minute dance for a dollar, seventy-five cents of it went to the house. And whereas a man couldn't drink a shot of whiskey

---

* It is indicative of the scarcity of goods in Dawson that winter that the charred nails were salvaged from the ashes and sold for $3.50 a pound.

every three minutes for too long, he could, and often did, dance for hours and dollars on end. Eddy was the "caller-off" at Pete's place, the man whose job it was to get the miners to dance as much as possible. In the evening, when the dancing was to start, he would yell out, "Come on boys, you can all waltz. Come on now for a juicy waltz." Or "Come on boys, we're gonna have a real fine cow-tillion." When Eddy had a few couples out on the floor he would turn to the orchestra—actually a trio of fiddle, flute, and piano—and shout, "Fire away!" Others would join in and the room would echo with a cacophony of raucous music, shuffling feet, laughter, and the yells of kibitzers. In winter the place would be kept hot and hardly ventilated, and the smell of rotten socks (for the miners often danced bootless, as they had in Circle City) mingled with the fumes of spilled whiskey, cheap perfume and cigar smoke. After a few quick circuits the music would cease abruptly, and each couple would promenade directly to the bar. There the man would have a shot of whiskey, and his partner would receive from the bartender a white ivory chip, worth twenty-five cents, her commission for the dance. The girls did quite well, often amassing one hundred and twenty-five chips by dawn, not to mention the 10 percent commission they got when they wheedled their partners into buying champagne at forty dollars a pint.

As at Circle City, the names the miners gave to the dance hall girls usually reflected some physical characteristic or biographical incident. Diamond-Tooth Gertie, for example, actually had a diamond anchored between her two front teeth; in fact, years later, when she was in financial straits she dislodged and sold it. The Oregon Mare whinnied as she danced, while the Grizzly Bear was a blonde mountain of flesh, one hundred and seventy pounds of it, who had lost one eye, it is said, doing combat with a colleague. Similarly, Nellie the Pig is reported to have bitten off a bartender's ear. Spanish Jeannette allowed as how she was from Castille, and of noble antecedents. Others were Dog-faced Kitty and Sunshine Sue, Minnie LaTour, Gussie LaMore, Josie LaVore and Lime Juice Lil, a teetotaler as the name implies, but a notorious roller.

There were two categories of women in the entertainment business in Dawson, those who "lived private," and those who lived on Paradise Alley just in back of Front Street. This was Dawson's first red-light district, but because the coal oil needed to light the red lanterns cost forty dollars a gallon, red curtains were used instead. Each girl had her "crib," a small square room with a big bed and a little gold scales. There were about seventy cribs in the alley; they were set out facing each other from opposite sides, and on every door appeared the name of the occupant. Customers would stroll up and down inspecting before they committed themselves. Many of these prostitutes were imported from Belgium by their *maquereaux* and were, in fact, indentured laborers. Some of them, the most enterprising, made business trips to the creeks; the fee was one ounce per man, there being a surcharge for home delivery.

In the spring of 1898 when Gene Allen came to Dawson and started the Klondike *Nugget,* he initiated a campaign to have the whores ejected from Paradise Alley. "One of Dawson's most important thoroughfares," he complained, is also "prominent in its display of red curtains. . . . It is certainly a most discreditable thing to see glaring signs of 'Jennie and Babe,' and wanton use of places and respectable business houses." Not long afterwards Colonel S. B. Steele of the Mounted Police decreed the eviction of the girls from Paradise Alley; they were shunted off to a more remote part of town soon known as Hell's Half Acre. Allen breathed a sigh of relief:

No longer may the woman in scarlet occupy the choicest city lots and flaunt her crimson colors on Dawson's crowded streets; no longer may the seductive window tap beguile the innocent prospector or hurrying man of business.

By 1898, Dawson was getting respectable, no doubt about it, and the change was reflected in the increased sophistication of the entertainment offered. Shakespearean plays were staged, and even *Faust* and *Camille.* There was a production of *Uncle Tom's Cabin,* with the roles of Eliza and Simon Legree skillfully interpreted, though the pack of pursuing bloodhounds, played by a single malemute puppy dragged on stage completely against his will by an "invisible" wire was less convincing. More common, of course, were Victorian melodramas on the order of *Jack the Ripper,* and the routines at the Combination. This pleasure dome, which opened during the summer of 1898, featured "A Bevy of Beauties in Title Roles," and then, a few months later, when it was rebaptized the Tivoli, billed "The Finest Formed Women on the Yukon." At the Novelty the leading attraction was Freda Maloof, "The Turkish Whirlwind Danseuse," at least until Colonel Steele had her hauled before the magistrate for indecent exposure. Twice Miss Maloof tried to prove to the magistrate, by demonstration, that there was nothing lewd in her act, and when he remained unconvinced, she took another tack, arguing that the dance she did was an integral part of the Turkish branch of Mohammedanism. The magistrate was still unmoved, perhaps because she was a Greek, and he fined her twenty-five dollars. There were also skits based on local events such as Swiftwater Bill's troubles with women, as well as wrestling matches, acrobatics, and "Tableaux of Famous Heroines"; and there was a variety act based on the career of Lady Godiva and a stunt routine in which a man nightly hanged himself.

Aside from stage shows, drinking, dancing and whoring, the most popular diversion in Dawson was gambling. Each saloon had its faro table, and its poker chips, and many of them had roulette wheels. The stakes were sometimes quite high, and not infrequently the gambling establishments themselves changed owners at the turn of a card. Swiftwater Bill, a faro man, was wont to fling his poke down on the table and yell, "The sky's the limit, boys. Raise her up as far as you want to go, and if the roof's in the way, why tear her off." One night William Haskell watched him lose five hundred dollars in a couple of minutes. "Things don't seem to be going my way," he observed, and ordered a round of whiskey and cigars for everyone in the house.

17 **1898**

THERE are two seasons on the Yukon, summer and the rest of the year. Summer begins with the river's breakup, and people in Dawson City customarily placed bets on the precise time that the ice would start to budge. After the turn of the century the ice pool became a well-organized lottery. Thousands of one-dollar tickets, each one indicating a date, hour and minute, were sold, and the resulting jackpot was worth a small fortune. To determine the exact moment when the breakup began, a stake, patriotically topped with a Union Jack, was planted on the frozen Yukon; from it a taut wire led to an electric clock in Charles Jeanerette's jewelry store and when the ice budged even a few inches the clock stopped. A gong then automatially sounded, announcing the news to Dawson, and within a few minutes every school and church bell in town was relaying the message to the surrounding countryside. In no time the entire population, leaving behind open safes, baking bread, warm beds, and incomplete sentences, would troop down to the banks of the Yukon and behold the arrival of summer.

By February or March the domain of winter on the Yukon has lasted so long and been so total that it becomes hard to imagine any other time of year; one begins to feel that not even half a dozen summers could seriously challenge its authority. Even before breakup, however, there are reassuring signs that winter, like all else, is transitory. On protected spots along the south-facing slopes tiny purple crocuses, the frailest of flowers, push forth from the dormant land, and along the watercourses yellow crowfoot

blooms. The first Canadian geese and sand-hill cranes form shifting skeins across the sky, and their wonderful wild music is un-
mistakably the song of a new season. The snow is wet and heavy
by day, and he who snowshoes or drives dogs must now travel at
night. Beneath the snow, drops and trickles are forming brooks
which feed into the tributary rivers of the Yukon. All winter the
Yukon has been subsisting on a reduced ration of ground water,
for during the six coldest months virtually all precipitation has
fallen as snow and accumulated on the land. During these
months the river's mean flow as recorded at the Eagle, Alaska,
gauging station, has fallen to 21,300 cubic feet per second, only a
third more than the annual average of the Hudson River. But
now, as the days grow longer and warmer, the snow melts and
the Yukon's fast ends. In May the mean flow at Eagle rises to
138,000 cubic feet per second, about five times the yearly average of the Colorado.*

At first the rising river does not carry its ice downstream, but
lifts it vertically. In the fall when this ice was first formed it fit a
river that was much smaller and much lower in its bed, so now as
the river swells, the ice no longer reaches all the way across
it. Open water appears in many places between the banks and
the ice itself, which floats free in a single sheet as long as the
Yukon. Along the channels of open water the Indians paddle the
tiny muskratting canoes they make from flattened five-gallon
cans, while on the river ice planes can safely land. As the days
grow longer and warmer the ice becomes soft and honeycombed
with fissures; it looks as though it had been riddled with worm

* The mean annual flow as measured at Kaltag, where the gauging
nearest the Yukon's mouth (though still 470 miles from it) is located, is
193,800 cubic feet per second, or 140,700,000 acre-feet per year. The
Yukon's discharge into the Bering Sea has not been measured, but hydrol-
ogists of the U.S. Geological Survey estimate that the annual mean is
216,000 cubic feet per second. By the criterion of flow, or volume, the
Yukon system is thus the fifth largest in North America. It is exceeded by
the Mississippi-Missouri system, the St. Lawrence, the Mackenzie and the
Nelson-Saskatchewan system, and followed by the Columbia. All these flow
calculations are based on measurements made during 1959–60.

borings, which is what prompted the oft-told tale of the Yukon ice worm.

So far the ice has withstood the onslaught of the sun above and the rising river beneath; it has remained intact and in place. Then suddenly it begins to move. It is a solid mass at first, a vast white section of the landscape slipping away downriver in an unbroken sheet. But it cannot withstand the shock of motion for more than a moment. It shatters like glass, and the sound of it breaks in upon the silence of a spring day with a groaning thunder audible for fifteen miles. The floes are five or six feet thick, weigh many tons, and move at seven to nine miles an hour. They hurtle into each other, are riven and cleaved, pound each other to bits, grind each other down. They gash the river's banks, are borne over them by the high water; they shave the spruce trees off islands and gouge out the earth. They become freighted with the debris of their work, and sometimes they carry away a doomed moose or caribou caught on the river when the ice began to move.

Then, without warning, the ice comes to a dead stop. It has dammed itself and the river behind a chaos of glistening blue-green chunks such as Coleridge might have seen in an opium dream. More water and more ice are impounded. The pressure increases, becomes unbearable. A slab that has acted as a key-stone hurtles skyward with a creaking groan. The mountain of ice collapses as fast as it was formed; the lake disappears.

Many towns on the Yukon have been inundated behind these ice-dams, and such floods are particularly perilous because they occur in a matter of minutes. Usually they do not last long but the dam that formed below Galena, Alaska, in 1945 was so sturdy that it barricaded the river for more than twenty-four hours and was dislodged only after a squadron of B-17's unloaded 168,000 pounds of bombs on it. The airfield there, one of a chain of bases used in ferrying lend-lease aircraft to Russia, was largely destroyed. To the inhabitants of the river below Galena the flood had its compensations, however, for it distributed a manna of lumber, boats, drums of oil, K-rations, even tinned candies, all along the way from the base to the Bering Sea. As of September

1966, residents of Marshall, nearly four hundred miles down-stream, were still digging drums of diesel oil from their sloughs.

In 1898 the Yukon ice began to move out on the seventh of May, and never before nor since did the event mean so much to so many people.

For Clarence Berry, Thomas Lippy, and a few hundred other rich claim owners it meant that frozen dumps were melting and could be sluiced. A winter's investment in the labor of burning, scraping, picking, shoveling and windlass cranking lay in these formless heaps, and now it remained only to extract the twenty-five tons of placer gold they would yield up that year. Soon Mike Bartlett, the muleskinner, would be up on these claims loading each one of his dozen pack animals with twenty-five thousand dollars' worth of gold sewn into canvas sacks a dozen layers thick. He transported the bullion to Dawson for seventy-five cents a pound.

For Tappan Adney the spring thaw meant, first of all, the inundation of his cabin. By May 3, a few days before the Yukon ice began to move, Bonanza Creek was running free, and far above its banks. The cold water, already silted from the first sluicing, unceremoniously entered Adney's cabin and covered the floor. It was only a few inches deep, but Adney was not pleased to have "to wade about the house in rubber boots, fighting mosquitoes, trying to cook a flapjack or make a cup of tea over the stove, and climbing in and out of a high bunk with boots on." He hiked off to Dawson in disgust, but soon the situation there was even worse. Shortly after the Yukon began to break up it deluged all of Lousetown and most of Dawson. Adney was forced to retreat to the flank of Midnight Dome where he pitched his tent and bivouacked for a few days. From this vantage point he had an excellent view of men sleeping on their cabin roofs, their boats tied to the eaves, and of taxi-boats working Front Street for fifty cents a fare.

The receding water left a thick coat of alluvial ooze on every-thing, but in exchange it took with it the last of the ice, and this was a cause for rejoicing. Soon the outside world would return to

Dawson, a little out of date upon arrival, perhaps, but to be welcomed with a profound joy and sense of relief. The first boats from Bennett Lake would bring, for example, two-week-old Seattle newspapers with their reports on the Spanish-American War; the persistent rumors of New York City's destruction by an enemy naval squadron would finally be laid to rest by news of Dewey's victory in Manila Bay. And there would be mail, letters from wives and lovers and mothers and friends, who had been left after a thousand precipitous leavetakings. From the passes, and also from St. Michael, fresh food would arrive, such extraordinary marvels of creation as the potato and the turnip. Already before the breakup Mr. R. J. Gandolfo, an Italian fruit vendor, was set to leave Bennett Lake for Dawson with eight tons of oranges, bananas, lemons and cucumbers. And before long Mr. H. L. Miller would be en route with Dawson's first cow, though at $30.00 a gallon, her product would be of benefit only to the city's well-to-do. The hundreds of scow and stern-wheeler loads of food and supplies that would reach Dawson that spring would bring prices down toward a more reasonable level. A fifty pound sack of flour, for example, had fetched between $100 and $120 in October 1897, but by June the price would fall to $3.00. The arrival of abundant fresh food would also put an end to the scourge of scurvy that had taken a heavy toll during the winter. Its more fortunate victims had filled every room and hall, and even the office, at Father Judge's hospital, while the less fortunate ones were discovered as blackened and toothless cadavers in their cabins on isolated creeks.

To the ten thousand stampeders at Bennett Lake the breakup in the spring of 1898 meant that the golden grab bag was now at arm's length. As usual the ice in the lakes lingered for a time after the Yukon itself was running free and the armada didn't get under way until May 29. Colonel Sam Steele, the chief of the NWMP in the Yukon, had spent the winter at Bennett Lake, and on that day he mounted the hill in back of his headquarters to watch the exodus. It was a grand sight. He counted no less than eight hundred boats on the half of the lake visible from his

vantage point. And when, a few hours later, he set out to follow
them to Miles Canyon, he was never more than two hundred feet
from his nearest neighbor. During May, June and July, 1898, the
police post at Tagish Lake recorded the passage of 18,631 people,* more than the total population of the Yukon Territory
today.

At first the boats were bunched together, as at the start of any
race. And this was indeed a race, for the peculiar fever of the
enterprise dictated the notion that to arrive an hour before the
next fellow would assure even greater good fortune. In the case
of men like Mr. Gandolfo the fruit vendor, and a number of
others who were piloting scows loaded to the gunwhales with
food and provisions, the haste made sense, for Dawson's absurd
prices would begin to fall as soon as a few of them arrived. But
most of the rest would find their haste sadly unrewarded.

Through Tagish and Marsh lakes the armada sailed, then on to
Miles Canyon, which claimed one hundred and fifty boats and
ten lives that season before Colonel Steele stationed a police cor-
poral there to enforce safety measures. Across Lake Laberge they
came, down the Thirty Mile River, past the Teslin, the Big Salmon, the Little Salmon, the Pelly, the White, the Stewart.

The sign that says "Entering Dawson City" to the river traveler
is a section of the face of Midnight Dome which has slipped
down leaving a greyish scar shaped something like a stretched
moosehide. It is visible for several miles upriver. By 1898 it had
been drawn and photographed hundreds of times, and had appeared in the dozens of hastily written pamphlets about the
Klondike. The stampeders knew what it looked like, even before
they left Kalamazoo and Coeur d'Alene. For how many months
had they waited for it to rise into their sight? No matter now; the
Promised Land lay right around the bend.

Dawson City, just drying out from the Yukon's flood, was inundated by the hordes of stampeders early in June. Their boats,
often two or three deep, formed a solid rim along the river from
the north side of town to the Klondike, and across it to Louse-

* According to Pierre Berton in *Klondike* the total by the end of the
navigation season rose to "more than 28,000."

town—one and three-quarters miles solid with boats. Their tents turned the hillside back of Dawson white as snow, they blossomed on both banks of the Klondike and the overflow on the far side of the Yukon. Adney counted two thousand eight hundred tents from the hill behind where he was bivouacking, and estimated that each one housed three to five people.

At this time the creeks of the Klondike were producing more gold than ever before. Charlie Anderson was about to push his total to three hundred thousand dollars, and Berry to raise his to twice this. On some claims, such as Eldorado Sixteen, owned by an ex-YMCA coach named Thomas Lippy, it was becoming clear that every running foot of the five hundred was worth an average of three thousand dollars. And so it went; Eldorado was the jackpot, but Bonanza, though more spotty, yielded three million dollars, and Hunker and Bear creeks, which empty into the Klondike upstream from Bonanza, each produced over one million dollars. So too did Sulphur, Dominion, and Quartz, streams originating near the Klondike placer creeks, but flowing south to the Indian River.

It is logical to assume that the mother lode from which the placers of the Klondike and the Indian were eroded was roughly equidistant from the two rivers, in an area a few miles wide and perhaps twenty miles long. Every major creek draining this area was found to be rich, while none arising elsewhere contained any exploitable gold whatsoever. In the course of time the gold was moved down by water, and distributed along the creeks in an expanded area roughly twenty-five by thirty miles and bounded on one side by the Klondike. Outside this area there was nothing. Along the Klondike itself, for example, the north bank was devoid of gold in all places, and the south bank contained gold only along the lower fifth of its length. The placer ground of the Dawson region was by no means unlimited.

By June 1898, when the greatest of the stampeder armies marched on Dawson City, about two hundred and thirty miles of five hundred foot claims had been staked and registered in the Recorder's Office on Front Street. Near the proven placer creeks every gulch, hollow, pup and trickle showed the blazes of a

claimant, and each, whether a worthless "skunk" or an Eldora-
dito, was baptized with a hopeful name. There was Too Much
Gold Creek (a "skunk"), All Gold Creek, Gold Run, and Ready
Bullion, Orogrande Gulch, Mint Gulch and Nugget Gulch, Eu-
reka Creek, Deadwood Creek and Australia Creek. And up on the
hillsides, where the old placers were deposited before the geological upthrust, smaller "bench" claims covered the ground like the
patches of a quilt. These bench deposits had been first discovered
in July 1897 by cheechakos, most of whom even then could find
no good creek ground to stake.

Tappan Adney was back in Dawson City from a trip to the
White River when the stampeder invasion reached its peak. He
watched as they tied their boats to the sterns and sides of other
craft on the crowded waterfront. They were exhilarated; their
voices loud, their gestures expansive. They bounded from their
boats and trotted with an eager stride up from the water's edge to
the town. On Front Street they talked to other newcomers, to old-
timers, to men in the bars where they went to celebrate their
arrival, to anyone. What was the local situation? Where should
one prospect? Where could one wash out the five hundred dollar
pans they had heard about? By what alchemy—for the Klondike
was a magic place—could a Denver millhand be transmuted into
a Dawson millionaire ere the Arctic summer died?

And, slowly or quickly, depending on their conversations and
their will to believe, they joined the growing throng that had
already learned the answers. They trudged aimlessly now, their
voices quieted. Their ardent quest for news was now only a half-
hearted search for some slight shred of evidence that the expectations they had held since Topeka and Tacoma were not just a
crazy dream.

Who is there [writes Adney] that can describe the crowd, curious,
listless, dazed, dragging its way with slow, lagging step along the main
street? Can this be the "rush" that newspapers are accustomed to
describe as the movement of gold-seekers? Have the hard, weary
months of work on the trails exhausted their vitality? or is it the heavy
shoes that make them drag their feet so wearily along the street? . . . It

is a vast herd; they crowd the boats and fill the streets, looking at Dawson. . . . The old-timer (we are all old-timers now) is lost. The mere recognition of a face seen last winter is now excuse for a friendly nod and a "How-de-do?" . . .

They arrived to claim their reward and found that it was claimed already; there was no good ground left to stake and thousands to stake it.

Probably between fifteen and twenty thousand people reached Dawson City during the navigation season of 1898, and it is estimated that a third of them departed within six weeks of their arrival. So many outfits were being sold that the price of flour dropped below what its buyers had paid for it in San Francisco. For a while everything under the sun was for sale and Front Street looked "like a row of booths at a fair." Miners' wages, which had been fifteen dollars a day that winter, fell to seven in August, and later there was unemployment. Some took to sleeping in the saloons, and Colonel Steele made provisions for the indigent to chop wood in exchange for meals.

Dawson's newborn government services sagged under the onslaught. At the post office, generally the first place a newcomer headed, tons of unsorted mail lay in heaps, and the chaos defied the feeble organizational genius of the two totally inexperienced police clerks assigned there. One stampeder, who had arrived after incredible hardships along one of the "All-Canadian routes" (the White Pass and Chilkoot trails, of course, began in Alaska), waited at the post office for seven hours to learn he had no mail. He then went to the Recorder's Office where the crowds were even worse. If he had had gold dust he might have hired a "stander," as others did, to queue up for him, but he had none so he waited in line every day from Monday to 3 P.M. Friday. When his turn finally came he was told by an official that "every likely spot within fifty miles is staked out." It was the end of the week, his first in Dawson City. He went to the North American Trading and Transportation Company's office, bought a ticket for St. Michael, and sailed on the *John G. Healy* a few days later.

Years later, of course, men like this could laugh at their Klon-

dike experiences, turn them into a moving saga for their grandchildren, and reminisce with other stampeders at the Sourdough
Conventions in Seattle. But now, as their dreams came crashing
down around them, they brooded over their ill luck, their poor
timing, the expectations that had defrauded them, the Klondike
that had deceived them, the madness of their journey from the
beginning, the houses they had mortgaged, the seniority they had
lost, the savings accounts they had withdrawn, the wives they
had left.

But hope dies hard, and in its terminal agonies it is not particular about its sustenance. In Dawson City in 1898, for example, a
wild stampede into the circumambient bush would do. Weekly,
even daily, these occurred: a man waits in line at the Recorder's
Office; he is grizzled and grimy, obviously just back from a prospecting trip to some remote place. He records his claim, then gets
some tools and supplies and starts back to work it. All along he
has been carefully watched by dozens of the claimless throng on
Front Street. So when he leaves they follow one after the other;
some in fact have kept packs of grub and blankets at the ready
for just such an occasion. After hours or days of slogging through
the trailless wilderness, the Pied Piper leads them to a dismal
creek in a boggy willow jungle where he has his discovery claim.
It is a miserable place, alive with mosquitoes all summer and
dead with cold all winter; and they stake it from source to mouth.
Then they all scramble back to Dawson City to record. Next day
they will all be seen shuffling up and down Front Street again,
hoping against hope that the Pied Piper, who remained to sink a
shaft, will find gold on the creek. And even before the word gets
around that he discovered only mica and pyrites, they are off
again on another wild goose chase. It was said at the time that
shipping companies started stampedes up or down the Yukon
from Dawson to augment traffic, that roadhouse keepers whispered news of bullion-paved creek beds nearby when business
was slack, but it is improbable that the stampeders needed any
inducement. Certainly no steamboat or roadhouse was involved
when they staked the moosehide scar on Midnight Dome, just in
back of Dawson, nor when they tried to claim Dawson itself, or
the islands in the middle of the Yukon.

Not everybody who came to Dawson in 1898 came to grief. Most who prospered there, however, had come in search of markets instead of mines. Mr. Gandolfo sold his oranges and apples at a dollar apiece, and one of his competitors brought in a watermelon, Dawson's first, and got twenty-five dollars for it. In August a man arrived with a cargo of cats and kittens. He suffered the ridicule of his trailmates en route, but he sold the animals for ten dollars each; they were just the thing for the lonely miner in his mouse-ridden cabin. One merchant parlayed his profits on a load of ten-cent cigars he sold for a dollar fifty each into a fortune of many thousands. "These mines in Dawson can be worked winter and summer," he commented, and he never saw a placer mine the whole time, nor ever hoped to see one.

The rough census made by the police in midsummer, 1898, indicated that Dawson City had a population of seventeen thousand to eighteen thousand, with another four to five thousand on the nearby creeks. It was the biggest city in northwestern Canada. Buildings stretched solidly back from Front Street and Second Avenue all the way to Ninth Avenue. Beyond that, on the flanks of Midnight Dome, was a suburb of tents. From George Street, on the north end of town, to Craig Street, by the Klondike, it was well over a mile, and every one of the blocks William Ogilvie laid out in between was now occupied. Corner lots on Front Street went for as much as forty thousand dollars. On the banks of the Yukon it was rare not to see three or four sternwheelers tied up at any given time between May and October, for a grand fleet of sixty now plied the river. The ACC⁰., for years represented only by the tiny *Yukon,* dead weight tonnage about thirty, now ran a fleet of seven, three of them over a thousand tons. Dawson had by now three newspapers, two banks, a telephone service, a brewery, and two sawmills which ran night and day and were still behind on orders. The Roman Catholics were joined by the Anglicans, the Presbyterians, the Salvation Army, the Masons, and the Odd Fellows. There was an establishment offering "Russian, Turkish, Medicated and Plain Baths: Vitality Restoring" and dozens of stores, one of which advertised

DRUGS   DRUGS
Rubber boots, Shoes, Etc.
Bacon, flour, rolled oats, rice, sugar, potatoes,
onions, tea and coffee, fruits,
cornmeal, german sausage,
Dogs Dogs

Clearly, Dawson City had come of age.

18   Gone to Gnome

He is a word in the wind, a brother to the fog. At the scene of his activity no memory of him will remain. The gravel that he thawed and sifted will freeze again. In the shanty that he builded, the she-wolf will rear her poddy litter, and from its eaves the moose will crop the esculent icicle unafraid. The snows will close over his trail and all be as before.

—Ambrose Bierce in The San Francisco *Examiner*

DAWSON CITY was born in 1896, rushed through pubescence and adolescene in 1897, reached adulthood in 1898, middle age in 1899, and old age at the turn of the century. The years of its vigor thus number three, and the years of its decline some sixty-eight.

By 1899 many tales of disillusion had reached the Outside and what had been a torrent of gold seekers the year before dwindled to a trickle. The very meaning of the word "Klondike" underwent a drastic change: whereas in 1898 the phrase "It's a real Klondike" was a popular way to describe any particularly bright prospect, two years later the phrase, "Oh, go to the Klondike!", meaning "Go get lost," was current. And where the word didn't acquire connotations of hoax, it was simply forgotten, buried under the excited chauvinism of the Spanish-American War.

As the influx slowed, the exodus of the disappointed quickened. The easiest route home, and the cheapest (for many were broke),

217

was via the Yukon to St. Michael, and thence to the West Coast
by steamship. Thousands made this trip in the summer of 1898,
and many more followed the next year. George Pilcher, a gold
seeker *manqué* who ran a wood station for the stern-wheelers on
the lower river, noted the exodus in his diary:

Tues. Aug. 2, 1898: I talk to many Klondikers all tell a hard story
and are more anxious to get out than was to get in. . . . Am camped
with three Austrilians [sic] from Klondike. They say its [sic] a farce
500 miners rush to Stuart [sic] river and not one color of gold
found.
Thurs. June 8, 1899: Clear and pleasant. Hundreds returning in
Rowboats bound for Home and only one man a Californian. Impressed [enough so that] he will return.
Sunday, June 18, 1899: Dozens of Discouraged people in small
steamers and rowboats. One took supper with me; he is an old miner
and dead broke . . . muskitoes getting bad I am a trifle *blue.*

Then, during the summer of 1899, the first reliable reports of
the new placer strikes at Nome reached Dawson. Here was a
second chance, a hope of salvaging a foundering enterprise on the
golden beaches of Norton Sound. Perhaps there, at least, not
everything would be staked. Signs saying "Gone to Gnome" were
hurriedly tacked up on cabin doors and during the single month
of August 1899 some eight thousand people left Dawson. Many
more left in the next two years, and the 1903 stampede to Fairbanks, Alaska, drained Dawson still further.

Even without the disillusion or the new Alaskan placer fields,
Dawson was bound to dwindle. Already before the turn of
the century agents of the big New York and London mining
companies were buying up whole blocks of claims on the
Klondike creeks. Within a few years they would have millions
invested in hydraulic and dredging machinery that could
process more gravel in an afternoon than a couple of old-
fashioned miners could handle in a whole winter. By 1910,
miles of rich creekbed had been acquired by the Guggen-
heim interests, locally known as the "Guggies," who controlled
the Yukon Gold Company. The hand miner working only with

a pick, a shovel and a strong back was becoming as obsolete as the proverbial shoemaker of the Industrial Revolution.

Socially as well, the old-time prospector was beginning to find himself out of place. He was an anarchist at heart, but Dawson was settling down to conformity, respectability, and class distinctions. How was he to feel in his element at the balls now regularly given at the ornate, Edwardian Commissioner's Residence, with its pillars and chandeliers, its walnut-paneled drawing room and gilt wallpaper? As a guest arrived there he dropped his engraved card on a silver salver, and, after the grand march, joined discreetly with his partner for a dignified quadrille. Between dances he refreshed himself with pineapple sherbet and stuffed olives. The women were dressed in Paris gowns from Mme. Aubert's dress shop, and the men were expected to wear tails.

Tails? What the hell are tails anyhow? Why you sure didn't need them when the M & M was still going. There all you had to do was plunk down your poke and go into action when Eddie hollered, "C'mon boys, grab yourselves a girl and we're gonna have a nice juicy waltz." Tails? Why you didn't even need to keep your gumboots on at the M & M. And between dances you devoted yourself to The Juice of the Snake, while afterwards you could rent your partner's body for the night.

Of course a miner of the old school wouldn't be invited to the balls at the Commissioner's Residence, for these were the social entertainments of the elite that had now jelled at the top of Dawson society. The commissioner (territorial governor) and his wife were the leaders of this elite, and it included the upper echelon Guggies, the commander of the mounted police, the town's doctors, bankers, lawyers, and the wives of all of these.

Needless to say, Dawson's upper crust, especially its female ingredient, took a dim view of the daughters of Lilith, and in due course had them evicted again, this time to Lousetown, clear across the Klondike River. One of the advantages of the new location was that, in the perpetual light of summer at least, an errant husband could be quickly spotted as he crossed the bridge that led over from Dawson.

For a while prosperity followed the girls to Lousetown, in spite of the bridge. Laura Berton, who arrived in Dawson in 1907 to teach kindergarten, was piqued by curiosity about this now forbidden, thrice-exiled demimonde. One summer's day she and a fellow teacher crept stealthily up to the flank of the hill overlooking Lousetown. The scene below reminded her of a Breughel canvas.

At the back doors of the tiny frame houses, the whores, laughing and singing, calling out to each other and chattering like bright birds, were making their toilet for the evening. Some were washing their long hair—invariably bright gold or jet black—drying it in the sun and leisurely brushing it out. Others were just reclining langourously and gossiping with their neighbors. Some were singing lyrically. All were in their chemises. Our eyes started from our heads as we gazed down on them, for these garments were quite short, scarcely down to the knees. . . . The chemises were also sleeveless, which seemed equally immodest, and cut with a low round neck. As they were made of colored muslin—pink, blue and yellow—the effect was indescribably gay.

Within a few years Dawson was no longer able to support the brothels of Lousetown. One after another the little frame houses were boarded up and each season further faded the names painted on their doors. Most of the girls left, while a few countered the slump by becoming honorable, even prudish, wives. Even Diamond-Tooth Gertie was deemed thoroughly reformed and socially acceptable to the elite after she married one of Dawson's leading lawyers. At first, it is true, there was a torrent of Victorian outrage, but after this subsided, Gertie's dental gem shone brightly o'er the long polished dinner table at the commissioner's.

Obviously Dawson City was no longer a remote mining camp lost in the taiga, no more a bivouac of émigrés from the workaday world. By 1900, Front Street was paved and bordered with sidewalks. The buildings along it were made of planed lumber according to architect's specifications; there were no log cabins, no windows of pickle jars or green moosehide, no lettuce gardens on the roofs, which were now of galvanized sheet iron.

At the Regina Hotel the printed menu listed *langouste à la*

Newburgh, and *petits pois au beurre,* which were served on Limoges porcelain while a five piece string orchestra played. Neither beans nor sourdough bread were to be had there. And at the Fairview there were potted ferns and Belgian carpets in the lobby. At St. Andrew's Church (Anglican), the organist Mr. Searelle could count on a good turnout for his evening concerts of Handel and Gabrieli.

In July 1900, the White Pass and Yukon Route Railway was completed so that freight and passengers could be quickly transported from tidewater at Skagway over the Coast Mountains to Whitehorse, the village that had grown up at the head of river navigation just below Miles Canyon. From there it was four hundred and sixty miles by stern-wheeler to Dawson. In 1897 it had taken Tappan Adney over two months to make the journey from Skagway. Now anyone, no matter how feeble, could do it in three or four days; and the railway traveler could catch glimpses of the whitened bones and abandoned outfits in Dead Horse Gulch between puffs on his cigar. In the old days news of the Outside reached Dawson as a muffled echo; in 1897, for example, Bob Fitzsimmons' victory over Gentleman Jim Corbett was three months old when Dawson learned about it. Now, at the turn of the century, communication with the Outside was instantaneous, at least when the telegraph lines weren't down. In Dawson itself, and even in Lousetown, there were telephones and electricity.

In 1900 gold production in the Dawson Mining District reached its peak of $22,000,000. By 1911 the figure had fallen to $4,100,000, and a decade later to $1,200,000. Since the production of bullion was the city's sole *raison d'être,* the population showed a similar trend. In 1901, Dawson had 9,142 inhabitants, about half the total enumerated in the unofficial police census of midsummer 1898. During the next decade the population declined to 3,013, and a decade after that, in 1921, it stood at 975. Each fall those who could afford to spend the winter in more salubrious climes would board the last river boats outbound from Dawson. Invariably they all swore that they would be back, and just as invariably some were missing when the spring boats arrived. Dawson's population was "trickling from it like water from a leaky barrel," wrote Laura Berton, who observed the process over many years. Abandoned buildings—homes, hotels, saloons, churches, stores, even Lowe's Mortuary—came to outnumber occupied ones, and good houses could be had for a song. In 1897 Tappan Adney could not afford the $1,000 being asked for an unfurnished one-room log cabin, while fifteen years later Mrs. Berton and her husband bought a large frame house complete with china, rugs, furniture and bedding for $700. As the town shrank, the Dawson *News*, the only paper left, went triweekly. The Methodists and the Christian Scientists gave up the good work and departed. The Fairview and the Regina hotels were boarded up, the last dance hall closed. In 1916 even the Commissioner's Residence was closed, though its fine crystal and silver plate were not sold but stored away against a time of renewed prosperity that never came. Ninth Avenue, the street farthest in from the Yukon, was consumed by invading alders, and on Eighth, Seventh, even on Fourth, the growing gaps between buildings were filled with rampant fireweed and tall grass.

By the end of the First World War, Dawson no longer had enough residents to populate two social classes, and the rigid distinctions that had come with respectability were forgotten. The townspeople became one big family, though a poorer, smaller, and older one, increasingly ingrown, and given over to gossip. The democracy of the Gold Rush returned, though without the overtures of anarchism, or any of the grand flamboyance of those old lost days. The reigning Kings of the Eldorado were English shareholders now (for the Guggies too had left), and they did not come to Dawson, much less broadcast gold dust like grass seed over its muddy flood plain. Those whose places they had usurped were gone too, nor did many of them have any gold dust left to fling; most were back in rubber boots, and toiling as before they had ever heard of Dawson, and the interlude of patent leather and leisure time was but an incredible memory among them.

On August 17 there was always a parade in Dawson City. George Carmack, Skookum Jim and Tagish Charlie had staked their claims on Rabbit Creek that day in 1896 and in a way this was the town's beginning. By 1930 the Discovery Day Parade had become so short it could no longer reach the full length of a 450-foot Dawson block. The paraders, many of them, had snow white hair now, and stooped shoulders, and their stride was slow and stiff. They marched bravely up Front Street from the old Commissioner's Residence. Then, at the corner of King, they turned right in the direction of Ninth Avenue, long since obliterated. They trudged slowly past the old Auditorium Theatre. It had been boarded up for nearly two decades now: a mute mausoleum with no Turkish Whirlwind Danseuse to swirl the thickening layers of dust, no Oregon Mare to whinny back at the silence. And when the parade ended some of the marchers went back to the Hospital of St. Anne. It was primarily an old age home now.

19 Missionaries

> They treat the Fathers wonderfully, especially
> Noidolan, a pious woman. . . . When the Fathers
> reached Koyekasten in their canoe, she addressed
> them as follows: "I have washed my house beau-
> tifully for you and arranged it so that God may
> grant me that I may wash my soul well through
> confession and contrition."
>
> —Nulato House Diary, Sept. 23, 1902
> [in Jules Jetté's hand]

> Even now I hate hearing confessions, and still
> more giving communion, for fear of profana-
> tions: I cannot bring myself to believe that they
> are sincere, except a few, of course . . . but the
> bulk of them is a *massa damnata*.
>
> —Jules Jetté to Father Provincial
> [dated Kokrines, Dec. 19, 1907]

DAWSON CITY was not the last placer boom town on the Yukon,
though it was by far the largest. Deep within Alaska the town of
Ruby blossomed from nothing in 1911, and down near the river's
mouth, where the tundra begins, Marshall sprouted a few years
later. Neither is quite a full-fledged ghost town today, but like
Dawson, both have their rotting board sidewalks that no longer
lead anywhere, their tilted, empty buildings, and stranded old
miners who pan a meager subsistence from memories and old age

assistance. Like Dawson, these towns declined after a few frenzied seasons, and this of course was their obvious destiny, part of the natural life cycle of such places.

Gold, like all minerals, is what economists call a "nonrenewable resource," and placer gold especially is snatched quickly from the earth. Each time it was discovered on the Yukon men rushed in, scraped, scoured and scarred the landscape, built towns like Forty Mile, Dawson and Ruby, and imported the trappings of civilization into the wilderness. So for a time the river teemed with the comings and goings of men, and its old silence was hushed. But these men did not come to the Yukon to be the progenitors of a local race, they came to seize what they sought and take it away with them. They were no more renewable than the placers, and gone just as quickly.

The missionaries brought more abiding concerns to the Yukon. They brought truth and salvation, as they conceived of these, and they found error and evil to be inexhaustible human resources. They were on the river before the first placers were discovered; they watched the miners come and build towns; and they saw the miners leave and the towns crumble. They stayed on, and are still there today.

Exactly when the first missionary reached the Yukon is uncertain. A letter is preserved in the Orthodox Church archives in Sitka in which Innokenty, Bishop of Kamchatka, the Kuriles and Russian America, informs the Holy Ruling Synod in Moscow that he plans "to establish a new mission on Kuikpak [Yukon] River," and that "Priest Jacob Netzvetov, as one of the most experienced and best missionaries, will be sent there." The letter is dated February 10, 1845. Unfortunately the surviving records give us only the most fragmentary sketch of Priest Netzvetov, the first Yukon missionary. We know that he was a creole, and that he graduated from the seminary in Irkutsk, Siberia, in 1826, a surprisingly early date considering that the Russian-American Company had been chartered only twenty-seven years before. He had served on Atka, one of the Aleutians, where he translated the Gospel of Saint Matthew into the Aleut tongue. He was a careful

observer and a good writer, and reading his fascinating account
of Russian life and sea otter hunts on Atka makes one regret all
the more that the journal of his Yukon experiences has not survived.

The site chosen for the new mission was the Eskimo village of
Ikogmut* about two hundred miles from the mouth of the
"Kuikpak." Priest Netzvetov probably first went there in 1846 or
1847, but it was not until December 1851 that, in Bishop Innokenty's words, "the wooden church built on the northwest
coast of America at Ikogmut village . . . was consecrated to the
glory of the Holy Life-giving Cross." Shortly after this Netzvetov
established a school, the first one on the Yukon. The Russian-
American Company had a trading post at Ikogmut, established
by Glazunov in 1836 or 1837, and Netzvetov's first pupils were
company employees. In time, however, native children were enrolled, a fact that may help to explain the deep roots the Russian
Church struck there.

Orthodoxy is still a vital force in Ikogmut; indeed, it is about
the only living vestige of the Russian presence that remains on
the Yukon. The church on the hill back of the village is topped
with a diminutive blue onion dome and three double crosses.
Father Vasili Chungsak, a pure-blooded Eskimo, preaches in his
native tongue, chants in English, and reads Scripture from a huge
Church Slavonic bible. From the church walls saints look down,
bearded and benevolent, from darkened paintings brought over
in the days of the colony. On either side of the altar a standard
bears the image of a swarthy, full-fleshed Slavic Christ.

The great days of the village are the feast days of the Orthodox
calendar, especially Christmas which falls during the first week of
January. Preparations begin weeks before. Men arrive from Outside aboard the bush plane, or merely from their trap lines.
Women bake and mix up washtubs full of *agudak*, an Eskimo
delicacy made of berries, seal oil (or, more and more, Crisco),
shredded whitefish or pike, and sugar. On the afternoon before
Christmas, Father Chungsak supervises the lighting of the lan-

* Now called Russian Mission.

terns which will burn at all recent graves for the four days of the feast. Later that day, about eight, the priest rings the church bells to summon his flock for the first of many Christmas services. The women wear their best dresses and, since their heads must be covered, bright new railroaders' handkerchiefs knotted under the chin. The men too are in their most formal clothes, and, for the lucky ones, this means the uniform of the Alaska National Guard. Next day, after the morning service, the villagers gather in groups to go from cabin to cabin caroling in Russian and Eskimo. They carry a large, sparkling star, symbol of the star of Bethlehem, and their songs announce the birth of their Saviour. After a few carols outside a cabin they are invited to enter and enjoy a feast of dried salmon, *agudak*, Spam, porcupine, moose noses—anything that the host can provide. Like the caroling, the banquet is solemn; voices are subdued and there is no drinking or jovial laughter: Christmas is more serious in Ikogmut than in most American communities.

By the time Netzvetov left Ikogmut, in June 1863, both the Anglicans and the Catholics had appeared on the Yukon. The Russian priest could not have known of their presence, however, for they came west from Canada and confined their activities to the upper river. William Kirkby, an Anglican, was the first to arrive, reaching Fort Yukon with the annual supply boats of the Hudson's Bay Company on July 6, 1861. He stayed only a week and did not know the Takudh language, so one wonders what to make of his claim that

Medicine-men openly renounced their craft—polygamists freely offered to give up their wives—murderers confessed their crimes and mother told of deeds of infanticide, that sickened one to hear. Then all earnestly sought for pardon and grace. Oh! it was a goodly sight . . .

Deacon Robert McDonald, another Anglican, found in his many years of combat against them that ancestral practices were not so easily changed. McDonald came to Fort Yukon the year after Kirkby, as did Father Seguin, a French-Canadian Oblate.

Seguin was thus the first Roman Catholic missionary on the Yukon, but he left after a single winter. McDonald on the other hand spent nine years around Fort Yukon and the best part of four decades in the adjacent part of Canada. He married a Loucheux Indian girl, and his grandchildren still live in Old Crow, a village on the Canadian section of the Porcupine River. He became fluent in the Takudh tongue, and his translations of the Gospels are still in use. An expert dogdriver, he traveled widely in the Fort Yukon area, visiting remote Indian bands that would not see another priest for a generation. Years later, in 1905, another Fort Yukon missionary named Hudson Stuck came upon such a band. He was amazed to find that the people had preserved as valuable treasures the prayer books McDonald had translated and given them, and that one of their number conducted regular services, as the deacon had taught him.

They were still praying to Our Sovereign Lady, Queen Victoria, and Albert Edward, Prince of Wales [writes Stuck], and I suppose are still; for though I took a lead pencil and struck out these prayers, and tried to explain that they were living under the Government of the United States, and that Queen Victoria was dead, I doubt if my remarks made much impression against what they had been taught by Archdeacon McDonald, whose memory they revere. And I cannot blame them much; they owe us little enough—I was the first missionary of the American Church [that is, Episcopal as opposed to Anglican] who had visited them.

Robert McDonald left Fort Yukon finally in 1871, two years after the Hudson's Bay Company had been ordered to depart, and from then until the late 1880s there were no missions on the river at all save those of the Orthodox. However, several Catholic missionaries made voyages through the region. The most notable of them was the Right Reverend Charles Seghers, who, as Bishop of Vancouver Island, was responsible for Roman Catholic missionary activities in Alaska. He reached Nulato from St. Michael in the summer of 1877 and spent the following winter evangelizing the Koyukon Indians of the area. Finding them quite receptive to his teaching, he decided to establish a permanent mission there in the future. He returned to the Yukon in 1886, this time via the Chilkoot Pass, to begin work on the new mission of Our Lady of the Snows, as he had already decided to call it.* Seghers was accompanied by Fathers Tosi and Robaut, both Jesuits, and Frank Fuller, a lay assistant. The Jesuits wintered on the upper Yukon, planning to go on in the spring to Nulato. There they would rejoin the Bishop and Fuller who had continued on down-river without them. Even before the party split up, this man Fuller had occasionally acted in a very peculiar manner. On Bennett Lake, for example, he had shot a bear; long after it was dead he ran around screaming and pumping bullets into it. In Miles Canyon he got drenched in the spume and loudly accused the priests of wanting to drown him. Later on, as he and the Bishop approached Nulato, the latter penned the following entries in his diary:

Nov. 19. Fuller asks me how it can be that I encourage the Indians to make fun of him. For five years the Indians did the same thing in the [Rocky] Mountains [he says].

Nov. 20. Fuller asks me why I sent one of our Indians ahead to burn the sleigh and himself, Fuller.

Nov. 25. Fuller says that Walker [a trader they had encountered at the mouth of the Tanana] predicted to him that I would give him a bad name.

When Seghers wrote the entry for Friday, November 25, 1886, he was only two days from Nulato; he planned to arrive on Sunday in time to celebrate Mass for the converts he had made there nearly a decade before. It was his last entry. After writing it he

---

* He chose this name because of the following incident: One morning during his 1877–78 sojourn in Nulato a band of Indian fishermen came to visit his camp. He took the opportunity to explain Christian doctrine to them, and was much pleased with the the attentive response. The lesson done, the Indians departed and the Bishop did not expect or even invite them to return. That afternoon, however, they reappeared, asking to hear more of his message. He was profoundly moved, and since the date was August 5, the feast of Our Lady of the Snows, he decided on this name for the mission he planned to establish.

lay down to sleep in a bearskin robe. Very early the next morning
he was suddenly awakened. Fuller stood over him. He shouted
paranoid accusations and brandished his rifle. A few seconds later
he fired point-blank at the Bishop's chest. The Bishop slumped
back on his bearskin and died. Fuller's bullet had pierced his
aorta. Several weeks after this Fuller, in the custody of a miner
and two Indians who towed the Bishop's body on a sled, reached
St. Michael. Fuller announced to the ACC⁰. district manager,
Henry Neumann, "I have brought Bishop Seghers." "Where is
he?" asked Neumann. "He is on the sled," Fuller replied calmly.
"I killed him."

Because of Bishop Seghers' death, the Roman Catholic mission
at Nulato was not started until the fall of 1887. During the summer of that year the Episcopalians arrived at Anvik, one hundred
seventy-five miles farther down the Yukon, and so to them goes
the credit for establishing the first American mission on the river.
The moving spirit behind this mission was John Wight Chapman,
a soft-spoken, self-effacing New Englander who came to Anvik in
his twenties and left in his seventies. The mission he founded is
still going today, and the older people in Anvik still cherish the
memory of "The Doctor" and "the man who spoke Indian better
than us." The conditions under which Chapman worked, the
problems he faced, the joys and disappointments he experienced,
were much like those of other early Yukon missionaries. As with
the early Anglicans and Catholics, a profound religious sense led
him to accept—and come to love—a primitive, uncomfortable,
often dangerous life. And though deeply religious, he was no
pietist, and surely would have accepted the maxim of his Jesuit
neighbors upriver to "act as if everything depends on you and
pray as if everything depends on God." As other Yukon missionaries in these pre-ecumenical days, he was a sectarian, though he
avoided the extremes to which some of them went.*

_____

* In his very first letter from Fort Yukon, the Anglican Deacon Robert
McDonald has harsh words for the Catholics, accusing them of trying to
make Indian converts by intimating that Queen Victoria had been converted
to "Romanism." Jules Jetté, S.J., who served for many years in the Nulato
area, described Protestantism as a "body in decomposition, breaking up into

"To a man brought up in Vermont, as I have been," Chapman once wrote, "no other country looks quite right." And Alaska, when he first beheld it, looked "as abnormal as anything could possibly be." His preparations for the voyage had not even included a perusal of the scant Alaskana of the times—the books of Whymper, Dall and Schwatka, and Ivan Petroff's report for the Census of 1880—and he had never ventured much west of the Green Mountains. Before he arrived his conception of the territory was based on such impressionistic fragments as the Tlingit totem poles he had seen in the Museum of Natural History while a seminary student in New York City. "They were not reassuring," he noted. "They made one think of that iron statue of Moloch in the valley of Hinnom."

Chapman debarked from the ACC⁰. steamer at St. Michael on June 26, 1887. There was only a handful of whites at the old Russian post, and one of them was Frank Fuller. Each Friday, Chapman was told, he would fly into a violent paroxysm and shriek that he had to be in Nulato in time for Sunday Mass. Early in July, Chapman watched as a detachment of marines from the revenue cutter *Bear* hauled him out of his tent and shackled him; he was being taken to Sitka where he would be convicted of manslaughter and sentenced to ten years' hard labor. Chapman heard about other cases of insanity in the Yukon valley. "The lonely surroundings were such that we could easily believe these tales," he wrote. "We considered the question, whether the nature of our errand were such that it would safeguard us against such a fate. We believed that it would." Alaska was an ominous as well as an abnormal place; perhaps the totem poles had faithfully captured its spirit.

---

various offensive compounds," and Orthodoxy as "an embalmed mummy." The Orthodox, for their part, spread a rumor according to which the Jesuits fed native children to caged serpents they housed in their boarding school. This situation has changed greatly in recent years, and Protestant-Catholic relations are generally cordial. At present, Francis Gleason, Catholic Bishop of Northern Alaska, and William Gordon, Episcopal Bishop of Alaska, are co-chairmen of a joint missionary committee on native socioeconomic problems.

The second person of the "we" in the above passage refers to the Reverend Octavius Parker. He had been sent out the year before by the Episcopal Board of Missions (which sponsored Chapman as well), to establish a mission somewhere in the vicinity of St. Michael. Some Ingalik Indians from Anvik had come to trade at St. Michael, and they invited Parker to visit their village. This he had done in March 1887. The Ingaliks wanted him to settle there and treated him with great kindness. One morning, for example, Parker awoke to discover that one of the villages had erected a shelter of poles and cloth over his sleeping form when it had started to snow the previous night. Before the end of his visit, Parker decided to establish his mission there and purchased two log buildings from the departing ACC[0]. trader. He then went back to St. Michael to wait for the *St. Paul* to arrive with the supplies he would need at Anvik. Chapman was one of the ship's passengers. His own orders were indefinite; he had considered going up the Bering coast to work among the Eskimos, but he readily accepted Parker's invitation to join him at Anvik. The missionaries bought an old boat at St. Michael, patched it up, and loaded it with a year's supplies. They arranged to have a stern-wheeler tow them upriver to Anvik.

We reached the village on the 21st day of July, 1887 [writes Chapman]. The natives were all out to see the arrival of the boat, the old men sitting in a row at the top of the high sand bank, knees drawn up to their chins under their parkis, the empty sleeves fluttering in the wind; little children [ran] about and the young men were ready to carry our goods up to our cabins. . . . Something of a sense of loneliness came over me as I landed among a strange people, who spoke or understood hardly a word of English. . . .

This was the first day of the first of forty-three years John Wight Chapman would spend at Anvik.

The eldest son of a pious Vermont sheep farmer, Chapman was just twenty-nine then. Until a few years before, he had regarded the ministry as an "inferior profession" and was bent on an artistic career, but a change of heart sent him to the General Theological Seminary in New York. He was drawn to missionary work, and to Alaska particularly, because of the total neglect his church, the nation's richest, had shown for the territory. Early in 1887 he became engaged to the daughter of one of his professors at Middlebury College, Mary Seely. Shortly thereafter he was ordained by the Bishop of Vermont, and the next day he took a train for San Francisco en route to Alaska. He would not see his fiancée again for six years, but he wrote her frequently. In these letters he describes his experiences at Anvik in much detail; it is as though he sought to assuage his loneliness by sending her fragments of his life. Chapman's son, Rev. Henry H. Chapman, has kindly made these letters available, and much of the rest of this chapter is based on them.

Upon arrival in Anvik, Chapman and Parker moved into one of the two cabins the latter had purchased that spring. It was a relatively large building, and by the time Chapman refitted the doors and rechinked the walls he could describe it to Mary Seely as "one of the most magnificent log houses that ever was." Later, when the cold weather came, three quarters of an inch of ice formed on the windowpanes, blocking out what little daylight there was, and the 15° inside temperatures made life precarious for Mr. Parker's much-coddled geraniums. In general, though, their living quarters were as comfortable as could be expected.

Domestic chores were divided equally between the two missionaries, at least in principle, but Chapman, Parker's junior by some years, seemed to end up doing the laundry each Saturday, and chopping most of the wood. He also did the baking, and boasts to Mary Seely that his bread "almost raised the roof off the house." In the long winter evenings the missionaries read aloud from Tolstoy, Goldsmith and Shakespeare, though they did not omit to study the Gospels in the original, nor to take "a dose of History daily."

Chapman had not come to Alaska to improve his literary culture, however, but to teach the Gospel of Christ—and that of hygiene, literacy, prophylactic medicine and aboveground housing. It is indicative of the importance he and Parker gave to this

second kind of gospel that their spare cabin was made into a
schoolhouse within two months of their arrival, while Anvik had
to wait six years for its first church. Already by mid-September
1887, Chapman could write to Mary Seely that

> Our school for the past week has been quite satisfactory. The at-
> tendance has been irregular, but we usually have half a dozen, and
> their interest does not flag. . . . They are now familiar with the
> alphabet, and all count to ten, and some, to twenty, and they are
> beginning to recognize words when they see them.
>
> We adopt Mr. Squeers' principle, and when a scholar has learned
> the name of a thing we have him make a rude drawing of it under-
> neath; and this, all his own work, he takes home and we take it for
> granted that the whole family will in time learn the names of such
> things, and that the scholars will learn by answering the questions
> of those at home.
>
> They like these drawing lessons, and some make neat outlines, while
> some are terrifically ridiculous. One little fellow cannot have the pa-
> tience to distinguish between a boy's hat and his face, and locates the
> eyes, nose and mouth in the hat, while the face appears underneath as
> a huge collar.

Chapman himself was the best pupil in his school, for here he
had a chance to begin his study of the Ingalik language. To learn
it was absolutely essential if his work in Anvik was to mean
anything, for the people of the village knew only this tongue and
a little of the mongrel Russian that still served as the *lingua
franca* on the lower Yukon. Chapman never had an interpreter,
and though he made many ludicrous mistakes at first, at least he
avoided the problem that Bishop Seghers had had when he was
first in Nulato in the late 1870s. The Bishop discovered, but only
after some time, that his interpreter could not figure out how to
translate "Holy Ghost" into Koyukon, and so was spreading the
notion of a trinity of Father, Son and . . . Mother. Chapman, who
was a good linguist and grew very fond of Ingalik later on, found
it to be "one of the most fiendishly ingenious dialects known to
man." To say "Thank you" something approximating "Nox-
woquorcrigudastcet" was required, while to pronounce a more
difficult word, Chapman advises that

you first take out your larynx and scrape it,—then you put it back after having turned it inside out;—then, placing the root of your tongue against the wisdom teeth, and grasping a stove, or anything solid, you breathe gently, and you have the word and the sensation. It is a little hard at first, but . . . after it is over, you feel all right.

In time Chapman spoke Ingalik as well as anyone in Anvik. He translated the Apostles' Creed, parts of the Book of Common Prayer, and the Gospels into it, and he translated the folk tales of Anvik into English for the American Ethnological Society.

There was a more fundamental barrier than that of language, however, and in the first years Chapman sometimes doubted strongly if he could surmount it. It was a cultural barrier, a wall of incomprehension between two very different ways of doing and thinking. The Ingaliks, for their part, must have often sensed its presence and insurmountability as keenly as the missionary.

An earlier chapter has attempted to give a picture of life in Anvik at the time of Andrei Glazunov's arrival. Some things had changed in the half century since then, but many had not. The Ingaliks now used guns instead of bone-tipped arrows, and they cooked what they shot in metal instead of bark vessels. The quest for wild food still dominated their lives, however, and it still required them to be seminomadic. When they were in the village many still lived in subterranean dwellings as in Glazunov's time, and they still bathed in urine and relished rotten fish-egg soup. The shamans retained their power, and the body of beliefs on which this power rested was still largely intact.

Since Glazunov's visit the Ingaliks had had considerable contact with white traders, especially after 1869 when the ACCº. established a post in Anvik. Their view of the outside world was still very circumscribed, however, and they thought that San Francisco, the headquarters of the ACCº., was synonymous with the United States. To them the missionaries were strange men from an incredible world, an impression fortified, no doubt, when Chapman showed them some photographs of New York City he had taken in his student days. Until the missionaries came, a white man meant a trader, looking for pelts. Why were these men settling among them? What were they looking for?

The missionaries, for their part, found the Ingaliks just as strange and very primitive. For Chapman and Parker, after all, the Stone Age had ended five millennia, not five decades, ago; for them writing was as old as the hieroglyphs of the First Egyptian Dynasty, while for the people of Anvik none existed until Chapman reduced the Ingalik language to syllabics in the late 1890s. The tradition of the missionaries included Greece, the Renaissance, and now Victorianism with its rigid concepts of morality, cleanliness, and God.

"Cultural shock," as it is called nowadays, was never anything abstract for John Wight Chapman. It was a matter of tastes, sights and especially smells, of failures in communication that turned innocent actions into wilful insults, meaningless gestures into promises later broken. The most common way of avoiding the wrenches of cultural shock is to convince oneself that the strange people one is among are not really humans at all, only so many wogs, Kaffirs, A-rabs or chinks. But Chapman felt compelled, both by his creed and his humanity, to love the people he had come to serve. At the same time he was occasionally filled with loathing for them, and this conflict writhed within him. "Made in the image of God?" he once questioned in his diary. "I wonder." And in one particularly bleak and rambling passage he writes:

I sometimes wondered whether I was destined to spend my life crawling these narrow tunnels [of Anvik's underground houses] on my hands and knees, choking in the smoky interiors . . . where disheveled creatures—hair uncombed, eyes bleared from . . . smoke . . . sun . . . and snow blindness—sucked their fingers after eating their meal of boiled fish, tucking away the remnants . . . under the wooden platform upon which they sat by day and slept by night. . . . I saw many things of which I do not care to tell. Vermin life was abundant and some of its manifestations were especially revolting.

Chapman was fond of writing poetry, and some of his poems reflect this same melancholy:

> What tempts thee, o unwilling soul,
>   To these dark heights where sunset lies?
> Why chase a dying vision bright,
>   That robs thee of thy earthly prize?
>
> What special joy hath Heaven for thee,
>   To lure thee from thy quiet home,
> To drive thee from thy chosen hearth,
>   A pilgrim on the earth to roam?

Cultural shock had its humorous side as well, especially in retrospect, and Chapman had a good sense of humor. In Africa the natives used a pot of boiling water to accommodate missionaries, but in Anvik he found they employed the kashim, the underground communal house of the Ingaliks. Each afternoon the village men congregated in it for a sweat bath, and one winter day during their first year Chapman and Parker happened to be there as the bath was being readied.

Knowing what was coming [Chapman relates], I tried to persuade Mr. Parker to leave the Kashime with me until the bath was over. He insisted upon staying with our stuff, so I sat down on the floor at the entrance where the inrush of cold air insured safety, expecting to see him driven out by the heat. The fire was kindled, the blast of cold air poured down through the tunnel [which served as the entrance] and sent the fire roaring up through the smoke hole in a column of flame and smoke. The room was so full of smoke that I could not see my companion, and became alarmed. I started back to find him. The naked men lying on the shelf and already gasping for breath shouted at me to go back, to take off my parki, to lie down, and what else I do not know. When I reached Mr. Parker, I found him lying on the floor, stripping to his underwear and shrieking, 'Yith! Yith!' meaning snow. Friendly hands did for me what they had done for him. My clothing was stripped off and I was told to keep down upon the floor. The heat increased and soon became almost unbearable. My lungs were filled with smoke and I felt as though I were inhaling flame.

I found a crack between two planks and obtained some relief by putting my nose down into it. The air became a trifle cooler and I hoped that we would get through alive.

When it seemed that the end of endurance had been reached, the fire went down, the curtain was lifted and the cold air came rushing in.

Mr. Parker left Anvik after two years, and Chapman ran the mission alone for the next four. The loneliness of his situation is evident in his letters to his fiancée, but the main impression they give is of a man who has found a definite purpose and place in life which he would exchange with no one. Despite the mosquitoes of summer and the cold darkness of winter, he describes to Mary Seely "a glorious, beautiful, sunny country" which he loves "rapturously." He tells her of the delight he feels one day on the portage trail to St. Michael when the Indians first accept him as an accomplished dog driver, and again in summer when the village children bring him an armful of wild flowers on his birthday. His daily round of teaching, holding services in his cabin, and tending to domestic chores left him little time for brooding, and even woodchopping had its compensations, as when he found a phosphorescent log out of which he carved a cross to hang above his bed. And his loneliness was only for Mary Seely and others of his own kind, as he usually had a half dozen boys—orphans and the sons of Indians out on their trap lines—sharing his cabin with him.

What really sustained him, however, was the progress of his work. Christianity could not be suddenly grafted onto the Ingalik spirit, but through Chapman's patient efforts it slowly began to take root. By 1891 he had baptized most of the village children, and solemnized the unions of their parents and even grandparents. As his reputation spread up and down the Yukon, Chapman was often invited to Indian camps far from Anvik. Some of the people he visited had had no real contact with Christianity, and he was sometimes surprised to find how receptive they were to his message. On one such visit he was greeted with the utmost courtesy and hospitality, but at first his hosts would not tell him why they had summoned him. Only after a banquet of native delicacies did the leader, an old man, suddenly turn to him and command, "Now tell us what you have come to say."

The abruptness of the challenge [writes Chapman], and the con-
sciousness . . . of my own inadequacy produced in my mind a kind of
bewilderment. What could I say? What were my listeners prepared to
hear?

At that moment I seemed to see a picture of an eager multitude
waiting for the words of a greater prophet than any other. . . . I
thought, how can I do better for these poor Indians, who sometimes
have scarcely enough to live upon, and who often are called to mourn
the loss of their dear ones, than to tell them the words which the Lord
himself spoke to just such poor people.

So I told them that when the people came to Jesus to hear Him, He
said, "Blessed are the poor for God's city in Heaven is for them.
Blessed are they that mourn, for they shall be comforted. Blessed are
they that hunger after righteousness, for they shall be filled."

When Chapman finished speaking,

. . . the old man leaped to his feet and crossed the room and sat down
literally at my feet. He called to the young men to come and listen.
"There," he exclaimed, "Listen to this. This is what I wanted to hear!"

Chapman felt the material progress and physical well-being of
the Ingaliks to be nearly as important as their conversion to Episcopal Christianity. He was no doctor by formal training, but he
literally practiced medicine until he was able to practice it with
considerable skill. Soon after his arrival he appealed to friends
back home to send medical manuals, and when they came he
pored over them. They are still in Anvik today, fat tomes faded
from red to pink, and coated with the decades of dust they have
collected on the top floor of the old mission house. Nowadays the
Public Health Service takes care of Anvik's sick in a modern
hospital in Bethel, but in the 1880s and early '90s these books
made Chapman into the best doctor for hundreds of miles
around. He learned to diagnose the more common diseases, set
bones, sew up axe and gunshot wounds, even repair a smashed
skull. He had no hospital, and his patients stayed in tents, or,
often as not, in his own cabin. Chapman was also Anvik's dentist
and ophthalmologist, though his duties in the latter capacity were

not too demanding: he would simply send a handful of used eye glasses (out of the three bushels donated to the mission) to any Indian with failing vision, and request the return of all unsuitable pairs.

Brought up in a prim white Vermont farmhouse, Chapman was shocked by Ingalik standards of housing. In the fall of 1887, shortly after his arrival, he wrote to his fiancée:

I will tell you of a piece of experience we had yesterday, and you will see from what we have to rescue these people. A few rods from the house a man put up a hut just before winter set in. It was six feet high, and ten feet square, and from the outside it looks like a mound of earth just about as high as my head. We thought it must be a temporary sleeping place for some one who was a member of an overcrowded family. It took but two or three days to make. . . . We were called to see a sick woman, and found that this hut is being occupied for the winter by a young man and his wife, his brother of about 16 years, his wife's daughter of 17 or 18, and her brother of 12, children by a former husband, and two smaller children. . . . The bare statement of this is enough.

Shortly after this "piece of experience," Chapman wrote jokingly to his father that he would rather have a sawmill than one of the placer mines then being discovered up the Yukon at Forty Mile. His father, who made no more than a modest living from his flocks of Merino sheep, took the jest to heart and sent a small portable sawmill to Anvik. Chapman was "amazed and somewhat dismayed" when it arrived. "I could use a jackknife, but putting up a sawmill with a steam engine was another problem." With the help of a passing miner he managed to get it operating, however, and from then on he turned out lumber not only for mission use but for the planking, doors and window frames which the Ingaliks needed in order to replace their underground dwellings with solid, dry cabins.

In September 1892, Chapman began work on Christ Church. He needed help in cutting the logs and rafting them to Anvik, and in the following letter he tells Mary Seely how he finally got the village men to volunteer.

When I wrote . . . yesterday, I was feeling as near despondency as I have been since I came into the country, because an appeal to the men who are with me to do something toward building the church without pay had failed, and that partly through my manner of presenting it; but today after dinner I appealed to them straight, addressing them as younger brothers, for they are all young men, and reminding them of God's love and providence, "How many grouse He has given us—and our food since we were children." . . . At last they all gave way at once, after one and then another had agreed, and so it was arranged that we are to give tomorrow 'cutting for God' and it will doubtless result in a good big raft. . . . I looked up, and it did seem as though I could understand a little of that "New heavens and a new earth, wherein dwelleth righteousness."

The raft was big, and there were others. By winter all the logs were cut and ready, and in May 1893 Christ Church began to take form on a high piece of ground next to Hawk Bluff.

Chapman took his first furlough later in 1893. Mary Seely had waited for him for six years, and that October they were married in Vermont. The following summer the couple returned to Anvik, where they lived and worked almost continuously until 1930, the year of Chapman's seventy-first birthday. When they departed, they left behind a prospering mission. The chapel, which had been one room in Chapman's old cabin, had long since been replaced by the church, complete with bell and steeple; and it had recently been set on firm foundations of concrete. Anvik's boarding school which began with a student body of six boys, all living with Chapman, was now housed in a three-story building and looked after by a staff of six. It even had electric lights, a fact Chapman was fond of pointing out to his kerosene-burning Vermont relatives. For Chapman, of course, the real accomplishments of a life's work were the changes in Ingalik life he had helped to bring about. In 1930 Anvik was a village of Christians, and increasingly, of literates. The younger people no longer knew what an underground house looked like, and Doctor* Chapman,

---

* He still had no M.D., but Middlebury College, his alma mater, had awarded him the honorary degree of Doctor of Divinity.

aided by the mission's registered nurse, had put the shamans out of business.

In 1887 when Chapman came to Anvik there were three stern-wheelers on the Yukon; a dozen years later three of them often passed Anvik in a single day. By 1930, the year he retired, there were hardly more than at the beginning. The placer towns they had supplied were fast being claimed by fireweed and silence. The men they had carried were gone. That year Chapman turned over Christ Church to his son, the Reverend Henry H. Chapman.

20 The Native People II

The wonderful catch of fish, the good hunting of beavers and land otters . . . and foxes in the vicinity provide all the necessities of their life.

—Lieutenant L. A. Zagoskin,
Account of Pedestrian Journeys in the
Russian Possessions in America in 1842,
'43 and '44

There's nothing for them here.

—Andrew Demoski, President of
the Town Council, Nulato, Alaska

As WE have seen, Bishop Seghers' destination in 1886 was Nulato, and his objective was to found a Roman Catholic mission there. He was murdered just the day before he would have arrived. The two Jesuits who accompanied him for the first part of the trip had stopped to winter on the upper Yukon, planning to rejoin the Bishop in Nulato the following spring. Naturally, they expected to find him at work on the new mission there. Instead they found his body in a dark corner of St. Michael's old Orthodox church; it lay in an ice-packed coffin awaiting shipment to Victoria, B. C., for proper burial. One of the Jesuits, Father Pascal Tosi, took the first steamer out of St. Michael to bear the news to the outside world. Tosi was a veteran of many difficult years in the Rocky Mountain missions, and it was characteristic of him, both as a man and as a Jesuit, that as soon as he had delivered his sad

message he set out to do what Bishop Seghers had been prevented from accomplishing. He recrossed the Chilkoot and again descended the Yukon. He reached Nulato in October 1887, and from then on the mission of Our Lady of the Snows has been active there. Today the staff consists of a Jesuit priest, Father Hargreaves, who conducts services in a neat little yellow church, two Sisters of St. Anne, who teach in the new grade school, and Brother Fox, a great bear of a man who is diesel mechanic, carpenter, boatbuilder, dog musher, and plumber, among other things. Of the staff members Brother Fox has served longest in the Alaskan wilderness, and his one regret is that he didn't come "before it got so darn civilized up here."

The mission complex is located just downstream from the village, and the two share a boggy little valley opening out on the Yukon. Back from the river, to the west, the valley gradually gives way to a range of hills. They are worn and low, hardly suggestive of the dramatic ecological frontier they delimit. On the far side of them begins the tundra of the Bering Sea littoral, the barren ground of Eskimos, caribou, lichens and lemmings. The coniferous forest that covers nearly the entire Yukon valley comes to a scraggly stunted end at this divide. Beyond it the

moose, the marten and the beaver go only as strays. And the Athapascan Indians, who inhabit the country all the way from the Mackenzie River, go no farther west than Nulato.

Across the Yukon, to the east of the village, the Kaiyuh Flats stretch away across a level and monotonous landscape. A hundred and thirty years ago, when the Russian explorer Malakov reached this region, the Flats teemed with beaver, and it was mainly because of this that he built his fur trading post at Nulato. Today they are getting scarce and the Alaska Department of Fish and Game has set a quota of fifteen beaver per trapper per season. Enforcement is another matter, however, and one Nulato man explains that this regulation doesn't bother him because, even in a good year, he can never catch fifteen quotas anyway.

Although there are sixteen hundred acres of Alaskan land per Alaskan inhabitant,* Nulato's log cabins, doghouses, caches, smokehouses and outhouses are clustered together nearly eave to eave. Inside the cabins the crowding is even worse. In one of them, a single room affair, an unofficial census turned up thirteen Koyukon Indians of three generations, an arrogant young Cana-

* Compared to the United States average of 11.3 acres per person.

dian goose, a robin and two small dogs. The goose, according to
its owner, would serve as the family pet only until Thanksgiving.
In the narrow alleys between the cabins scrofulous children
splotched with impetigo while away the brief summer at play
with their pals and their puppies.

The muddy river beach in front of town is cluttered with
weathered flat-bottom plank boats, fish nets, drying racks where
dog salmon hang like orange laundry, chained dogs, and drift
logs snatched from the river as they floated by. In winter the
town's refuse is dumped on the river ice; but the spring breakup,
which acts as garbage man, is quite unreliable and sometimes
shunts the refuse raft in to the beach where it melts out from
under its burden. The beach is littered with rusting tin cans once
full of Hawaiian Punch and Carnation Evaporated Milk, as good
a sign as any that the people of Nulato no longer live off the
land.

The change from self-sufficiency to nearly complete depend-
ence on the outside world is the paramount fact of recent history
in Nulato, as in every other native village among the Yukon. The
Hawaiian Punch came from faraway, and so did Nulato's language, religion, laws and tools, as well as many features of its
social organization, mores and outlook.

In Nulato there is a particularly good record of the changes
that have taken place in the last three quarters of a century. The
missionaries were naturally much concerned with these changes
and, beginning with Father Tosi, every priest who served there
entered his account of day to day events in what the Jesuits call a
house diary. The following excerpts from the Nulato House
Diary, translated from Latin and kindly supplied by William
Loyens, S.J., sketch the transformation that has taken place.

Jan. 16, 1891: After a few words [of a sermon] about shamans and
the necessity to rely upon God alone for help . . . Guzota (he is the
shaman) began to speak loudly. The father told him to stop & keep
still. But the impious man said: 'Though I prayed a good deal, I never
got anything from God.' The priest told him to go outdoors; he uttered

more blasphemy & finally went out, trying to bring all the people with him.

March 24, 1892: N.B. We found out for sure, that the Indian feasts for the dead cannot be allowed to those who want to be Christians. It is truly a superstitious practice, & we must keep our Christians away from such matters.

Dec. 13, 1892: Trial of catechism at Korkorine's place [a little village upriver from Nulato]: people very badly disposed. Did not want even to have their children baptized.

Aug. 11, 1900 [At the height of the great influenza epidemic]: In the morning we hear of the deaths of Kosal'o, an old woman who once was shaman, and of Paul Ugara. . . . Care of the sick. About 2 P.M. death of Kasaya, wife of Kerilka, with church rites. At Nelnorotalotem, at about 4:30 died also Kokesa . . . strengthened by sacraments and prayers. . . . we minister to the sick until late at night. The news of the death of Daniel is confirmed.

Dec. 25, 1912: We were told that the Indians were preparing a big potlatch in honor of the dead and were going to dress a girl around whom, while stripped, they were to dance. The Indians therefore were told that we would have no Christmas celebration unless they promised to give up that horrible practice. They did not want to promise, so we had no midnight mass. . . .

Jan. 9, 1914 [This is part of a letter from the priest in charge to the Jesuit Father Provincial]: . . . I doubt whether there is any other spot on earth where our efforts could be so fruitless. [Our converts] are, without exception, still semipagan, weak, ready to relapse into gross superstition, and for the most part hypocrites. They are neither honest, nor moral.

——— 1926 [This was written by one of the Sisters of St. Anne]: Sewing and cooking lessons for the older girls resumed. In order to instill cleanliness and order, we visit the homes regularly every week and see that the lessons received are put into practice. A nice dish of cinnamon rolls was just taken out of the oven the other day when we stopped into a cabin. Another family had a very appetizing rabbit stew steaming hot for supper. The table was well set. But what we are most proud of is the home made bread which four girls have tried with success . . . a bait for all future husbands.

May 8, 1936: Some of the Indians came in today and proceeded to get drunk. Hardly one was able to walk.

June 16, 1936: Disorder reigns supreme. The sale of liquor to the

Indians continues unabated. Representations to the proper authorities in Juneau have been made—but so far to no avail.

Jan. 16, 1939: Isidore Mountain, 22 years old, shot himself in the head while in a drinking craze and committed suicide.

March 28, 1963: Had a village meeting to see whether Nulato should be [incorporated as] a city.

April 16, 1963: They voted to become a fourth class city today.

Oct. 6, 1963: Two men from The Golden Valley Electric Co. came to help our men set up their light plant.

Feb. 5, 1963: Stick dance tonight [this was part of the Feast for the Dead so much opposed by the Jesuits in the past]. . . . No one, even the old people, knows just what the dance is all about. Both Father and Brother watched for a while.

Oct. 28, 1964: Archie Thurmond and Andrew Demoski put up our basketball backboard.

Dec. 18, 1964: Fred Sommer brought the Husski [a gas-powered snow traveler] from Galena.

Jan. 14, 1965: Men and women sponsor a "Wood Drive" for the church, school, etc. The men used dog sleds, snowcats, hus-ski, etc. The women prepared coffee and lunches.

Jan. 20, 1965: BIA [Bureau of Indian Affairs] welfare man Gerald Ousterhault arrived from Koyukuk to check on cases and give information on the "Anti-Poverty Program."

Feb. 12, 1965: Valentine's Party for children in Sister Colleen Ann's room.

Feb. 22, 1965: National Guard Meeting at 7:00 P.M.

One might conclude from these entries that the Koyukon of Nulato, a primitive heathen people in Tosi's day, have since become typical modern Americans. Such a conclusion would be true, and also false. Today the Koyukon are neither primitive nor modern, yet they are both. It is their lot—and their anguish—to live out this central ambiguity. Theirs is a world in which lemmings descend from the same sky where artificial satellites are visible at night, a world of moon phases and punched timecards, imperatives of the chase and of the computer, potlatches and National Guard Meetings, raw fish washed down with Coca-Cola.

Let us first consider the modern, typically American aspects of life in Nulato, and the changes that have brought them about.

Such changes are significant because, with minor variations, they have occurred among all the native people of the Yukon. And, it must be stressed, the Indians and Eskimos constitute the overwhelming majority of the population along most of the river today. The 1960 census indicates that, with the exception of Whitehorse and Dawson City, 4,765 people reside permanently along the whole 1,800 mile course of the Yukon. Of these less than 300 are whites.

Language

In Father Tosi's time the people of Nulato spoke their ancestral Koyukon language, though they had adopted such loan words as "gussek" (from the Russian, Cossack) to mean "white man," and "massi" for "Thank you" from the French-Canadian ACC⁰. traders. Father Jules Jetté, S.J., perhaps the greatest Alaskan linguist, came to Nulato in 1898 and mastered Koyukon well enough to preach in it in less than two years. By 1914, however, he was again preaching in English sometimes, because already there were "a few that lack the Indian tongue." Today few people under twenty-five can converse in Koyukon, and Andrew Demoski, the chief of the village council, does not know it at all. Koyukon proper names have largely disappeared: Demoski's name is Russian, and the families of Missouris and Kentuckys are the legacy of a white schoolteacher who was so exasperated by Koyukon phonetics that he named each of his pupils after a state. How the Wholecheeses came to be called by such a name is uncertain.

Religion

Traditionally the spiritual world of the Koyukons was much like that of the neighboring Ingaliks downriver at Anvik. There was no one god, but everything of importance—people, fish, animals, nets, snares, the sky, particular places—had its spirit, or *yega*, that was at least as important as its visible aspect. The world was pervaded by intention, for each *yega* was an active force; and the Koyukon, like the Ingalik, had a complex set of rituals and taboos to ensure that the *yega's* intention was benevolent. As in Anvik, sickness and death were caused by the *yega's* wandering from its body, and the shaman was a powerful figure because he alone know how to coax it back. As we see from the early entries in the House Diary, the shamans still had considerable influence during the first years of the mission.

Today Nulato is a village of practicing Roman Catholics. For decades now the Jesuits have baptized the children and buried the dead. Nearly all marriages are celebrated in the little yellow church, though many of them are actually solemnizations of common-law arrangements. The Jesuits have taken over the shamans' role as the dispensers of spiritual power and protection. Nowadays before a man goes out on his trap line or away to Bristol Bay to work in a salmon cannery, he almost always goes to Mass, confesses, and receives communion. Instead of the old bone amulets, he will take along a new rosary or crucifix. In the cabins of Nulato it is common to see little bottles of holy water which is rubbed in sore places and fed to ailing babies.

In much the same way that the early Christians transformed an old Roman feast into Christmas, the Jesuits transformed the Koyukon Feast for the Dead, which had fortunately been celebrated in midwinter. As we see in the House Diary, the missionaries strongly objected to this ceremony. In the entry for March 24, 1892, for example, we find them learning "for sure" that participation in it is incompatible with Christianity. The ritual, after all, helped the deceased on the way to an eternity where no judgments of good and evil were made, and where saints and sinners alike fornicated and feasted. At present the only part of the old ceremony still celebrated is the stick dance, and it has lost so much of its old significance that in 1964 we find the priest himself attending. The dance honored those who had aided in the burial of the deceased, and since the priest had conducted the funeral he received a fine new pair of knitted gloves.

Nowadays the winter's most important ceremonial occasion is the midnight Mass celebrated on Christmas Eve. In the afternoon before it, the villagers decorate the church with panels of ice frozen from brightly dyed water. During the service the building is packed, for everybody in Nulato attends. Next day a Santa

Clause, complete with red uniform and flowing beard (though a true Indian Santa should properly be quite beardless), distributes presents in Sapiry Hall, the square log community house. The event is sponsored by the Nulato Woman's Club, with the help of the Sisters of St. Anne.

Economy

When Father Tosi arrived, Nulato was a place where semi-nomadic people congregated periodically for ceremonial occasions and trade. They would remain a few weeks, a month perhaps, and then each family group would go its separate way. The quest for food determined where a family might go, just as it determined the whole rhythm of Koyukon life. Today the people of Nulato live in fixed residences and their largest source of income is wages; in both respects they are like most other Americans.

In a sense this profound change began back in the spring of 1838 when the Russian explorer Malakov bartered the first iron knife to the Koyukons of Nulato. Ever since then, and at a constantly accelerating rate, these people have been more and more concerned with procuring the goods of the white man and less and less with deriving all they needed from the land.

At first the white man's goods were obtained by trapping furs for barter and this did not alter Koyukon life very much because it fitted in with the traditional food quest. But with the Gold Rush came woodcutting and steamboat jobs, and from then on cash from wages became an increasingly important way to procure these goods. Even those who continued to hunt, fish and trap for a living became more settled and dependent, for the white man's tools made these pursuits much more efficient. The fishwheel and the outboard motor are good examples. The former, a trap mounted on a raft and rotated by the river current, made it possible for a single man to catch more salmon than a dozen could have with the old willow fiber nets. And the outboard, first mentioned in the House Diary in 1913, allowed the fisherman to live in Nulato and go out each day to tend his wheel. Remote camps were given up, and since the summer salmon catch was so much larger, fall and spring fishing expeditions were no longer necessary.

Because they made traditional tasks so much easier, the white man's goods quickly changed from luxuries into necessities. Even before Tosi's time the Koyukon had forgotten how to use a fire drill or make a spear point from the caribou's tibia; matches and guns were thus essential. As time went on these goods became more complex and expensive—an outboard for tending a fish-wheel, for example, as opposed to one of Malakov's iron knives. Furs were Nulato's one salable product, and while they had sufficed to barter the knife, they often did not suffice to purchase the outboard, the chainsaw and the wardrobe pictured in the Sears catalogue. So while living off the land became physically easier, it became economically impossible. Wage employment was the only alternative. Thus, in increasing numbers, the Koyukon were forced not only to depend on the white man's goods, but to enter his world, on his terms, to get the wherewithal to buy them. Self-sufficiency had all but disappeared in Nulato.

In the village today income from furs accounts for a little more than a fifth of the total, and the value of *all* products of the land for under one third. Since there are only two full-time salaried jobs in Nulato, and almost no seasonal work, wage earners must leave the village. For many of the men this means going down to Bristol Bay on the Bering Sea where the salmon canneries are busy in June and July.° Later in summer and during fall some work as forest fire fighters for the Bureau of Land Management. A few get summer-long construction jobs in Fairbanks or Anchorage.

Education

The Jesuits opened Nulato's first school in 1891. Father Judge, known a few years later as "The Saint of Dawson City" for his

---

° This is also the salmon season at Nulato, but since the men are away the catch is now small. Salmon was always the staple of the Koyukon diet, and the decreased catch means that the villagers are now more dependent than ever on imported food.

hospital work there, was the first teacher. The student body numbered twenty all told, but attendance was erratic. Most children still accompanied their parents as they moved to their fishing camps, caribou grounds, and trap lines, and for Judge's female pupils there was the additional impediment of the menstrual taboo. Menstrual blood was thought to be particularly dangerous because, being the essence of femininity, it would emasculate a man on sight or on the slightest contact. At her first menstruation a girl would be covered with a hood and sequestered in a corner for a whole year. Her mother would bring her food and water which could be drunk only through a swan-bone straw. The porcupine, known—rather surprisingly—for its ease in giving birth, provided the only fresh meat she could eat, and if possible her mother would obtain a pregnant one so that the girl could slide one of its fetuses down inside her clothing. By doing this she imitated, and thus acquired for the future, the porcupine's parturitional talent. The Jesuits managed quite early to convince the Koyukon that secluded girls could come to school if they carefully avoided paths used by the village men. Later even this precaution was forgotten.

In 1899 the school at Nulato was taken over by the Sisters of St. Anne, and they have run it ever since.* There are eight grades, and the students completing them go on either to the Catholic boarding school at Glenallen, Alaska, or to the Bureau of Indian Affairs school at Mount Edgecumbe, near Sitka. In Nulato, as elsewhere in America, every child now receives some formal schooling, and two villagers are presently enrolled in the University of Alaska.

Views of the World

The traditional world of the Koyukon was a small place. Even heaven was right on the Yukon River, though farther upstream than anyone from Nulato had ever ventured. Downstream were

---

* The presence of the school, and, later, the law making education until age sixteen, or grade eight, compulsory, have perhaps contributed as much as changing economic pursuits to making Nulato a permanent settlement.

the sea and the Eskimos, and somewhere beyond was the place where the white man lived. Of their own little world, however, the Koyukon had an incredibly intensive knowledge. He knew the spirits of all the things around him that mattered, and if he had the right "song" he could talk to them. He knew about the stars in the heavens, that they were the size of the opening in a kayak and inhabited by a race of tiny, vaguely malicious men. He knew of ancient cosmic strife and how it caused the seasons to be divided as they are. He knew what brought about sickness and death, and just what to expect in the hereafter. He knew that if his hair turned white prematurely it was because, as a child, he had eaten the head of a snowshoe rabbit; that if, out on the trap line, he came upon copulating beavers, his wife was being unfaithful to him.

In this small, familiar world nothing happened by chance, and nothing happened according to abstract laws such as those on which modern science and civilization are based. No event was without personal meaning. The traditional Koyukon explanation of things might seem absurd to an outsider, but it served the crucial function of imposing coherence on what the Koyukon experienced; it made his sensory world make sense and lent meaning to the events of his life. Randomness, meaninglessness and chaos, after all, excite the most profound human aversion. Every society on earth has its walls and bastions—and its well-guarded castles in the air—to defend against them.

In Nulato today the old defenses and explanations have largely been supplanted by those the white man uses to explain and defend *his* world. The missionaries instill the idea of an order based on moral purpose, and in school the Koyukon learns that the universe is governed by natural laws. Abstractions have more and more replaced the intimate, concrete perception of things, and the Koyukon view of the world is more and more like that of other Americans. The globe tilts on its axis to cause the seasons now, and the rocks no longer speak.

Health

We have seen from the House Diary entry for August 11, 1900, how an epidemic could devastate the Koyukon before the advent of modern medicine. On that day five deaths were recorded, and by the end of the summer sixty-six people, one out of every five, had succumbed to influenza. Farther downriver the situation was even worse. George Pilcher, a woodcutter, accompanied several priests who went from camp to camp to lend what assistance they could. His diary entry for Sunday, September 19, 1900, reads:

Lovely Autum Day   It doubtless frosted last night . . . visited the village 1½ miles Distant whar I witnessed more death and Desolation than I ever before beheld. First was a man lying Dead in the jungle under his up turned canoe. near by lay his wife covered with grass Next was a hut with one corpse then a tent containing 4—one man two women and one child. The nekt [next] held a dead man while his wife lay 50 paces a way in the brush covered with grass Next tent held man wife and Child. here I stopped as the stench was awfle. But the missionaries toiled on fifty yards whare they discovered four more corpses . . . Since they wer two putrid to be handled I proposed making a bond fire out of each. this not being acceptable to the natives I quit with plenty to meditate on.

Influenza was a white man's disease, and so was the smallpox that *totally* depopulated Nulato the fall after Malakov's first visit. But other diseases, typhoid and scarlet fever for example, were endemic. Together with periodic starvation and a high infant mortality rate, they kept the Koyukon population small.

There have been no epidemics in Nulato in the last quarter of a century. T.B., which took an enormous toll in the past, is now much less common and seldom fatal. Partly because most of the Nulato's babies are now born in the Bureau of Indian Affairs hospital in Tanana, the infant mortality rate has been reduced to a fraction of what it was in Father Tosi's day.

We have considered the changes that have taken place in five important areas: religion, language, economy, education and health. It is obvious that in each area the people of Nulato have come much closer to the norms of the American nation. Like the typical American, the Koyukon now speaks, reads and writes English, lives in a fixed location, receives modern medical attention, embraces the Christian religion and derives the largest part of his income from wages.

But let us take a closer look.

We have maintained that the Koyukon is a wage earner. What does he earn? Father William Loyens, S.J., who has worked both as a missionary priest and a social anthropologist in Nulato, calculates that the village's total income from wages and salaries amounts to $52,800.* This means that the average family, which has six members, receives $976.00 a year. There are, however, other sources of income. The sale of furs brings the average family another $434, and government programs such as unemployment insurance and relief amount to an additional $943. The land still supplies moose meat and salmon, and wood for cabin building and fuel, but the value of such products probably does not exceed $200 per capita. The sum of income from these four sources, $3,553, is the yearly total of the average village family. This figure must be adjusted downward, however, because of the high prices that prevail in Nulato as elsewhere in rural Alaska.** At a conservative estimate, goods cost the Koyukon 40 percent more than they cost the average American, which means that his dollar is worth only sixty cents. Income therefore falls to $2,132. The average Nulato family with its six members thus lives on considerably less than the average American *individual*.†

The people of Nulato and of the Yukon generally are so poor because on the one hand there are very few jobs available locally, and on the other they seldom leave their villages and go to places

* This figure, as others in this section, is for 1965.

** At Sommer's, the bigger of Nulato's two stores, a five gallon can of outboard gasoline costs $5.00, a dozen eggs, $1.25, a loaf of bread 70 cents.

† In 1965 average per capita income in the United States stood at $2,727.

where jobs are plentiful, except on a temporary basis. There are no farms or factories in Nulato, nor any place else along the Alaskan Yukon. It is no longer possible to live by cutting wood for the stern-wheelers, for they have long since vanished from the river. Jobs as mail carriers no longer exist because airplanes have replaced dog teams. Trapping is less profitable each year because competition from fur farms and synthetic furs has depressed prices, and at present the catch is legally restricted for reasons of conservation. There are only two full-time salaried employees in the village, the tall, gaunt postmistress who operates from her cabin so she can keep an eye on numerous children, and the agent for Wien Air Alaska who makes sure passengers, cargo and the twice-weekly bush plane get together at the unpaved airstrip up beyond the graveyard.

A number of Nulato men do leave the village to get jobs, but these jobs are nearly always seasonal. The Bristol Bay canneries, Nulato's biggest employers, provide only six or eight weeks of work and few men return from them with as much as twelve hundred dollars. Fighting forest fires, the second most important source of work, is also seasonal, and undependable as well. A very few get steady summer jobs as construction laborers in Alaskan cities. By October nearly everyone is back in Nulato, and in most families the only real hedges against starvation are unemployment insurance, relief, and other government assistance.

Most men in Nulato view unemployment as their major problem. "Without jobs we've got to depend on welfare," explains Andrew Demoski, head of the village council. "We don't like it; we'd rather help ourselves. But we have to live." Demoski, a soft-spoken, greying man with a crewcut, works in a cannery at Chignik down on the Alaska Peninsula. He usually brings home about $1,100, and he manages to supplement this with money from fire fighting, trapping, and a part-time job in Nulato's Public Health Service clinic. In all his yearly income may come to the village adjusted average of $2,132. He has nine children, the oldest of whom is fifteen. Demoski, who left school during the eighth grade, hopes they will go to college and find permanent jobs outside. "There's nothing for them here," he says.

A few villagers—a total of five out of a population of 325—

have found steady, year-round jobs away from Nulato. They earn much more money than those who stay, and, materially at least, their lives are much easier. Why then don't more follow suit? The answer to this question is complex, as the Bureau of Indian Affairs has found in the course of a generally unsuccessful program designed to resettle village people in areas of high employment. There are two factors involved: the appeal of life in the village, despite the poverty, and the unhappiness of life in the cities of the white man, despite the jobs and higher income.

Much has changed in the village, but much has not. Life is still relaxed. If the weather is bad the hunt is postponed. Time is continuous and hence irrelevant, while in the cities it is dissected into minutes and eight hour shifts. In the village a man's prestige is still closely related to his ability to give away his possessions, but in the cities it is based on his ability to acquire and keep them. Both the Eskimos and the Indians are intensely communal people; there are no strangers in the village. In the cities of the white man there are nothing but strangers, nor are they always sympathetically disposed. "Indian children are dirty," says a Dawson woman, "they go to the bathroom just anywhere." "All they want to do is drink," says a Whitehorse store manager. "Why, do you know I've got to keep my vanilla extract locked up? They'll even swipe hair tonic for the alcohol in it." For most Yukon natives the only good thing about the cities is the money one can make, and this is not enough to counterbalance the unhappiness of living in them.

"I'd rather stay right here in Nulato. This is where I was born and raised, so this is where I'd like to live. I been Outside, in Anchorage, but I didn't like it. Too much rush all the time. Here you don't make much money, but I manage. . . . Something always comes along. I got friends to hunt with and talk with." The speaker is a man who, at twenty-two, has his whole adult working life ahead of him; it could be any one of the hundreds of young native* men on the Yukon. The passive fatalism of "something always comes along" allowed these people to survive for

---

* The term "native" has no pejorative connotation in Alaska; it is frequently used by Indians and Eskimos in referring to themselves.

centuries in an incredibly tough environment over which they had no control. It is the antithesis of the modern American mentality with its stress on mastery of the environment, individual assertiveness, economic competition and the strict regimentation of time and energy. The old outlook "worked" in Nulato; it does not work in Anchorage. And yet it is impossible to switch off attitudes that were probably old when the ancestors of the Koyukon came out of Asia; it is also painful to see them held up to ridicule and failure.

A small number of natives have managed to carve niches for themselves in the white man's world; among them are some of Alaska's best bush pilots, the senior operator at the Barrow radio station, a newspaper editor, a number of successful commercial fishermen and a few dozen entrepreneurs. But success is not as common as failure. Of those who fail, many return to their villages after a short time. Others linger on, frequently joining what Father John Fox, S.J., a missionary of nearly forty years' experience on the lower Yukon, refers to as "the human scrap pile that so many natives of this area help to build in the larger cities." Concerning this scrap pile of ruined lives, suffice it to say that the crime rate in White Horse, Y.T., is three times that prevailing in southern Canada mainly because of the Indian contribution to it, that the incidence of alcoholism among the natives in Fairbanks is probably as high as that of any group on earth, and, finally, that while only 20 percent of Alaskans are natives, they accounted for 56.2 percent of the patients in the Alaska Psychiatric Institute as of 1966. In short, many Indians and Eskimos who leave the economic dead end of their villages arrive at a social and psychic dead end in the cities. From the standpoint of village poverty, however, the essential fact is that few leave at all.

As we have seen, the people of Nulato, like other Yukon natives, now go to school. Two village girls are presently in college, and several young men have attended technical schools. The average level of education is extremely low, however, and it lags as far behind American norms as does income. The most recent census reveals that the average Alaskan Indian or Eskimo of twenty-five or older has received 6.6 years of schooling, under half the national average. The situation has improved markedly in the last few decades,* but even today the majority of native students do not complete the eighth grade, and only a third of them enter high school. Among the native students enrolled in the University of Alaska, the very cream of the crop, one half do not stay to complete the freshman year.

The native village of Alaska exists on the margin of American society, and education is the obvious route leading from it to real participation in the work and abundant rewards of that society. That very few follow this route is a matter of clear statistical fact, but the reasons why this is so are much less obvious. In an effort to elucidate some of them, the University of Alaska made an extensive study** of attitudes toward education in Alakanuk, a Yukon delta village of three hundred Eskimos. Until recently Alakanuk was more isolated than practically any other Yukon village. River traffic had always bypassed it, entering and leaving the Yukon by the Apoon delta channel thirty miles to the north. No gold stampeders entered the region, and despite its proximity to Siberia, no military or radar facilities were ever built there. Most river villages have their share of white man's genes, manifest as brown or blue eyes and Caucasian facial bones, and English is used in nearly every household. Alakanuk, on the other hand, is a village of pure-blooded Eskimos who converse almost exclusively in the Yupic dialect.

There was no school at all in Alakanuk until the early 1950s, and no full-time modern elementary school until 1960. That year the census revealed that two thirds of the villagers had not completed the third grade, while nearly half had had no formal education whatsoever. Since the Bureau of Indian Affairs constructed the new school the educational level has risen. The University of Alaska report concludes, however, that it has risen much more slowly than it would have if lack of modern facilities were alone responsible for its being so low in the first place. Other factors are

* In 1939 the average was 1.9 years.
** *Alaskan Native Secondary School Dropouts: A Research Report* by Charles K. Ray, Joan Ryan, Seymour Parker. University of Alaska, 1962.

obviously at work, and by far the most important of them is the attitude of the villagers towards education. Though Alakanuk is an extreme case, similar attitudes persist to some degree in every native community on the Yukon. As a result, village mentality often prevents education from serving as an exit from village poverty.

Fishing is still the basic economic activity in Alakanuk, though most of the catch is now sold to the local cannery rather than consumed in the old subsistence pattern. Seasonal wage labor in the canning operation is also important, and so, to a lesser extent, are trapping and hunting. A child in Alakanuk is surrounded by people engaged in these pursuits; he seldom sees anyone with any other livelihood, and he naturally expects that when he is older he too will follow them. The most common motivation for education in Alakanuk, as elsewhere, is the desire to better one's economic position. Yet in Alakanuk formal education beyond a minimal level is viewed as being totally irrelevant to the pursuit of economic well-being. A scholar with Ph.D.s from Harvard and Heidelberg could catch no more, and probably less, salmon than a functional illiterate who dropped out of the fourth grade. There is no visible justification for undergoing the sacrifices that higher education entails. A few years' schooling, on the other hand, has a practical value in Alakanuk. A young woman expresses a typical view in explaining that her children should complete a few elementary grades

To learn English so they can write for checks and read and speak to the white men. There are more white men coming around here, and some of the older people feel bad when they can't speak to them. Also, if you want to order things in the catalog, you have to read and write.

But beyond an elementary level, education is not only viewed as irrelevant to the tasks of life, but actually inimical to them. When a student returns to Alakanuk from a secondary boarding school

. . . he is like a gussok [white man]. He doesn't even know how to put on his boots. You can't even let them go out alone in the winter to get wood with the dogs because he will freeze. He doesn't know how to take care of himself like an Eskimo does. . . . We always said a man should remain in the country where he is going to make his living.

Needless to say, most villagers expect to make their livings right in the village.

Except in matters concerning the traditional quest for food, Alakanuk attitudes run strongly against anybody who is outstanding. To be average is the ideal; if one attempts to be better than average he is "just trying to be superior." The white owner of the village cannery once rewarded a particularly efficient worker with a pay increase. Shortly thereafter a deputation of workers announced to him that they would strike unless he either extended the increase to everybody, or rescinded the one he had awarded his efficient worker. The owner did the latter. Everyone was equal again and the matter was forgotten; the intended recipient was as happy as anybody with the outcome. This rigid egalitarianism has a strong influence on attitudes toward education, for he who gets more schooling than others is subject to scorn. One of the two high school students in the village was asked how he felt about his status.

Well, I don't like to feel important. Maybe I would like to be like everyone else around here. Some of my brothers and sisters, they feel that I'm getting too much education and am getting to be different from them. I don't know—maybe they are jealous. People around here are like that. They know that I want to go away later on, so they think I'm trying to be better.

It is doubtful that many white middle-class American children would finish high school if doing so were discouraged by their parents, scorned by their peers and unrelated to any increased economic opportunities in their communities. Especially if the middle-class child, as the Yukon native, had to attend a faraway boarding school run by strange people with strict, unfamiliar regulations. The Indian or Eskimo who graduates from the University of Alaska—and some do each year—is indeed a remarkable person.

The people of Nulato now benefit from modern medicine, as we have seen, and the same is true of all the native people of the Yukon. They are much healthier than in the past, but they are still much less healthy than the average American. T.B., for example, is twenty times as common among Alaskan natives as among Americans in general, and the infant mortality rate on the lower Yukon is more twice the U.S. average.* T.B. is responsible for many fewer deaths now, however, and if the infant mortality rate is still high, it has declined by a third since 1950.

For any populations to survive, birth rates must at least equal mortality rates. In the past both were very high among the natives of the Yukon. But in recent decades mortality rates have declined dramatically, while birth rates have risen. The result is a population that is exploding at a faster rate than that of any nation on earth. In 1950 the crude annual rate of natural increase among Alaskan natives stood at 2.37 per cent; by 1960 it had climbed to 3.84 percent, and it is still rising. At the 1960 rate the native population would have doubled in just under nineteen years, less than a generation.**

The implications of the population explosion are evident in Nulato. The village has not grown quite as fast as others on the Yukon, but there are seventy-seven more mouths to feed than there were a decade ago, and two thirds of the 325 villagers are under twenty years old. At the same time, Nulato still has only two full-time jobs to offer. The salmon canneries are no busier than a decade ago, nor are there more forest fires to fight or

* That is, 6.3 percent of live births compared to 2.5 as of 1964.

** To bring these figures into focus consider that in the United States as a whole the crude rate of natural increase in 1960 was 1.5 percent, in India 2.0 per cent, and in Mexico and El Salvador, two of the most demographically explosive nations on earth, the rates were 3.51 and and 3.40 percent respectively. In the United States in 1960, 24.2 babies were born for every thousand people, in India 41.0 per thousand, in Egypt 40.3 per thousand, and in the Yukon valley approximately 48 per thousand.

beavers to trap. Government subsidies are part of every Nulato family's income; they alone have increased as the population has grown. If the people of Nulato are any better off now than they were a decade ago—and they may in fact be poorer—it is solely because of government money.

The economic consequences of the population explosion are similar in all the native villages of the Yukon. Even in the few of them where aggregate income has shown a marked increase, per capita income has not been able to follow suit. "If we define economic progress in terms of per capita income growth," states Dr. George Rogers, Alaska's leading economist, the "rates of population increase [among Alaskan natives] far outstrip even the most optimistic projections of rates of economic output for the State." Thus, even if the natives were equipped to take full advantage of anticipated future economic growth in Alaska, which they certainly are not, they would still face an exceedingly grim economic future.

The natives of Alaska are one of the very poorest groups in the nation. Without question they are poorer than the hill people of Appalachia or the Negroes of urban ghettos. And they must be about the only group of Americans whose per capita income is either not growing or actually shrinking.

Poverty along the Yukon is manifest in every physical aspect of life. It leaks through the roof during the spring thaw and whistles in under the tar paper in winter. It is placed before a growing child as a tin plate of pure starch. It follows a woman to the river to haul water from a hole in the ice at forty below. It lurks in the deep shadows of a cabin where the dim light of a single Coleman lantern cannot hope to dispel it. It reeks from a five-gallon gasoline can half full of excrement. At night it follows four children to a single mattress on the cold floor.

A recent survey concludes that the statistically typical lower Yukon house is fifteen feet wide by eighteen feet long and thus contains two hundred and seventy square feet of floor space. If it has "rooms" they are made by hanging blankets from wires, but usually it doesn't even have these. Six people live there, so each is statistically entitled to a seven by seven section of unplaned board floor. The house is heated by wood, and lit by a gas lantern. There is no electricity, running water or sewer, which means, among other things, that the owner is not eligible for federal home improvement loans. In Appalachia outhouses are becoming quaint symbols of the past; at Kaltag, a village a few miles down the Yukon from Nulato, they are just now being installed: an outhouse is a great improvement over a gasoline can set in the corner of the cabin. Nulato itself has had electricity since 1963, and outhouses since long before that, but nine of the village cabins house ten or more people each. Mrs. Marie McGuire, who toured the lower river region in her capacity as Commissioner of the United States Public Housing Administration, was shocked by what she witnessed. "I've never seen anything like it," she said, "even in the worst slums of our major cities."

If Father Tosi could be resurrected and taken on the same tour, he probably would be elated. The people Mrs. McGuire saw are Christians, after all, and the good father would note with satisfaction that no shaman is to be found practicing his devilish arts among them. Doctors visit from time to time, he would observe, and woodcutting is certainly much easier now that they have chain saws. The children attend school, even if only for 6.6 years. There is money around, though not too much, and as long as the social worker is on his toes nobody starves.

Standards change. By those of today the natives of the Yukon are compared to (and increasingly compare themselves to) Americans in general. They are unlike them in many ways, typical only of the natives of Alaska and the wretched of the earth elsewhere. They live on the farthest tattered fringe of American civilization, out beyond its abundance, its work, its challenges, even its decent concern. They are marginal people.

21 The Native People III

Only the appearance is better, but the Eskimos' minds are not better. The way they think is not so good as before.

—A Frobisher Bay Eskimo

SENATI was a great hunter and a great rogue. He could kill caribou, it is said, when others could not so much as find their tracks. Of bears, even grizzlies, he had no fear; and when a bull moose charged he stood his ground and calmly took aim: if he brought it down before it got to him, well and good; if not, he merited being trampled to death. His vanity was as great as his bravery, and his discourse was marked by a "super-extra allowance of boasting and self-praise," according to Alexander Murray, the founder of Fort Yukon and the first white man Senati ever discoursed with. To his guile there was no limit, and though he killed many men he never once resorted to honorable means. He had "at least eighteen wives," says Dall who met him at Fort Yukon in 1867. This may have been an exaggeration, for a story still told in the region relates that he had ten, but murdered one and thereafter never had more than nine. Deacon Robert McDonald's estimate is even lower, though it should be noted that when he made it Senati was still acquiring additional wives. Wrote the Deacon in 1865:

Sehnyate has . . . caused me much anxiety through his pernitious determination to take, in addition to five wives which he previously possessed, two widows of the chief Kweyate, who died last winter. I reasoned, pleaded, and expostulated with him, threatening him with the anger of God but all without effect. . . . His conduct will I fear have an ill effect on others who may be of the same disposition as himself. May God mercifully overrule and control all for good!

Senati was chief of the Kutcha-Kutchin Indians for nearly half a century. A hero during his lifetime, he endures to this day as the folk hero of many tall tales told by the old people of Fort Yukon. Knavery and polygamy are good story material in any culture, and perhaps Senati owes his posthumous life to them. They did not gain him the chieftaincy, however. This came his way because he was the best hunter in a society where hunting was the most important activity. In Senati's time everything depended on the hunter, for he was by definition *the* provider. If he was successful his family prospered; if not, it was threatened by starvation. Naturally, a man's prestige and self-esteem depended on his ability to fulfill this essential role of hunter-provider.

The following letter, written a few years ago by a Fort Yukon boy, illustrates the extent to which all this has changed.

Dear Daddy,
Since you have been in jail we get 190 dollars a month. Things are going very fine now that you are in jail.

Daddy's family would be more secure if Daddy had simply died, but even a short jail term is some help. Illness would serve as well, in fact even better if Daddy had some long-term disease like T.B. And blindness or permanent paralysis would be as good as death itself.

There is no reason to believe that Daddy's boy does not love his father. His letter has nothing to do with filial disaffection. It is a simple comment on the economic facts of life at Fort Yukon today. One of these facts is that Aid to Dependent Children checks from the Alaska Division of Welfare amount to more than

Daddy ever earned. Another is that when he comes back the checks will be cut off. Daddy at home and working is the bane of his family's material prosperity.

If Daddy had followed the example of many Fort Yukon fathers, he would never have received such a letter. His mistake was marriage. As a legally single man his illegitimate children would have been eligible for the same ADC payments they are now allotted only because he is in jail. His common-law wife would get $80.00 a month for the first child, and $30.00 for each additional one. If he had sired four children she would receive $170 a month. This is big money at Fort Yukon where the 1960 census estimates that the average family—6.7 members—has an income of $135 a month. Daddy could have stayed right at home and enjoyed the prosperity while his children enjoyed his presence.

In Fort Yukon illegitimate children are such an important pillar of the community—more so, probably, than the old, the blind, the crippled, the sick and the jailed put together—that less than half the village's households contain married couples. The ADC checks arrive like clockwork near the beginning of each month. It is frequently a time of celebration, and in Fort Yukon to celebrate means to get drunk. At the end of the spree there may be enough money left over to buy food and clothing for the children, the intended recipients of the checks. This is not always the case, at least to judge by the following letter which was sent by a Fort Yukon woman to the Bureau of Indian Affairs office in Fairbanks:

Dear Miss Towne:

WRITING a Few Lines ABout These Two persons who get this BIA [money]. They DON'T use it Right LIKE They Should. Spend IT ALL on Liquor.

[One of them, call her X] when first Check Came, Ordered bunch of wines and MALT SYROP—Been on a drunk for 3 or 4 wks.

[Y and Z] Both SAME Too, when Check Comes, They BOTH goes on a drunk for wks. & wks, maybe buy $5.00 worth of Grocery and drink up the rest. They get Lots of MALT Syrup and keep on making home MADE Beer—Drunk ALL time. That is sure NOT a WAY To use The money.

Some peoples used iT right WAY They THINK of Their Childrens.

Since the mothers receive the ADC checks, it is up to them to give what they will to the fathers of their children, or whoever else might be living with them at the time. Thus the grandsons of Senati, who not only provided for his many wives but ruled them with an iron hand, are now mendicants vis-à-vis their women.

Old attitudes and values die slowly, much more slowly than old economic arrangements. So the grandsons of Senati are stuck with a prestige system based on fulfilling a once essential role that no longer exists. From what, then, do they derive their self-esteem, their identity and purpose in life? From nothing at all, is the answer, their answer. They no longer possess these. "You goddamn whites, you pretend we don't know what's going on here, how we live now," snarls a middle-aged man, his emotions loosened by alcohol. "We know what's happening to us." He is asked who he is. "Nobody," he snaps. "I don't have a name." Who is this man? Once he knew, once he was somebody. And when the cases of bootlegged Gallo's wine arrive from Fairbanks (Fort Yukon is legally dry), he and his fellow specters are there to meet them. It is not surprising.

The situation in Fort Yukon is economically, socially and psychologically so demoralizing that some, the least demoralized, have left to escape it. A few years ago six or seven families struck out far up the Porcupine River to build a new village in the wilderness. Because of the village's remoteness they had to do without electricity, medical attention and all the shiny wares on the counters of the Northern Commercial Company's store in Fort Yukon. Their standard of living dropped sharply. The village is still a going concern, however, because the standard of *being* there is so much higher than in Fort Yukon. The men hunt and trap, build cabins and boats, drive their dogs in winter, and fish in summer. They are the providers and heads of their families; in short, they are once again Kutchin men, once again able to derive pride from the one standard that can give it to them.

More commonly the undefeated go in the other direction, toward the cities. Some fail to establish themselves there, but others succeed, and they do not return to live in Fort Yukon. The effect of this emigration, as of that to remote new villages, is to drain away Fort Yukon's most constructive citizens. "This filtering of leaders will continue unless there are jobs here," according to the Reverend Murray Trelease "and as it goes on the situation at Fort Yukon is bound to get worse." Trelease, a former jet pilot who has been in charge of the Episcopal Mission in Fort Yukon for the last eight years, counsels anybody who thinks he has even a slim chance of success away from the village to leave. "There's nothing here," he says, "it's just like a feather mattress—no real demands. . . . Some join the service, but it's a mistake for them even to visit here after that. They arrive back sharp and active, but, boy, this community can sure change someone overnight. Somebody who makes a go of it outside is scorned here. And in Fort Yukon people are extraordinarily sensitive to public opinion."

How do people at Fort Yukon and elsewhere along the river view themselves and their prospects? The answers to this question are oblique and partial. Many people are still hopeful and cohesive, looking and working forward to a better future. Fort Yukon is not an exclusive colony of the defeated, but it is they, mute figures in a passive but crushing tragedy, who concern us here. They are the problem, and perhaps even the majority. They are the concern of the undefeated among them as well.

Martha Taylor, the old woman in Dawson who related the tale at the beginning of this book, is asked how the younger generation of Indians is faring. "Oh, now days everybody just crazy around"; and then, after a pause, "Pretty soon there be no more Indian." A Fort Yukon man who has resisted the common degradation is asked how his village's problems might be solved. "It's simple. Get all the women knocked up and kill off all the men. Start with a clean slate." Another, Joe Ward, is a white man, not an Indian, but he has been around Fort Yukon for over half a century. Until a few years ago he and his Indian wife Ellen spent every winter trapping on the Porcupine River northeast of Fort Yukon. He was considered the best trapper in the entire region.

How have the people in Fort Yukon changed since Joe Ward came there from England in 1908?

Now all they do is drink. In the old days you wouldn't see a drunk Indian in twenty years. They never heard of relief—no such word, not here. They worked hard and made money, had darn good outfits too, and good boats. Take the Shuman family up on the Porcupine—never were better trappers or better people; they taught me all I know.

In general the women and the older men have suffered least from the defeated passivity that is so common among the natives of the Yukon. The woman's role in life remains intact; she bears and rears children as always, cooks, gathers wood and water. The older men have lived most of their lives, and acquired most of their habits of mind, in a time when the male fulfilled his role as provider.

Jake Aloysius is sixty-three and fat enough to have been put on a diet by the Public Health Service doctor in Bethel. He lives far down the river from Fort Yukon on the last great bend it takes before veering northwest into the Bering Sea. He is illiterate ("I'd learn to read but I'd be ruined by all them lies they write.") but loves to talk, and can do so in fluent Ingalik and Eskimo, and wonderfully ungrammatical English. He is gregarious, and meets every occasion for a smile with a loud deep-throated laugh. He's a little too old and a lot too fat to trap any longer, so in the winter he "don't do nothing, just eat and sleep like a bear" in the old Roman Catholic mission town of Holy Cross. Like the mosquitoes, he comes to life right after the breakup. He loads his family —he has sired nineteen children—and his movable possessions into his motorized houseboat and goes downriver to the ex-village of Paimiut. Until the grass fire of 1956 there were a church and a number of houses in Paimiut, but after that Jake alone rebuilt. Why? "Because it's a real good country here. Best King [salmon] fishing in Alaska's right out there in that back eddy. Moose all over the place, though nobody ever saw one when I was a boy. Good mink and marten country too. In winter a net under the ice'll take five or ten white fish every day, real fat ones."

It is evening. Jake shows a visitor around his place. The steep path from the landing where his houseboat is tied leads up to two well-built cabins, one for Jake and his wife, the other for the dozen or so children that happen to be at Paimiut. Down from the cabins is a refrigerator building in which salmon are frozen until a plane comes to take them to market. In the big salmon smoking shed by the river row upon row of dark orange strips of flesh hang from the blackened roof. Jake and his family have taken over two thousand Kings this year, and they will do well.

As night falls, one of Jake's sons, a boy of twelve, comes down out of the steep hills above Paimiut. He had a dead porcupine in one hand, a .22 rifle in the other. "Good boy," says Jake, and then to his visitor: "That's good meat, porcupine. Gussek don't eat it and he don't know what he's missing." Half an hour later an outboard motor echoes in the pitch darkness somewhere out on the Yukon. "Let's go down and see how they done," says Jake. When the boat is anchored to the side of the houseboat, two of Jake's older sons debark. A lantern reveals the gory mass of a half-butchered moose inside. "We got it up Paimiut Slough," one of the boys explains. "A big bull." Jake turns to his visitor: "See what I mean? It's a real good country here. You oughta stay here and live. Spend the winter. You can't write no book on the Yukon unless you spend the winter on it. . . . When my youngest kid's done school, I'm coming down to stay all year. It's one hell of a country."

These are rare words on the Yukon today, for more and more it is a river of defeated, passive and unhappy people. "There's a big difference with people now," says Jake.

They don't live like we did. Now everything comes to them like gravy. They don't have to do a darn thing. They don't trap no more for mink or anything, don't ever walk on snowshoes. They don't even go out of town. All they got in their head is booze and mischief—wrecking things, other peoples' things. Why they shot the hell out of that searchlight I got on my boat last winter—just for the hell of it. Nothing else to do. They never make things now, like boats and sleds. Don't want to work that much. Why, when I was young I worked for fifty cents a day packing freight up the Innoko [River, a tributary joining the Yukon about thirty miles up from Paimiut]. Now they get $1.75 an hour for loafing around like on that [Neighborhood] Youth Corps. All they do is dance, drink, chase girls—all kind of dirty stuff. They got no place to go. . . . They're no damn good.

Are these just the mouthings of an irascible old man? To an extent, perhaps. But more than that, they are the reflections of one who has a distinct role and identity, upon a younger generation in which these are lacking. Jake's position in the world and in his family is firm and solid; he is a Yukon salmon fisherman, and the autocrat of Paimiut.

It is characteristic of the American people, affluent and materialistic as we are, to believe that the solution to any problem can be *bought* about. It is only a question of the price tag, how much money is spent, not how it is spent. The Indians and Eskimos of Alaska are woefully poor? Then send them monthly relief checks. Their educational level is low? Then equip their schools with all the latest audiovisual gadgetry and fly in a few VISTA volunteers for good measure. What such an approach neglects, at least on the Yukon, is that the defeated, roleless male and the resulting unstable family prevent these people from really benefiting from such programs. The Bureau of Indian Affairs, the State of Alaska, and the Canadian Indian Affairs Branch have spent millions of dollars on the native people of the Yukon. Much good has been done in such areas as health and education. Nonetheless this charity has generally been cruel, and blind to its consequences. "The government is financing the degradation of these people," says a Fort Yukon man. "It's destroying them as human beings." Is he oversimplifying? Certainly the irreversible changes that have taken place in native life in the last century have made subsidies the only alternative to starvation in the villages or forcible resettlement away from them. But these subsidies need not take the form of a corrosive, self-sustaining dole.

Not until they have ceased to view themselves, and be viewed by others, as of marginal importance, can the men regain their lost self-esteem and confidence. This can occur only if and when they are once more the heads and providers of their families. Since the old subsistence economy is no longer viable, such a role can now be filled only through employment. Yet jobs in the villages scarcely exist, while for very understandable reasons the men are loath to establish themselves elsewhere. Welfare programs intervene between the horns of this dilemma. They permit continued physical survival in the villages, but only at the price of pride.

As we have seen, village housing is almost universally substandard, roads are lacking, and water and sewer systems nearly nonexistent. Projects to improve these conditions are being undertaken on a small scale by the BIA and other agencies. However, these projects are not only few but ill-conceived. Almost always they are viewed by those responsible as ends in themselves. If, let us say, an airstrip is to be constructed, it will be done by a contractor from far away who will bring with him a work force of outsiders. The only consideration is that the strip be completed according to certain specifications. Such projects are of value, but only to the extent that the finished product is. The basic problem of the river villages is not a lack of airstrips, or schools, but a lack of the means and skills by which the men can support themselves and their families. Public works projects should be greatly expanded, but they will not cure the basic ills until they are thought of as means, not ends. A road construction project, for example, should give as much importance to the making of road builders and wage earners as to completing the road. In such an undertaking the only nonvillagers employed should be teachers; that is, professional heavy-machinery operators, mechanics, engineers and so on who are hired to instruct as well as to build. The more adept native workers should be paid for learning on the job, and the project should last long enough to train competent bulldozer operators, welders, mechanics and similar tradesmen. After that, those who were proficient could be certified and recommended for jobs in other parts of Alaska. Those who did not take advantage of the training would at least have jobs.

Native men seldom leave their villages permanently, but as we have seen in the case of the Nulato salmon cannery workers who go to Bristol Bay, they are willing, often eager, to leave temporarily if jobs are available. Employment in Alaska is highly seasonal for all races; in winter there is a scarcity of jobs, but in summer, when all road construction is done, hundreds of workers are lured to Alaska from other states. With adequate training and job information, there is no reason why native men should not fill many of these jobs. A native bulldozer operator could make enough money in the four-month construction season to support himself and his family for the rest of the year, for though village prices are high, the cost of living is relatively low; the land still supplies meat, fish, fuel and building materials. If the project were not a road but a school or clinic, or some other structure, training could be provided for future carpenters, plumbers, masons and electricians.

Two of the main reasons for the phenomenally high drop-out rate among native students are the lack of relevancy of the curriculum to future economic opportunity, and the fact that high schools are located so far from home. The vocational training sponsored by such public works projects would avoid both problems, for it would be part and parcel of a present job set in the village itself. It would be aimed primarily at the more than 50 percent of teen-agers and young men who have not finished high school, for it is this group more than any other that is a lost generation.

The State of Alaska spends roughly $6,100,000 a year on welfare; of this about 80 percent goes to Indians and Eskimos though they constitute less than a quarter of the state's population. In addition the BIA budgets about $1,750,000 annually for welfare. Without doubt a comprehensive public works program designed to create employment and teach job skills would cost much more than this, nor could it immediately or completely end the need for welfare. But the taxpayers' investment in the future of men who can contribute their work and knowledge—and their taxes—to Alaska's advancement, who can support themselves and their families and take pride in what they are and what they do, such an investment is unquestionably sounder than the continued practice of subsidizing degradation. In the long run it would cost less as well. One thing seems clear: only after a drastic change in present programs do the native peoples of the Yukon stand a chance of being better off than they were in the days of Senati, scarlet fever, starvation, superstition, dignity and self-reliance.

22   *Moose Pasture*

> This was the river I had read and dreamed of,
> which had seemed as if shrouded in mystery, in
> spite of the tales of those who had seen it.
>
> —William H. Dall, *Alaska*
> *and Its Resources*

WHILE most of the native people of the Yukon live in Alaskan villages, most of the whites live in two Canadian towns, Whitehorse and Dawson. The two are separated by 460 miles of river, 335 of road, and by an era as well. Nothing so well reflects the changed preoccupations of white men on the Yukon as the contrast between them.

If you persevere for 918 miles north along the Alaska Highway the ping and clack of flying stones will suddenly cease. The silence is ominous at first for these sounds have become synonymous with motion itself. Is the motor exercising a well-earned right to conk out?

Not at all. You are entering the paved civilization of Whitehorse where the second half of the twentieth century sprawls over a flat plain for its one encounter with the Yukon. In a moment you will be stopping at traffic lights, dodging other pock-marked cars and stalking a place to park on Main Street.

Whitehorse is the capital of the Yukon Territory and the home of half its fifteen thousand people. It is a new town for the most part and much like a thousand others to the south. The buildings

277

are foursquare and functional, about as symbolic of the northern frontier as the Dairy Queen on the corner of Second and Elliot. Whereas in Dawson, the old capital, they built suburbs of log cabins and called them Lousetown and Moosehide, in Whitehorse they build them of pastel ranch houses, call them Riverdale and Crestview, and install barbecue pits out on the back lawns. Robert Service lived in Whitehorse in 1905, the year he came to the Yukon,* and he composed some of his most popular ballads of the untamed North here—in a cabin that has disappeared to make way for a used car lot.

Dawson was flamboyance, gold, madmen and then decadence; Whitehorse is cost-accounted business, bureaucrats, copper, and prosperity. Indeed, Whitehorse is now booming as only once before in its history. Like Dawson in the past, it is the base for an extensive prospecting industry, but the men involved are geologists, diamond drillers, engineers and assay technicians, and they shuttle themselves and their electronic gear around in helicopters. Companies with such names as Atlas Explorations, Ltd., Sphere Development Corp., New Privateer Mines, Golden Gate Explorations and Silver Pack Mines, Ltd. pursue their operations from temporary headquarters in rented store fronts. There is an air of excitement, of big things about to happen. Men meet for lunch at the Whitehorse Inn and the menu is forgotten under a sheaf of geological maps; the talk is hurried and hushed. In the phone booth a mining engineer holds an urgent one-hour technical conference with his Toronto headquarters. The Yukon Territory's first important new mine in decades has recently gone into production just south of town. This mine, which exploits a large copper vein, was developed thanks to capital from Japan. Nor was this the first Japanese contribution to the prosperity of Whitehorse.

Before the turn of the century Whitehorse was merely a portage camp on the route to the gold fields downriver, a place to dry out or despair (as Haskell and Meeker had done) after running the treacherous water of Miles Canyon and Whitehorse

---

* Thus, he of course had no direct experience whatsoever with the Gold Rush of 1898.

Rapids. In 1900 the railway from Skagway reached Whitehorse, and from then until 1942 it was a sleepy settlement where freight was transferred from trains to stern-wheelers. In that year the Japanese attacked the Aleutian Islands. An inland defense route to Alaska became an urgent necessity and since Whitehorse was the only place along the route connected by rail to tidewater, it became a major construction center. Before March 1, 1942, when work on the Alaska Military Highway began, Whitehorse was a village of eight hundred people at most; within two months fifteen thousand workers and innumerable bulldozers, trucks and earthmovers made it their base. The town's few hotel rooms were crammed with three or four men at a time sleeping in eight hour shifts, and vast barnlike barracks were thrown up overnight. The old, slow White Pass and Yukon Route Railway groaned under the burden until additional locomotives could be brought in from a Colorado gold mine, apparently the only enterprise in America using the same narrow guage as the White Pass Line. The Alaska Highway, 1523 miles of gravel road traversing the wilderness of the Northern Rockies, was passable along its entire length after only eight months; by 1943 it was finished. The exodus of the construction men must have seemed like the rapid ebb of another gold stampede, but there was a crucial difference: Whitehorse was now on the road map of North America. This fact, along with the already existing railroad, would give the town a permanence and a durable prosperity that no placer field could ever have provided.

By 1953 Whitehorse had so far outstripped Dawson that the territorial capital was moved there. Since then government has been Whitehorse's biggest business, and with the bureaucrats have come a solid, depression-proof economic base and a large drab Federal Building the color of anemic coffee. The structure is the essence of modern functionality, the antithesis of Dawson's old Edwardian capitol with its crystal chandeliers and gold-plated radiators.

Despite its Dairy Queen, its dry cleaners, its nine-to-five office jobs, its diaper service and home-delivered Southern-fried chicken, Whitehorse is no Toronto in miniature, no subarctic

Saskatoon. The wilderness still begins in the hills just across the river and as in most frontier towns its population is young* and predominantly male. There are too few neckties and inhibitions, too many beards and oaths for Whitehorse's packed bars to be mistaken for those of Ottawa. And the rouged Indian girls in beehive hairdos and stretch pants who wait for someone to happen outside the Taku Inn bar on Saturday night would surely look out of place in Toronto. Edmonton, the nearest Canadian metropolis, is thirteen hundred miles away, and the bureaucrats in the Federal Building get an "isolation allowance"—much to the annoyance of local residents.

People in Whitehorse are open, friendly, vocal, inclined to overstatement; their sense of humor is more slapstick than wry. Emotions are near the surface, expressed directly rather than through the sign language of decorum. Class lines are vague, though something of a self-conscious upper crust has congealed in the Riverdale Subdivision, and the Indians in the tar paper ghetto constitute a proletariat. People in Whitehorse are more like Texans or Alaskans than other Canadians. In good frontier tradition, they distrust central government. Ottawa, which governs them through a commissioner, is viewed as a distant, foreign place where their aspirations are unknown if not actively plotted against; it is the source of all evil, unredeemed by the fact that it picks up the tab for two thirds of the territorial budget.**

For decades the riverfront of Whitehorse was the heart of the town. The Yukon River was the territory's only highway, the only link between Dawson, the capital and leading city, and the outside world. Half a dozen stern-wheelers sometimes departed Whitehorse in a single day. Along the 460 mile stretch between that town and Dawson a score of settlements grew up. Some of the people in them mined, but many more made their livings by chopping wood for the steamboats, or by working as crew on them. In 1953 a spur off the Alaska Highway connecting White-

---

* Only 3.3 percent are over 65; in Dawson-the-Decrepit the figure is 9.3.
** The Dominion Government's contribution to the budget of Alberta, for example, is about one fifth the total.

horse and Dawson was completed. Road transportation was much quicker, cheaper and more reliable than river transportation had been, and so, one after another, the stern-wheelers were hauled out on the banks of the Yukon and left to rot. By 1956 all had ceased operation. The river settlements, such places as Big Salmon, Upper Laberge, Fort Selkirk and Stewart River, suddenly found themselves shunted from the main line to an unused siding. The boats that had given their inhabitants work and brought them supplies abandoned the river, so the people were forced to do the same.

At this time the Whitehorse waterfront became a bone yard. Once so busy, it is now only a muddy bank strewn with hulks long past hope or physical possibility of relaunching. The riverfront is a good indication of what the Yukon now means to the town. Another is the steel and concrete bridge that crosses the river just above it. And a third is the dam which has converted the rapids that gave Whitehorse its name and original reason for being into fifteen thousand h.p. of hydroelectric power. The Yukon now means an obstacle to be spanned, moving water to be blocked up. Men now intersect it only, they do not follow its course.

At the same time there are fewer people than in the past. Only recently has the population of the Yukon Territory grown back to *half* of what it was at the beginning of the century.* On the Alaskan part of the river even this fraction has not been regained, for although the native population has grown considerably, there are still fewer than three hundred permanent white residents.

The Yukon today is as it was a century ago, a silent river of cold water running through deep wilderness. Once more it is nearly useless to white men, irrelevant to their progress. It is wild again, the only big American river that is, and the only one that nature has so largely reclaimed from human enterprise. This, of course, is its appeal.

Bound downriver out of Whitehorse, the whole era from the

* In 1901 it stood at 27,229; in 1961 at 14,628; and in 1968 at about 16,000.

Gold Rush to the Riverdale Subdivision recedes into unreality behind the first sharp bends. There are signs only, the occasional fading footnotes to an obscured chronicle: rotting old pilings, for example, that once held a channel for the stern-wheelers, and rusty fifty-five gallon gasoline drums contributed by the White-horse Municipal Dump. The river, the Yukon as a natural phe-nomenon, an ahuman force, becomes the only reality; and one's encounter with it is as varied as its own encounter with the land: a new world lies around each bend.

Just upstream from the Yukon's confluence with the White, the meeting of land and water is abrupt, decisive. The banks rise up sheer and perpendicular in crenelated bastions and parapets of angular grey rock; the river is shunted into deep moatlike gorges. Above the mouth of the Pelly the meeting is less decisive: the banks rise gradually from river level and shade imperceptibly into old rounded hills, and the hills climb gently up to a soft horizon in undulating tiers. Time and the river have worn away all sharp contours, all traces of angularity. Bare humps of skree and dry grass, ochre, dun and burnt sienna, alternate with deep green splotches of spruce and paler ones of balsam poplar. If Cé-zanne had painted these hills with their panels of tone and tex-ture, he could have employed the utmost literalness for his style is already in them. Above the Pelly, in Minto Flats, the meeting of river and land is equivocal, ambivalent. The terrain is flat and the river sprawls among scores of shifting islands and innumerable sloughs. In spring the river rises, becomes aggressive, invades the low land; then, toward July, it can no longer sustain its offensive; it turns back in retreat and the land pursues it in a contest with-out term or issue.

Beyond the river's banks the forest stretches out hundreds of miles past the farthest visible horizon. To the northeast it ex-tends, nearly unbroken, uncrossed by roads or high tension wires, untraveled, even unexplored in places, to the tundra of the polar coast; to the south and west it is halted only by the glacial peaks of the St. Elias and Wrangell Mountains, and by the Pacific; and to the east it shades off into the barren ground of the Northwest Territories on the far side of the Mackenzie River. In all this wilderness there is only a handful of people now. On the 460-mile section of the river between Dawson and Whitehorse there are, aside from the 218 inhabitants of the sole village, Carmacks, only two families of permanent residents.

Lake Laberge, twenty miles below the Whitehorse riverfront, is much as it was in 1867 when the Fort Selkirk Indians described it to Mike Laberge and Frank Ketchum. It is once again the undisturbed summer home of scoters and bufflehead ducks, and bald eagles that bend the spruce tops horizontal as they scan the lake for dying salmon. Man, the great vagabond of this part of the earth, intruded for a season and then left, and the dumb inflexible wisdom of the scoters and eagles allowed them to outlast the intrusion. Now they have Lake Laberge all to themselves, have even inherited the ghost village at the south end. It is a beautiful legacy, this cluster of rotten cabins invaded by wild pink roses and indigo lupines that bathe in sunshine near the clear green water. Most of the sod roofs have fallen back down to the ground, and some of the cabins suffered when the last occupants used their departed neighbors' houses for firewood. A few still

stand, however. Tacked to the door of one of them is a note, "Gone Hunting RATS," the message no doubt of a muskrat trapper. It is not dated. Inside another one, the wall is pasted with the pages of a *National Geographic* photographic article on Washington, D.C., that appeared in the late 1930s. Next to the Lincoln Memorial a half-naked woman reclines lubriciously on the calendar of a Whitehorse trading company. The last month torn out from under her was February 1956. Is this the date of the final depopulation of Lake Laberge?

After its slow meander through the lake, the Yukon funnels its current swiftly through the twisting switchbacks of what the miners called the Thirty Mile River. The pilots who compiled the old river logs took a perverse delight in naming navigational hazards along this stretch after the stern-wheelers that came to grief on them. The river claimed the *Casca II* and the *Tanana* years ago, and by now it has partially demolished Casca and Tanana Reefs as well.

On the Thirty Mile River it is much less surprising to see moose than men. These animals, the largest of all deer, come down to browse on the brush-grown bars, and it is common to spot four or five of them in a day's drift. On the S-bend ten miles below Laberge a cow busily strips leaves from the tops of willow bushes. She remarks a strange form in the water, but since the boat is downwind from her, and silent, she pays no heed. Smell and hearing are her alert senses, not sight, and after the most perfunctory inspection she resumes her considerable daily task of supplying herself with forty or fifty pounds of browse. At thirty yards she stops munching and raises her heavy head; a willow stalk still dangling from her mouth gives her the air of some overgrown north country hick. Her long ears sweep forward to rigidity, and her big bulbous nose wrinkles with concentration. Her altered behavior, and perhaps a low grunt, brings her light brown calf out to join her on the bar. He imitates her with utmost precision—and without the slightest idea of what she is reacting to. Mule-eared and colt-legged, he too stands staring. She strides a few yards to a better vantage point near the bank; he follows as exactly in her hoofprints as his short strides permit. Then, as the boat drifts across some invisible fear perimeter, the cow trots off into the bush. Her speed and the fluid grace of her motion are remarkable for such a high-shouldered, ungainly looking creature. Her long, strong legs carry her effortlessly over a tangled chaos of driftwood. Her calf, however, trips on the first log, falls, thrashes in panic.

The calf is entrapped for a full two minutes, and in such circumstances one might think him a perfect target for a wolf or bear. But his mother has stopped to wait on the far side of the tangle. She will return if necessary, and no American mammal excites greater respect from a predator than a cow with calf. Even the bigger, antlered bull is less dangerous. Wolves will attack her only if driven by extreme hunger, and when they do, her front hoofs are likely to cost the pack casualties. Several instances of cows in full pursuit of fleeing grizzlies are reported by Adolph Murie, the great Alaskan naturalist.

Moose calves, about half of them twins, are born in May or early June. Helpless at first, they grow extremely fast; during the second month they gain as much as five pounds a day. By August they can generally keep up with their mothers, both on land and in the water. The moose is a strong and frequent swimmer, and though slower than the caribou, can outdistance most canoe paddlers. Animals have been seen ten miles from the nearest shore, and they sometimes completely submerge while foraging on aquatic plants. It is an odd sight to round a bend and suddenly see the head of an unsuspected moose emerge from the depths a few yards away. On land an Alaskan cow has been clocked at thirty-five miles an hour.

The bull enters the family life of the moose only as a sire. In summer, while the cow cares for her calf, he puts on fat and cares for his tender antlers. Since early spring he has grown a brand-new pair of these, perhaps more than six feet across, and useful only for sparring with other bulls; they are a sort of grand intraspecific vanity tree, for he, like the antlerless cow, uses his front hoofs to fend off predators. By the end of August the bull has rubbed his antlers clean of velvet, uprooting and debranching small trees in the process. Now his summer of indolent gluttony comes to an end. He grows restless, browses in fits and starts only: his sexual appetite overshadows his appetite for willows, and he has no alternative but to grow steadily leaner until the rutting season ends in October. He roams ceaselessly, emitting guttural grunts, and keeping his ears cocked for the low, wailed response of a cow. Distraught and unpredictable, he will charge a man he would normally run from, or demolish an alder he would otherwise stop to crop.

If the bull's nervous quest leads him to a solitary cow, he will usually stay with her for most of the rutting season, defending his rights against other bulls in sparring matches. Much has been made of these contests. In countless paintings for sporting magazines and beer calendars they are depicted as life and death battles. Never was nature so red of tooth: the bulls charge ferociously and there is a subliminal hint of fire issuing from their nostrils. Surely they will not disengage until one has died. In the background a cow waits submissively for the victor. In fact, the sparring matches usually amount to nothing more than cumbersome shoving contests in which one, usually the challenger, backs off if the "battle" shows no signs of an easy victory. And, as for the cow, she wanders about at will; it is the bulls who do the pursuing.

The moose of the Yukon basin, *Alces gigas,* is larger than that of lower Canada, Maine or Montana. Big bulls sometimes weigh well over three quarters of a ton and stand six feet at the shoulder; the record antler spread is six feet five and five-eighths inches. Like much of the Yukon's fauna—the caribou, salmon, sheefish, grayling, wolverine and ptarmigan, for examples—the moose is circumpolar in distribution. He still lives in Siberia and Scandinavia, and probably crossed the Bering Land Bridge to America during the Pleistocene Age.

The Thirty Mile section of the Yukon ends at the ex-settlement of Hootalinqua. The old Mounted Police post still stands there, partially hidden by alders, but this is about all that's left. Just below the post the pilothouse and stacks of the stern-wheeler *Evelyn,* once of Dawson, peers out over a thicket of poplars. She was drawn up here years ago, even before the Whitehorse-Dawson road supplanted the river as the region's vital artery. Now, at least, she no longer has to suffer the humiliation of having her sister ships puff proudly past.

The Teslin, which arises in the Rockies to the southeast, joins the Yukon at Hootalinqua, and their confluence has created a large rounded cove of nearly still water. It is an ideal place for insects to hatch, and this probably explains why Arctic grayling congregate there in such numbers. The cove is directly in front of the police post, and no doubt off-duty mounties used to fish it. Perhaps at that time the grayling learned to be wary, but nobody fishes the cove now and they have long since forgotten any lessons they might have learned.

A tiny Black Gnat on a number sixteen hook falls on the still water. Not two seconds later a swirl breaks the mirror surface where it lies. The fish has missed his target, as grayling often do. He changes tactics, leaps clear out of the water six inches from the fly. A marvelously graceful arc sends him down upon it. The line tightens. He jumps again, dances on his tail, but cannot shake the hook. He runs for deeper, faster water. But soon he begins to weaken. He is drawn toward shore, cutting semicircles with the 3x leader on the water's surface. Two feet from the bank, fear and adrenalin allow him another run. Only now, with land and a fisherman in sight, does he realize the enormity of his fate. But he is nearly exhausted. In a moment he is landed.

A small fish, barely fifteen inches long, he is not small for a grayling; the record is only twenty-four. He is laid on the grass the mounties once kept scythed. The sun catches his side, iridescent blue-violet dotted with spots nearly as big and jet-black as his extraordinary eyes.* But his chief marvel is the swept-back, saillike dorsal fin that gives him his Latin name, *Signifer*, or standard-bearer. The fin's outer edge is rimmed with salmon orange, the rest a fantastic pattern of deep blues and blacks

---

* It is because of these eyes, I suppose, that grayling are the only fish I know that disturb me to catch. When one is about to be landed, his big eyes seem to express such astonishment at being deceived, such violated innocence, that I feel like a sadist.

flecked with light red. Isaac Walton tells us that some people believe "he feeds on Gold, and that many have been caught . . . out of whose bellies grains of gold have been taken." His looks suggest such a habit, though at Hootalinqua his belly contains only half-digested terrestrial insects.

The Arctic grayling is not the scrappy fish he is often described as being; he tires quickly, having none of the stamina of a trout or the sheefish. Nor is he hard to catch; no other fresh water fish takes more readily to a fly. And though he is a good eating fish, he is not to be compared to the two chars of the Yukon, the Dolly Varden and the lake trout. Still, he is a symbol of the northern wilderness, of cold, clear streams that have never been cut over nor even fished.

Grayling leave the Yukon to spawn in small streams just after the ice goes out, but in a few weeks they return. Then, in July, they reascend the streams following the King salmon whose eggs they prefer even to insects.

The King salmon is the largest of the Yukon's fish and the largest of the world's salmon. His proper name is *Oncorhynchus tschawytscha*, but even ichthyologists shy away from pronouncing it and he is known variously as the Chinook, Tyee and Spring salmon. Now that dams block the Columbia, the Yukon is probably his most important spawning river.

A biologist, or perhaps it was a cynic, once observed that an organism was simply a sex cell's way of producing another sex cell. Even to cynics, the roundaboutness of the means of production must appear one of evolution's greatest marvels, and on the Yukon there is no organism more marvelous in this respect than the King salmon. By September, when the grayling again return to the Yukon, the Kings have spawned and died. Bears and bald eagles have cleaned up the carnage and grown fat on it, and the stench is gone. But by then the bottoms of swift, shallow streams conceal a new generation. Tiny, helpless embryonic fish lie buried in the gravel deep within North America. They are fed now only by the yolk sacs attached to their bellies. Yet they will later cruise the coast of Asia devouring octopus and herring. And then, somehow, they will return to these same stream beds to leave the sex cells of another generation and the carcasses of their own.

The bright red eggs of the King salmon are deposited in mid-summer and begin to hatch in the fall. During the cold months the embryos develop slowly because of low water temperatures, and only in spring do they absorb their yolk sacs, wriggle up through the gravel and become free-swimming fish. By then insect life is plentiful in the streams and they feed actively. For several weeks they remain in the vicinity of the spawning beds, growing rapidly in size and agility. Then, when they are about an inch long, they begin gradually working their way down the streams to the tributary rivers and on to the Yukon itself. By the end of the first summer of life (though sometimes not until the second) they pass out of the Yukon estuary and become fish of the high seas; they will never again swim in fresh water until the spawning migration. As marine fish they range far out into the Bering Sea and to the North Pacific. Systematic tagging indicates that some Yukon-born specimens go as far west as the coasts of Japan and Siberia. The sea is rich in food, and like all anadromous fish, King salmon grow much faster in it than in fresh water. They sometimes attain weights of well over a hundred pounds, though the average is much less.

Usually after five years at sea (though sometimes after four, six or even seven), the fish reach sexual maturity, and no doubt the biological clock that now dictates their return to the river has much to do with the hormonal changes resulting from this. During the last winter before spawning the Kings begin migrating towards their natal rivers, which include the Sacramento, the Columbia, the Fraser, the Stikine, and the Amur in Siberia, as well as the Yukon. How they navigate over hundreds of miles of open sea is not known. A "sun-compass" hypothesis has been put forward, but the salmon have so little respect for it that they swim by night as well as by day, and are apparently not bothered by the weeks of overcast skies they often encounter. During this migration they do not travel in schools, but once they approach the river's estuary they begin to do so. Here fish born in one spawning tributary segregate themselves from all others, and form compact, exclusive schools. At this time the salmon of the Porcupine River, for example, will be separate from those of the Pelly.

At some time between May 20 and June 15, the Yukon Kings begin to ascend the river. They swim night and day, traveling about two and a half miles an hour vis-à-vis the current, but less than half this in actual speed; they average about thirty miles a day. The salmon must reach their spawning beds when the water level and temperature are optimal if they are to reproduce successfully, and for this reason precise timing is necessary. Since some races have much farther to go than others, they must begin the upriver journey earlier. Salmon of Nisutlin River, for example, must travel nearly two thousand miles, while those of the Anvik merely five hundred.

The Nisutlin rises farther from the Yukon's mouth than any other tributary. It flows southward through the Rockies to meet the Teslin, about 150 miles above Hootalinqua, where the latter river meets the Yukon. To reach it the salmon must not only have the stamina to swim constantly for over two months against a strong current; they must perform a remarkable navigational feat. As they ascend the Yukon, which, because of its silt, must appear as black as night to them, they are confronted with countless wrong routes and never more than one correct one.

How do they manage to make the right choices? While there is no definitive answer to this question as yet, there is at least a reasonable hypothesis. Basic to it is the observation that the waters of different streams are chemically different. Every watershed has its own particular geology and microclimate, and because of this its flora and fauna are distributed in unique proportions and concentrations. It is these organisms and their decay products that give to each stream a distinctive odor, or "bouquet" as one investigator calls it. It has been shown in laboratory experiments that salmon, like other fish, can distinguish one stream's bouquet from that of another. Physically, this perception results from contact between the vast array of complex organic compounds making up the bouquet, and the acute olfactory receptors located in the salmon's nose pits. It has also been proven that salmon can remember a given stream's water over extended periods. Recognition of a particular bouquet is not inborn, but learned, as is shown by numerous experiments in which fertilized eggs have been transported from the streams of deposit to ones far away. Invariably, the adults return to their adopted, not their natal, watercourses, and in this way researchers at the University of Washington have developed a race of salmon for which the "home stream" is an experimental hatchery inside the city limits of Seattle.

According to the bouquet hypothesis* the odor of the natal stream is imprinted on the salmon as they hatch and develop into fry. Later, as they descend towards the sea, a further imprinting takes place so that the fish retain a memory of the river as a whole in which the natal stream's water has become too dilute to smell.

If this theory is correct, the Nisutlin salmon recognizes the odor of the Yukon as he approaches its estuary. Upon entering he picks up the scent of the Teslin, or perhaps simply of water from the upper river. This he follows in the direction of increased concentration, much like a hound. Since neither the Koyukuk nor the Tanana nor any other tributaries flowing into the lower Yukon contain this smell, he does not enter them. As he ascends the river the smell of the Teslin grows more distinct because it is less diluted and he is able to bypass the Pelly, the Stewart and other upper Yukon tributaries. He will not pass the Teslin's mouth, however, because the scent leading him on would be lacking. As he veers up the Teslin, and perhaps even before, the bouquet of the Nisutlin becomes perceptible, and this too he follows. Entering Teslin Lake, into which the Nisutlin flows, he perceives that the scent is strongest on the northeast side, and so is directed there to the river's mouth. Once in the Nisutlin, he picks up the oldest and most deeply imprinted odor, that of his small natal stream. He enters it, and ascends until this odor reaches maximum concentration. At this point he has arrived at his final destination.

When the King salmon reach the Nisutlin they have been swimming against the current night and day for over two months. They have not eaten since before leaving salt water, and on each

---

* For which Dr. Arthur D. Hasler of the University of Wisconsin is primarily responsible.

day of the upriver migration an average fish, weighing twenty pounds, has expended three hundred calories, the equivalent of six tablespoons of sugar. At the same time the females have been expending themselves ripening thousands of protein-rich eggs, and the males in producing millions of sperm cells. At the beginning of the journey body fat is consumed, but as this is used up, energy is supplied more and more by the breakdown of vital tissues. The liver shrivels, and the glucose content of the blood, a constant throughout life until now, drops to as little as 25 percent of normal. As with starving people, the blood becomes acidic with the end products of body protein digestion.

When the Kings leave the Bering Sea they are perfectly shaped and a beautiful silvery blue. They are so fat that in frying them one pours off oil rather than adding it. When they reach the Nisutlin River, or the headwaters of the Porcupine, or the Chena above Fairbanks, or the streams which give rise to the Pelly, their bodies are deformed by starvation, splotched with grotesque patches of fungus and irregular red-purple blotches resembling varicose veins. Their dorsal fins are frayed and the integument between the rays broken; their tails are tattered and stumplike, and their sides scarred, battered and infected. During the migration the male has developed a hideous jutting lower jaw studded with irregular dogteeth. The last part of the journey is the hardest; in poor shape now, the fish must enter shallow water, leap falls, and scrape themselves as they scuttle over bars on their sides. The King, unlike some other salmon, must spawn in swift, shallow water; without it the eggs will not be sufficiently oxygenated. The salmon's drive to reach his spawning grounds is implacable. On the streams flowing into the Nisutlin driftwood jams sometimes block passage, and the migrating fish collect by the hundreds just below them. They literally fight to death to leap over, and for weeks the stench of dead fish pervades such places.

On reaching the section of stream bed on which she was born, the female begins digging out a pocket, or redd, in the gravel. By repeated thrashing with her tail and body, she agitates the finer pebbles which are washed downstream. The bottom of the redd, usually about six inches deep, must be lined with coarse gravel so that the eggs can fall down into the interstices. As she digs she pauses at intervals to lie in the depression and feel it with her ventral fins. When it is satisfactory, she crouches down inside it, facing upstream, and opens her mouth.

The male has been hovering nearby as she dug, and her posture is a signal to him. He swims to her side. Then, right against her, he quivers. His motion is violent, a series of rapid paroxysms swirling the water. In response to him, hundreds of red, sticky eggs spurt from her to the bottom of the nest. At the same instant the male ejaculates a milky cloud of milt containing countless sperm cells. The eggs adhere to the gravel, the milt descending on them like a shower. In minutes they absorb water, become less sticky and fall into the spaces between the pebbles.

By then the male has departed to resume hovering a few yards away. If another male, or an egg-devouring grayling or Dolly Varden trout, comes near he will give chase, snapping with his grotesque lower jaw.

Meanwhile the female is digging again, this time at the upstream rim of the redd. As she works, gravel is washed down to cover up the eggs she has just laid. She continues to thrash after this is done, so as to dig out an upward extension of the redd. Again she tests the bottom with her ventral fins, and when it is ready she crouches as before. The male returns, shudders, and more sperm and eggs are liberated. This cycle may be repeated half a dozen or more times before all her eggs (as many as twelve thousand) are expelled.

When she covers the last of her eggs the redd is finished. Spawning is done. A new generation lies in the gravel. Still, she hovers over her redd for hours or even days longer. But she is near spent. To hold her own against the current she is burning her vital organs as fuel, consuming herself fatally.

After a while she is swept downstream. The current rolls her onto her back, shunts her through a little riffle. Still she fights, and in a moment regains control. At colossal cost the dying fish struggles back up to the redd. Again she hovers, but she can not keep from wobbling. The current mercilessly pries her head upwards toward the surface. Again she is washed down, and this time a hundred feet and a little falls separate her from the redd before she can reassert herself against the moving water. She struggles upward, but can only lurch at the base of the falls she leaped without effort two weeks before. She loses ground, drifts again. Then she is swept into the slower water of a back eddy. She manages to right herself again and waits. In a few minutes even this nearly still water becomes too much for her. She no longer resists. She floats to the surface, her empty fungus-grown belly upward. Her only movement is an occasional gasping flexion of the gills, now half out of water. Then this too ceases.

The Yukon stream that brought her wriggling upward to life six years before, that carried her toward the sea and back, now strands her on a bar to rot in the hot August sun. And as the stream lays her there it brings the first signs of life, tiny black dots that will be eyes, to her eggs.

The salmon of the Yukon return generation after generation to the places of their birth, but what of the men along the river? Where are the people born at Upper Laberge, Hootalinqua, Stewart River, Nation and a dozen other ghost towns?

At Fort Selkirk there is at least a partial answer. Danny Roberts and his family are still right there. Of the village's hundred-odd inhabitants they alone remain, and for years now they have had the place all to themselves. Danny, a trapper, is a short, middle-aged man who wears a motorcycle cap replete with plastic rhinestones although he does his traveling by boat and dogsled. Danny used to work on the river boats, but now he runs his trap line in winter and "just rests up" in summer, except when the salmon are running. Since he was born in Fort Selkirk and is now the head of its only family, he has become quite proprietory about the place; he shows his occasional visitors around the sagging buildings with the air of a country gentleman showing off his fine barns and prize bulls to an acquaintance from the city.

"This is my school," he says, pointing to a one-room cabin half-hidden in the tall grass. "I learn English here."

Inside, the little open-top desks with their inkwells and attached bench seats are still in good shape. The students who sat in them were the children of the Han and Kutchin tribes, and perhaps to help them identify with Old Testament tradition the missionary teacher tacked up a map of the Holy Land showing the homelands of the tribes of Israel. In the years since teacher and pupils departed a curse has fallen on the lands of Issachar and consumed them utterly; Zebulon has been cast out from the bosom of Israel, even beyond Sinai, to the plank floor that lies below.

The Anglican missionary who ran the school lived close by in a solid house of seven-inch squared timbers. The building has not deteriorated much as yet, but the window in the study has fallen in and the wind has scattered reams of third grade compositions and yellowed back issues of *The Church Missionary Intelligencer*. Queen Elizabeth and Prince Philip gaze benignly down from the wall, faded a bit, but looking ever so young and not in the least perturbed by the mess strewn before them.

In 1938, eighty-six years after Robert Campell's post was pillaged by the Chilkats, the Hudson's Bay Company returned to Fort Selkirk. But by now the remains of this "new" post—a concrete foundation littered with bricks and rusted stovepipe—are hardly more imposing than the heaps of chimney rubble that mark the site of the old one. Besides these remnants and the mission buildings, Fort Selkirk consists of two abandoned stores, a machine shop full of cannibalized motors and junk, the old Mounted Police post whose tall white flagpole lies prone in the grass, a few tin-roofed warehouses, and a number of cabins. Each growing season the grassy clearing around Fort Selkirk loses further ground to the alders and poplars. Some of the outlying cabins are now completely hidden. Around others the brush comes only to the eaves where its tops mingle with the tall fireweed, grass and even trees that thrive on the sod roofs. Recently half of one cabin's roof fell in, so a thick mat of vegetation now grows next to the old iron bed and a spruce tree three inches in diameter pokes out of a sod-covered bureau. It would be a surprising sight to wake up to.

Before too long Fort Selkirk will no doubt disappear altogether unless it is maintained. Each winter's snow breaks the backs of a few more cabins, and each summer the rot moves a tier or two farther up the log walls. Then too, Fort Selkirk is sometimes used for fuel, though it has been officially designated an historical site. Danny Roberts may not be guilty himself, but he is a generous host. "You need wood for a supper fire?" he inquires solicitously. Pointing to a leaning structure he says, "Got plenty right over there. That's where my grandfather lived." And so granddaddy's house is diminished by a few more logs.

It is fall and the river is low. The reefs above Dawson must be treated with respect at this time of year. Nobody marks them any more, and to do so wouldn't be worth the bother anyhow. All the way from Fort Selkirk, 165 river miles upstream, the only boats to be seen were hulks stranded on the bank.

In the deep valleys west of Dawson the green-black spruce are splotched with pale yellow stands of poplar. Above, on the slopes, the tundra foliage of tarnished gold and deep wine-red shades upward into a dusting of new snow that will last till next June. The chief tasks of the year are done. Another tree ring has been added, another generation of geese is in the wedges flying south over the river. The caribou that wander the hills in small bands have come down from higher up and farther north, and their clove-brown coats have thickened in response to the first heavy frosts. The rut is nearly over, and the cows carry next spring's calves.

It is midday. Dawson basks in the last warm sun of the year. Nothing stirs. The tourists have driven their campers back down the Alaska Highway, and the more affluent of the town's residents have gone Outside to spend the winter. There is no sound. Suddenly a diesel engine coughs to life. A Caterpillar D-8 bulldozer chugs out from around a corner and clacks its way ponderously down Front Street toward Klondike at five miles an hour. Front Street is over a mile long, and the great yellow machine preempts the middle of the road all the way. A mongrel dog moves lazily out of its path, yawns, stretches, waits a moment, and lies back down in the gravel. Otherwise the bulldozer disturbs nothing but the silence, blocks no traffic of man or vehicle, all along its route.

In Dawson the grass grows tall where the dance halls stood and alders thrive on prone log walls. Frost-nipped fireweed has gained title to ten-thousand-dollar lots now worth twenty-five dollars plus back taxes, and a green belt, the envy of many a crowded city, separates the business and residential sections. But the most wonderful thing about Dawson, besides the fact that it still exists, is its angles. The permafrost has heaved with such a fanciful whimsy that there are no parallel lines left in Dawson, though still some straight ones. Take the telegraph line on Third Avenue, for instance. Each pole is straight enough, but some point up at the Kingdom of Heaven, though no two to the same province thereof, while others are content to aim at Midnight Dome, the Yukon, even Lousetown. Lowe's Mortuary is sway-backed, the old post office is humpbacked, and Madame Tremblay's big old store is both. In a good score of buildings the permafrost has squeezed the windows into secretive squints, sagged them into naive gapes, left them at midyawn; it has buckled door fronts into dramatic masks both tragic and comic. It has heaved the board sidewalks into contours such that a sober man is led to doubt his sobriety and a drunk to fear for his life.

Dawson City has great charm. It is an anachronism, aslant, askew, ajar, awry, a wonderful place to visit but not so good to live in these days. The people of Dawson are like an impecunious man who has inherited a vast ark of a house. He lives there in one tiny wing unable to afford either the upkeep or the demolition of the rest. And of course the servants have long since departed. Dawson, a town built for 15,000, now has 350 year-round residents. It can no longer support the services of a full-time doctor, beautician, barber, or baker, and has dispensed with dentist, druggist and magistrate altogether. There is no hardware store, and only one newspaper, *The Klondike Korner*, mimeographed sporadically by public-spirited ladies. On the other hand, social organizations abound, for Dawson has inherited these along with the surplus buildings. There is a curling club, an historical society, the Yukon Order of Pioneers, the Brownies, Cubs, Guides and Scouts and a whole raft of others. Why so many continue to exist in such a small town is perhaps explained by the case of the Rebekahs, a women's organization: at the meeting called to vote the club's dissolution it was discovered that there were not enough members left to form the quorum stipulated in the charter.

The gold creeks around Dawson have always been a mirror image of the town itself. Large scale mining, begun during the winter of 1896–97, when William Haskell arrived, came to a halt in 1966. That November the Yukon Consolidated Gold Company, heir to the old hand miners and the Guggenheims, left its dredges squatting in their ponds and closed up shop. This was only the latest in a series of setbacks that began in 1899, though the worst for the town's economy since the territorial capital abandoned Dawson in 1953.

Perhaps things in Dawson will pick up one day. There is still gold in the creeks, even after they have yielded a quarter of a billion dollars' worth, and if the price rose substantially the dredges would be resuscitated. On Clinton Creek, a tributary of the Fortymile River northwest of Dawson, an asbestos mine has gone into production recently, but it's too far from town to do much good. Intensive prospecting is underway in the region; maybe some new bornite bonanza will fill Dawson's blocks once more and pump new low life into Lousetown, now completely abandoned. If not, the town's fine green belt may soon include the present business and residential sections instead of separating them. But perhaps Dawson has suffered too many deaths to ever really die.

From Midnight Dome, the high hill just back of Dawson, there is an excellent view in all directions. To the south the Yukon flows forward motionless from around a bend, a band of silver-blue shimmering in the October sun. In the foreground the clear water of the Klondike enters it as a dark streak hugging the east bank, wide at first, then tenuous, then as strands waving like water grass that are engulfed by the silted Yukon just below Dawson. Farther down the big river veers off to the northwest. Its valley is a deep trench worn between rugged hills, and the river seems old beyond imagining. In the distance the trench narrows, and the Yukon crosses over into Alaska through a slot in the far horizon—a fine silver thread in a minute wrinkle of the earth's ancient face. The hills through which the Yukon carves its way northwest of Dawson are the lower slopes of the Ogilvie Mountains, a rump of the northern Rockies. On a clear day many of the taller peaks of this range are visible from Midnight Dome. Ridge upon ridge of jagged sawteeth thrust up, cold, snowy and remote, little visited and poorly mapped, still as they were before any man saw them.

In the opposite direction from the Ogilvies, due south of the Dome, the eye is led straight up into the valley of Bonanza Creek. There nothing has escaped human refashioning. Whole hillsides are simply missing, lopped off sheer and clean by hydraulic mining. The valley floor, a boggy thicket when Carmack slogged his way down it to record his claim, appears naked of all vegetation. Long regular heaps of dredge tailings crawl across it, one against another, like dun-colored worms; they creep along every contour, frighten away every living thing.

The appearance of Bonanza valley from the summit of Midnight Dome is deceptive, however. At closer range it ceases to be a total wasteland. Willows crop out of the sides of tailing piles, and though their roots encounter nothing more fertile than cobblestones and gravel, each year they manage to advance farther up the heaps. In places they have become so thick that it is difficult to avoid tripping on the discarded dredge cogs and cables concealed underneath.

In the days of Forty Mile and Circle, the Klondike creeks were considered mere "moose pasture" and not worth the serious prospector's attention. Even Arthur Harper was of this opinion, and neither he, nor Jack McQuesten, who spent years just downriver at Fort Reliance, ever seriously prospected them.

The course of Bonanza, like everything else in the valley, has been altered in many places, but it still flows through Carmack's claim in the old bed. On the claim itself the tailing heaps have been leveled and a little commemorative plaque implanted in a rock. Not ten feet from this plaque the moose have cropped the willow and left deep hoofprints in the gravel.

Larger Tributaries of the Yukon

(based on data in Army Corps of Engineers, *Yukon and Kuskokwim River Basins, Alaska,* Interim Report Number 7, Washington, D.C., April 1964)

Name	Miles from Its Confluence with Yukon to Yukon Mouth	Drainage Area (in sq. miles)	Length (in miles)	Rank (by length)
Andraefsky	94	1,360	105	
Innoko	280	10,900	463	4
Anvik	325	1,700	126	
Nulato	495	866	73	
Koyukuk	515	32,600	554	2
Melozi	596	2,700	249	
Nowitna	637	7,200	283	
Tozitna	706	1,700	103	
Tanana	720	44,500	513	3
Chandalar	1,013	8,180	113	
Porcupine	1,034	46,200	555	1
Kandik	1,177	1,194	112	
Fortymile	1,306	6,562	56	
Klondike	1,355	4,100	102	
Sixty Mile	1,396	1,523	83	
Stewart	1,416	20,500	390	6
White	1,427	18,500	177	
Pelly	1,520	20,275	457	5
Little Salmon	1,625	1,340	116	
Big Salmon	1,663	1,993	136	
Teslin°	1,696	13,900	253	
Takhini	1,760	2,370	105	

° The Nisutlin flows into the Teslin 147 miles above the latter's mouth; it is 150 miles long, and thus arises 1,993 miles from the mouth of the Yukon.

The Yukon Compared to Some Other American Rivers

	Length from Farthest Source to Mouth (in miles)	Drainage Area (in sq. miles)
Colorado	1,440	244,000
Columbia	1,214	258,000
Hudson	306	12,200
Mackenzie	2,635	682,000
Mississippi-Missouri	3,860	1,243,700
Nelson-Saskatchewan	1,600	444,000
Rio Grande	1,885	172,000
St. Lawrence	2,100	565,000
YUKON	1,993*	330,000

* There is wide disagreement about this distance, even among respected authorities. The U.S. Army Corps of Engineers, in the study cited in Appendix I, has arrived at the figure of 1,993. According to the Geological Survey of Canada, the river distance from the foot of Marsh Lake, where the main stream of the Yukon begins, to the Bering Sea is 1,979 miles. This would mean that the distance from the headwaters of the Nisutlin River, the tributary most distant from the sea, to salt water is roughly 2,200. I have listed the Corps of Engineers estimate in the above table because it probably reflects more careful study than does the Canadian one. It was arrived at in the course of extensive investigations of the Yukon basin made to determine the feasibility of a huge dam the Corps proposed building near Rampart, Alaska. Other estimates of the "length of the Yukon"—just what is meant by this phrase is not specified—range from 2,300 miles (*American Peoples Encyclopedia*) to 1,800 (*Rand McNally World Atlas*).

Bibliography

I. The physical setting and prehistory of the Yukon; general histories.

A. GEOLOGY, HYDROLOGY AND CLIMATE

Brooks, Alfred H., *Blazing Alaska's Trails*. Washington, D.C., College, Alaska, 1953.

Collins, Henry B., ed., *Science in Alaska*. Washington, D.C., 1952.

Dawson, George M., "The Narrative of an Exploration Made in 1887 in the Yukon," in *The Yukon Territory*, London, 1898.

Hendricks, E. L. and Lowe, S. K., *Quantity and Quality of Surface Waters of Alaska, 1960*. U.S. Geological Survey, Water Paper 1720. Washington, D.C., 1962.

Ogilvie, William, "Extracts from the Report of an Expedition Made in 1896–97," in *The Yukon Territory, op. cit.*

U.S. Army, Corps of Engineers, *Yukon and Kuskokwim River Basins, Alaska*. House Document 218, 88th Congress, 2nd Session; Interim report No. 7. Washington, D.C., 1964.

U.S. Army, Materiel Command, Cold Regions Research and Development Laboratory, *Illustrated Summary of the Geology of the Yukon Flats Region, Alaska*. Hanover, N.H., 1964.

Williams, Howell, ed., *Landscapes of Alaska*. Berkeley, 1958.

B. PREHISTORY

de Laguna, Frederica, *The Prehistory of Northern North America as Seen from the Yukon*, Memoirs of the Society for American Archaeology, No. 3; Menasha,, Wisc. 1947.

Giddings, J. Louis, *Ancient Men of the Arctic*. New York, 1967.

Leechman, Douglas, "Prehistoric Migration through the Yukon," *Canadian Historical Review*, Vol. 27 (Dec., 1946).

Macgowan, K. and Hester, J. A., *Early Man in the New World*. Garden City, N.Y., 1962.

Mac Neish, Richard S., "Men Out of Asia; As Seen from the Northwest Yukon," *Anthropological Papers of the University of Alaska*, Vol. 7, No. 2 (May, 1959).

C. GENERAL HISTORIES

Andrews, Clarence L., *The Story of Alaska*. Caldwell, Idaho, 1942.

Bancroft, Hubert H., *History of Alaska*. San Francisco, 1886.

Documents Relative to the History of Alaska. 15 Vols. Typescript copies in Archives, University of Alaska, and Library of Congress. Dated 1937.

Hulley, Clarence C., *Alaska, 1741–1953*. Portland, Ore., 1953.

Jetté, Jules, *Jottings of an Alaskan Missionary*. Unfinished, undated MS.

Copy in Archives of the Oregon Province of the Society of Jesus, Crosby
Library, Gonzaga U., Spokane, Wash.

II. The Russians

Chevigny, Hector, *Russian America.* New York, 1965.
Dall, William H., *Alaska and Its Resources.* Boston, 1870.
Documents Relative to the History of Alaska. Op. cit. Vols. 1 and 2.
Okum, S. B., *The Russian-American Company.* Carl Ginsburg, trans. Cam-
bridge, Mass., 1951.
VanStone, James W., ed., "Russian Exploration in the Interior of Alaska:
an Extract from the Journal of Andrei Glazunov," *Pacific Northwest
Quarterly,* Vol. 50, No. 2 (April, 1959).
Whymper, Frederick, *Travel and Adventure in the Territory of Alaska.*
London, 1869.
Zagoskin, L. A., *Account of Pedestrian Journeys in the Russian Possessions
in America.* St. Petersburg, 1847. Antoinette Hotovitsky, trans. Undated.
Mimeo copy in Archives, University of Alaska.

III. The Aboriginal People

Chapman, John W., *Ten'a Texts and Tales from Anvik.* Leyden, 1914.
Dall, William H., *Alaska and Its Resources, op. cit.*
Jetté, Jules, "Senati," undated MS. in Jesuit Archives, Spokane, Wash.
Kennicott, Robert, "Journal," Chicago Academy of Sciences, *Its Transac-
tions,* Chicago, 1869.
Loyens, William J., *The Changing Culture of the Nulato Koyukon Indians.*
Unpublished Ph.D. dissertation, U. of Wisc., 1966.
———, "The Koyukon Feast for the Dead," *Arctic Anthropology,* Vol. 2,
No. 2 (1964).
Murray, Alexander H., *Journal of the Yukon, 1847–48.* L. J. Burpee, ed.,
Archives of Canada, publication No. 4, Ottawa, 1910.
Osgood, Cornelius, *The Distribution of the Northern Athapaskan Indians,*
Yale Publications in Anthropology, No. 7, New Haven, 1936.
———, *Ingalik Material Culture,* Yale Publications in Anthropology, No. 22.
———, *Ingalik Social Culture,* Yale Publications in Anthropology, No. 53.
———, *Ingalik Mental Culture,* Yale Publications in Anthropology, No. 56.
Whymper, Frederick, *Travel and Adventure, op. cit.*
Zagoskin, Lieutenant L. A., *Pedestrian Journeys, op. cit.*

IV. The Hudson's Bay Company

Campbell, Robert, *Two Journals of Robert Campbell, 1808 to 1853.* J. W.
Todd, ed., Seattle, 1958. Limited edition.
*Charters, Statutes, Orders in Council & Co. Relating to the Hudson's Bay
Company.* London, 1931.
Murray, Alexander H., *Journal of the Yukon, op. cit.*
Parnell, C. "Campbell of the Yukon," *The Beaver,* June, Sept., Dec., 1942.
Pinkerton, Robert E., *The Hudson's Bay Company.* New York, 1931.

V. 1860–1885

Adams, George R., "Journal," *California Historical Quarterly,* Vol. 25, No.
4 (Dec. 1956).

Dall, William H., *Alaska and Its Resources, op. cit.*

———, "A Yukon Pioneer, Mike Lebarge," *National Geographic Magazine,* Vol. 9, No. 4 (April 1898).

James, James A., "Robert Kennicott, Pioneer Illinois Scientist and Arctic Explorer," *Papers in Illinois History,* Evanston, 1941.

Jetté, Jules, *Jottings, op. cit.*

Kennicott, Robert, *Its Transactions, op. cit.*

Kitchener, L. D., *Flag Over the North.* Seattle, 1954.

McQuesten, Leroy N., *Recollections of Leroy N. McQuesten: Life in the Yukon 1871–1885.* Dawson City, Y.T., 1952.

Mercier, François, "Le Fort Reliance," MS in Jesuit Archives, Spokane, Wash.

Petroff, Ivan, *Report on the Population, Industries and Resources of Alaska.* Washington, D.C., 1884.

Raymond, Captain Charles, "Reconnoissance [sic] of the Yukon River, 1869," in *Compilation of Narratives of Exploration in Alaska,* Senate Report 1023, 56th Congress, 1st Session (3896), Washington, D.C., 1900.

Schwatka, Lieutenant Frederick, *Along Alaska's Great River.* New York, 1885.

Sherwood, Morgan, *Exploration of Alaska, 1865–1900.* New Haven, 1965.

Whymper, Frederick, *Travel and Adventure, op. cit.*

VI. From 1885 to the Klondike Gold Discoveries

Archer, F. A., *A Heroine of the North: Memoirs of Charlotte Selina Bompas.* London, 1929.

Cody, Hiram A., *An Apostle of the North: Memoirs of the Right Reverend William Carpenter Bompas, D.D.* New York, 1908.

Dawson, George M., *Narrative of an Exploration, op. cit.*

De Windt, Harry, *Through the Gold Fields of Alaska to the Bering Strait.* New York, 1898.

Hamlin, C. H., *Old Times in the Yukon.* Los Angeles, 1928.

Haskell, William B., *Two Years in the Klondike and Alaska Goldfields.* Hartford, Conn., 1898.

Hayne, M. H. E. and Taylor, H. W., *Pioneers of the Klondyke.* London, 1897.

Kitchener, L. D., *Flag Over the North, op. cit.*

Ogilvie, William, *Early Days on the Yukon.* Ottawa, 1913.

Pike, Warburton, *Through the Subarctic Forest.* New York, 1896.

Sherwood, Morgan, *Exploration, op. cit.*

Walden, Arthur T., *A Dog-Puncher on the Yukon.* Boston, 1928.

VII. The Gold Rush of 1897–98 and Its Aftermath

A. EYEWITNESS ACCOUNTS

Adney, Tappan, *The Klondike Stampede.* New York, 1900.

Allan, A. A., *Gold, Men and Dogs.* New York, 1931.

Becker, Ethel A., *Klondike '98: Hegg's Album of the 1898 Alaska Gold Rush.* Portland, Ore., 1949.

Berton, Laura B., *I Married the Klondike.* Boston, 1954.

Black, Mrs. George, *My Seventy Years.* London, 1939.

Cantwell, Lieutenant John C., *Report of the Operations of the U.S. Revenue Steamer Nunivak on the Yukon River Station, Alaska, 1899–1901*. Washington, D.C., 1902.

Carmack, George W., *My Experiences on the Yukon*. Privately printed. Seattle [?], 1933.

Haskell, William B., *Two Years, op. cit.*

Hayne, M. H. E. and Taylor, H. W., *Pioneers, op. cit.*

London, Jack, "From Dawson to the Sea," Buffalo *Express*. June 4, 1899.

————, "Through the Rapids on the Way to the Klondike," *Home Magazine*, June 1899.

Lotz, James R., "The Dawson Area: A Regional Monograph," *Yukon Research Series*, No. 2. Ottawa, 1964 [?].

McConnell, R. G., "The Klondike Region," *Summary Report*, Geological Survey of Canada, Ottawa, 1899.

————, "Klondike District, Yukon Territory," *Summary Report*, Geological Survey of Canada, Ottawa, 1904.

Morgan, Murray, *One Man's Gold Rush: A Klondike Album*. (Photographs by Eric Hegg), Seattle, 1967.

Ogilvie, William, *Early Days, op. cit.*

Pilcher, George M., Diary. Unpublished. Archives, University of Alaska.

Rickard, T. A., *Through the Yukon and Alaska*. San Francisco, 1909.

Smith, Alden R., Diary. Unpublished. Copy in Historical Museum, Dawson City, Y.T.

Steele, Colonel Samuel B., *Forty Years in Canada*. London, 1915.

Thompson, Fred, "Diary," *Yukon News Magazine*, Nov.–Dec., 1966.

Walden, Arthur T., *A Dog-Puncher, op. cit.*

Wickersham, Hon. James, *Old Yukon: Tales-Trails-Trials*. Washington, D.C., 1938.

B. SECONDARY SOURCES

Bankson, R. A., *The Klondike Nugget*. Caldwell, Idaho, 1935.

Barbeau, Marius, *Alaska Beckons*. Caldwell, Idaho, 1947.

Becker, Ethel A., "Monument at Dead Horse Gulch," *Alaska Sportsman*, Vol. 23, No. 5 (May 1957).

Beebe, Iola, *The True Life Story of Swiftwater Bill Gates*. Seattle, 1908.

Berton, Pierre, *Klondike*. Toronto, 1963.

Brooklyn *Daily Eagle*, 1897, '99.

Davis, Mary L., *Sourdough Gold*. Boston, 1933.

Documents Relative to the History of Alaska, op. cit., Vol. 7.

Judge, C. J., *An American Missionary: A Record of the Work of the Rev. William A. Judge, S.J.* Baltimore, 1904.

Kitchener, L. D., *Flag, op. cit.*

New York *Journal*, July, Aug., Sept. 1897.

Rickard, T. A., "The Klondike Rush," *British Columbia Historical Quarterly*, July 1942.

Winslow, Kathryn, *Big Pan-Out*. New York, 1951.

VIII. Missionaries

Alaska Churchman, Vol. 21, No. 4 (July 1930); Vol. 38, No. 1 (Feb. 1938); Vol. 56, No. 3 (Sept. 1961).

Anon., "Robert Macdonald." Undated typescript in possession of Anglican Bishop of Yukon, Whitehorse, Y.T.

Archer, F. A., *A Heroine of the North, op. cit.*

Boon, Thomas C. B., "William West Kirkby," *The Beaver,* spring 1965.

Chapman, John W., *A Camp on the Yukon.* Cornwall-on-Hudson, 1948.

——, Letters 1887–1899. In possession of Rev. Henry H. Chapman, Asheville, N.C.

Chapman, Mary S., *The Ministry of John W. Chapman, D.D., at Anvik in Alaska.* Hartford, Conn., 1943.

Cody, Hiram F., *An Apostle of the North, op. cit.*

Documents Relative to the History of Alaska, op. cit., Vol. 3.

Dragon, Antonio, *Enseveli dans les neiges.* (Life of Jules Jetté, S.J.) Montreal, 1943.

Jetté, Jules, *Jottings, op. cit.*

——, "Sketch of Alaska Missions," undated MS in Jesuit Archives, Spokane, Wash.

——, Letters to His Superiors, 1907–14, in Jesuit Archives, Spokane, Wash.

Judge, C. J., *An American Missionary, op. cit.*

Loyens, William J., *The Changing Culture of the Nulato Koyukon Indians, op. cit.*

McDonald, Robert, Letters, 1862–78. Public Archives of Canada, Ottawa.

Steckler, Gerald, *Charles John Seghers, Missionary Bishop in the American Northwest, 1839–1886.* Unpublished Ph.D. dissertation, U. of Washington, 1963.

Stuck, Hudson, *Voyages on the Yukon and Its Tributaries.* New York, 1917.

——, *10,000 Miles with a Dog Sled.* New York, 1916.

Wright, T. G. A., "The Venerable Robert McDonald," typescript in possession of Anglican Bishop of the Yukon, Whitehorse, Y.T. Written in London, 1911.

IX. Native People in Transition

Anchorage *Daily News,* "Alaska's Village People"; series of eleven articles appearing between Dec. 5 and Dec. 16, 1965.

Cantwell, Lieutenant John C., *Report of Operations, op. cit.*

Chapman, John W., *A Camp on the Yukon, op. cit.*

Graham, Robert E., Jr., "Income in Alaska," *Survey of Current Business,* June 1961.

Hannum, Walter W., "The Social Situation of the Natives of the Upper Yukon"; undated typescript, copy in office of Bureau of Indian Affairs, Fairbanks, Alaska.

Jetté, Jules, Letters, *op. cit.*

Loyens, William J., *The Changing Culture of the Nulato Koyukon Indians, op. cit.*

——, trans., *House Diary.* Nulato, 1891–1965 (excerpts); copy in possession of translator, original in Jesuit Archives, Spokane, Wash.

Ray, Charles K. *et al., Alaska Native Secondary School Dropouts: A Research Report.* College, Alaska, 1962.

Rogers, George W. and Cooley, Richard A., *Alaska's Population and Econ-*

omy, *Regional Growth, Development and Future Outlook.* 2 vols. Juneau, 1962.

Shimkin, D. B., "The Economy of a Trapping Center: The Case of Fort Yukon, Alaska," *Journal of Economic Development and Social Change,* Vol. 3, No. 3 (April 1955).

U.S. Bureau of Census, *Census of Population, Alaska,* 1960, Final Report PC (1)—3 C. Washington, D.C., 1961.

X. Flora and Fauna

Alaska, State Department of Fish and Game, *Annual Report, 1965.* Juneau, 1966.

Black, Mrs. George, *Arctic Wild Flowers.* Vancouver, 1940 [?].

Brett, J. R., "The Swimming Energetic of Salmon," *Scientific American,* Vol. 213, No. 2 (August 1965).

Dufresne, Frank, *Alaska's Animals and Fishes.* West Hartford, Vt., 1946.

Fisheries Research Board of Canada, *Journal,* Vols. 21–24. (1964–67).

Hasler, Arthur D., *Underwater Guideposts.* U. of Wisconsin Press, 1956.

Mason, James E., "Chinook Salmon in Offshore Waters," International North Pacific Fisheries, *Bulletin,* No. 16, 1965.

Murie, Adolph, *A Naturalist in Alaska.* Garden City, N.Y., 1963.

Murie, Olaus J., "Alaska-Yukon Caribou," U.S. Biological Survey, *North American Fauna,* No. 54. Washington, D.C., 1935.

Osgood, W. H., and Bishop, L. B., "Results of a Biological Reconnaissance of the Yukon River Region, Alaska," U.S. Biological Survey, *North American Fauna,* No. 19. Washington, D.C., 1900.

Peterson, R. L., *North American Moose.* Toronto, 1955.

Peterson, Roger T., *A Field Guide to Western Birds.* Cambridge, Mass., 1941.

Sharples, Ada W., *Alaska Wild Flowers.* Standford U. Press and London, 1938.

Taylor, R. F., and Little, E. L., "Pocket Guide to Alaskan Trees," U.S. Department of Agriculture, Forest Service, *Handbook* No. 5, Washington, D.C., 1950.

Index

About the Author

Richard Mathews, whose articles have appeared in such periodicals as *The Saturday Review, The New Republic,* and *The Reporter,* is a free-lance writer. He and his wife, Ella, have traveled many miles of the Yukon and its tributaries. This is his first full-length book.